D1387732

Warwickshire College
* 0 0 5 1 3 8 4 6 *

712.60942
BRO

WITHDRAWN

THE ENGLISH GARDEN

THROUGH THE 20TH CENTURY

THE ENGLISH GARDEN

THROUGH THE 20TH CENTURY

JANE BROWN

GARDEN • ART • PRESS

LIBRARY

WARWICKSHIRE
COLLEGE

© 1999 Jane Brown
World copyright reserved

ISBN 1 870673 29 8

First published 1986 as *The English Garden in our Time from
Gertrude Jekyll to Geoffrey Jellicoe*
Reprinted 1987
Completely revised edition 1999

All rights reserved. No part of this publication may be reproduced, stored
in a retrieval system or transmitted in any form or by any means electronic,
mechanical, photocopying, recording or otherwise, without the prior
permission of the publishers

British Library Cataloguing-in-Publication Data
A catalogue record for this book is
available from the British Library

The right of Jane Brown to be identified as author of this work has been
asserted by her in accordance with the Copyright, Designs and Patents Act 1988

.·ARWICKSHIRE COLLEGE
LIBRARY
·SS No: 712.609
42
Acc No:
005138146

Published by Garden Art Press, a division of
the Antique Collectors' Club

Cover: *Craig y Parc, Gwent, house and garden 1913-14 by Charles Mallows.*
(RIBA Drawings Coll.)
Frontispiece: *Turn End, Haddenham, Peter Aldington's garden.* (Peter Aldington)
Title Page: *Oval jardinière by Quinlan Terry, West Green House, Hampshire.*
(The author)

Printed in England
by the Antique Collectors' Club, Woodbridge, Suffolk
on Consort Royal Satin paper
supplied by the Donside Paper Company, Aberdeen, Scotland

CONTENTS

Author's Foreword
to the First Edition

Garden design used to be such a certain art. We can speak confidently of Tudor knots, Queen Anne parterres, the English landscaped park and Victorian borders and carpeted beds. We can restore them, conserve them, dress up and dance in them, hold *fêtes-champêtres* in them, and on these occasions slip back into our pasts with ease. But what happens if we venture into our own century? 1910 or 1920? 1960 or 1970? We know the dress for these dates, but what about the settings? We know the interiors, but what kinds of gardens make the backdrop for modern living? Are gardens even important as expressions of personality or lifestyle any more? Because of these questions I have set out to put 20th century gardening ideas into perspective. That is my first reason for writing this book.

My opening chapter is about Munstead Wood; the closing chapter about Sutton Place. To those who know something of English architecture moving from Munstead Wood to Sutton Place may seem like a journey backwards in time, without even touching the 20th century. Munstead Wood was designed by Sir Edwin Lutyens and finished in 1897; Sutton Place was built by Sir Richard Weston in the early part of the 16th century. But to gardeners Munstead Wood is the home of Gertrude Jekyll, whose garden was established in the last few years of the 19th century and whose influence marked radical changes in attitudes to garden design which strike well into our times. Sutton Place, a few miles away and also in Surrey, is the repository for a garden of the 1980s by Sir Geoffrey Jellicoe, who stands without rival as the most significant garden designer of the 20th

Opposite: the Magritte Avenue, Sutton Place by Geoffrey Jellicoe. For the reverse view, see page 275.

Left: Munstead Wood, restored to blooming in the 1990s.

century. Sir Geoffrey has been present in the world of landscape and garden design since the 1920s, and his achievements at Sutton Place in the mid-1980s embody the best of the ideas he has gathered in that time. His work, I believe, answers many of those questions about the kinds of gardens that we now need. To attempt to fit his design philosophy into its context was my second reason for writing this book.

I wrote my first book, *Gardens of a Golden Afternoon*, about Gertrude Jekyll and her partnership in garden making with the architect Edwin Lutyens. Miss Jekyll was born in 1843. She was intelligent, well educated and hard working; she grew up and lived in a world of artists and artist-craftsmen, working at many arts and crafts herself, until she was in her mid-thirties and her eyesight began to fail. She had to turn to less demanding activities and she turned, with enthusiasm, to gardening. She bought her fifteen acres of Surrey heath and wood that was to become her Munstead Wood in 1883; in 1889 she met the twenty year old Lutyens, who built her house. They began a partnership that created over one hundred houses and gardens, mainly in the years up to the First War. After that they drifted into their separate ways, though remained good friends. Miss Jekyll published her first gardening book, *Wood and Garden*, in 1899. After that she wrote incessantly, books and articles, about her gardening, she ran her garden as a nursery business and she fulfilled some 250 gardening commissions of her own. She died in 1932. She looms over English gardening in this century rather in the way that John Maynard Keynes looms over economics. Everyone who has gardened since her time has owed her something.

Yet she did not live and garden in isolation. She was part of a movement, the Arts and Crafts Movement, and my second chapter traces some of the influence on gardens of the architects of this Movement who shared a dedication to English country building traditions and the English countryside. As with any movement peopled by individuals, there were variations in their interests and approaches as far as gardens were concerned, and I have tried to illustrate this. Lutyens was part of this Movement, and though he and Miss Jekyll together cannot but dominate the early part of my book I hope they are revealed as part of 'The Return to Englishness' rather than in splendid isolation. I have chosen to detail the garden at Rodmarton Manor as a symbol of the Arts and Crafts ideals because there was a purity and an earnestness about its creation that was characteristic of the Movement, though these are not epithets that I would apply to the Lutyens/Jekyll gardens.

Even within the Arts and Crafts Movement few gardens of the 20th century can escape the influence of Renaissance Italy. Neither George Sitwell, nor Vita Sackville-West, nor Lawrence Johnston, nor Geoffrey Jellicoe, would have made gardens without their Italian inspiration; others were more imitative and acquisitive. My fourth chapter explores this theme, but it is of necessity too brief; there is a whole book on the Italian garden in England to be written.

And then comes the revolution. The impact of the Bauhaus, of white concrete and International Modern Architecture on garden design was fleeting but unforgettable. That other country of the 1930s has now, for us, almost matched the aura of the Edwardian golden afternoon; they are both lost dream times. The 'thirties' brief dalliance with modern garden design holds us in an extra thrall because there are such close parallels between the 18th century theories of the English landscape movement and the 'modern' theories. Christopher Tunnard was capable of presenting us with what we most wanted, our finest landscape hour *in miniature*, garden size: to fit attenuated lives and spaces. But the Second War took him and others away, and when it was over we had to begin all over again.

Chapter six is devoted to the garden of Sissinghurst Castle because it was made in the face of war, and survived to become the most loved of English 20th century gardens. It was made by two individuals, Vita Sackville-West and Harold Nicolson, who brought their love of literature, art and architecture into their garden, and endowed it with wit, humour, more love and a sense of mystery. Because of the 'star quality' of its makers, Sissinghurst's classical spaces filled with perfect flowers lead double lives: they are obviously beautiful, but by what is unseen – the aura that hangs about the place – they exert an appeal to our subconscious. Quite by accident, Sissinghurst possesses what was to become the holy grail of artists and the best landscape designers (and, I presume, architects) in post-war Britain, what Barbara Hepworth had called the 'chosen perfected form' of expression that allows the power of the idea to shine through. This fact dawned on Geoffrey Jellicoe after the war, and it began to infiltrate his work, his writing and his lectures to landscape architects both here and abroad.

In the meantime, others were seeing gardens in different ways. The historical approach to gardening was introduced into post-war Britain with the foundation of the National Trust Gardens' Committee and the acquisition for conservation of Hidcote Manor and its garden in Gloucestershire. My chapter on Hidcote Manor and the 'New Georgian' gardens also attempts to contain a whole world within a few thousand words and fewer pictures. This is the world that John Cornforth described in *The Inspiration of the Past* where, spurred on by the National Trust's restorations and those of a few far-sighted private owners, distinctive houses, mainly 18th century but not always large, have been classically restored in present-day terms. Gardens were a natural corollary to these houses, but in fact many of the gardens had to be made anew because, of course, the English landscape style of the 18th century swept formal gardens away. Georgian gardens in 20th century terms mix beauty and use, flowers and herbs, flowers and vegetables, within ordered enclosures and walks ornamented by the works of Mr Chippendale or Quinlan Terry. Many (too many) of the gardens of the National Trust, which are those most seen by the general public, fall into this category. Georgianism in gardening means 'good taste' and has contributed greatly to the post-war

The troughery at Rodmarton Manor.

commercial success of gardening. It has, in theory, the added attractions of adaptability and of fitting into the smallest pocket handkerchief plot, though this must be done with restraint.

In the main the professionals, the landscape architects (who can deftly turn out Georgian gardens), have preferred to pursue classical design in more modern terms. Chapter eight's title, 'Quandaries', indicates just how difficult this has been in a society that neither has the resources to have its private gardens designed nor the wish to pay for the upkeep of those which already exist. The opportunities for good garden design are rare, but I believe that those by Sylvia Crowe, Brenda Colvin, Anthony du Gard Pasley, Michael Branch, John Brookes and Preben Jakobsen convey an effective message. The pity of it is, that in so much landscape design outside garden walls, where in theory we are still the same human beings with the same desires and needs, the precious human scale of gardens has been blatantly ignored. But that is another story.

My final two chapters are devoted to the work of Sir Geoffrey Jellicoe. Before I wrote this book I recorded conversations with him, at his London home, during the spring and summer of his eighty-third year, 1983. The purpose of those conversations was to hear him pinpoint the literary and artistic inspirations, stemming from the Constructivist Movement of the 1930s, that he had transmuted into landscapes and gardens. My explanation of this philosophy, in Chapter nine, 'Geoffrey Jellicoe and the Garden of the Mind', is too brief; he has explained everything himself in much greater detail, and I refer my readers to his own books, listed at the end of this chapter. What I have tried to do – and it is, as I have said, an important reason for writing this book – is to set him at the end of the 20th century road that he, and we, have taken. So many of the themes of this book meet in the garden at Sutton Place that it seems to be not only a representative 20th century garden but also to set us firmly upon a number of paths to follow for the future.

Jane Brown
Dogmersfield, April 1986

Hailey House,
Oxfordshire, a
garden of the
1960s by
Sylvia Crowe.

FOREWORD TO THE 1999 EDITION

If I could have one wish for this edition, it would be to prescribe it for new readers to be taken in small, regular doses, preferably before breakfast, on days to be spent visiting gardens, nurseries or garden centres, or actually gardening. I hope it will impart some assurance of a continuing tradition in gardens which embraces us all, or, for the innovatory, at least a tradition to kick against. The revised notes on books and gardens at the end of each chapter seek to extend these paths of exploration to the present, perhaps in the way of a guiding green twine, into the ravishing avalanche of books and gardens that are now available.

In the seemingly distant, chilly winter of 1985 when I wrote *The English Garden In Our Time*, the end of this century was hidden in the mist. Now it is so clearly upon us, some changes have needed to be made, but some have not. Gertrude Jekyll still looms over the gardening world. She and William Robinson employed all the planting moods and themes which have been so beautifully brought to life for us by Rosemary Verey, Christopher Lloyd, Beth Chatto, Penelope Hobhouse and Stephen Lacey, to name but a few. Chapter Two has been renamed 'The Arts and Crafts Garden', because that name has become accepted in recent years, for gardens of the period 1890 to 1914: happily Rodmarton Manor remains a family home which embodies the integrity of that tradition.

The four chapters that follow, on the Italian influence, the Modern Movement, the making of Sissinghurst Castle's garden and on Hidcote Manor and the New Georgians, remain the same. I see no reason to alter them here (though perhaps my own perspective has moved with the years – but that is another story). Chapter eight has accepted the inevitable – 'The Post-Modern Garden' – though this by no means follows slavishly the architectural definition of this term, nor is it in any settled state. Two major trends of the last fifteen years are that landscape architects have almost relinquished their interest in garden design to the new breed of garden designers, and that conservation and restoration have become a creative force. Education in garden design, pioneered in private schools such as the Inchbald School of Design and the English Gardening School, and by John Brookes's courses at Denmans and Kew, has now become a degree subject in the new technological universities: there is a flourishing Society of Garden Designers which publishes an excellent journal and is a lively forum for established and talented young designers.

No one was more delighted at this prosperity in gardening talents than Sir Geoffrey Jellicoe, who died peacefully in the summer of his 96th year, 1996. My two chapters on his philosophy seem more inadequate than ever, but they do place him in the context of his century, and it is with a smile

that I recall the delighted note he wrote to me after the first publication in 1986. I have not changed these chapters, except to add a footnote on the developments at Sutton Place.

As Sir Geoffrey has perhaps now taken his place with his heroes, Capability Brown and Humphry Repton in the Elysian Fields, so he has certainly become the source of inestimable inspirations to his successors, both for his subtly persistent Modernism and for the metaphoric delights his works display. Who could wish for a more prescient, or a more kindly, humanist guidance into the unknown regions beyond the Millennium?   *Jane Brown*

Orford, Suffolk. The Old Rectory designed by Lanning Roper. Tall trees form a backdrop for Henry Moore's 'Seated Woman'.

Munstead Wood. The house designed by Edwin Lutyens and completed in 1897, seen through flowers once again in its 1990s restoration by Stephen King.

ONE
Munstead Wood

Twentieth century English gardening begins at Gertrude Jekyll's Munstead Wood in Surrey for three especially good reasons. First, her garden was at its best from 1890 until 1914; she took hundreds of photographs throughout this period, and it was no coincidence that the last was dated August 1914, the month in which Britain declared war on Germany. Ever practical, she gave her time over to knitting socks for soldier boys; she would soon have to turn to the designing of the gardens round their graves. There is that awful sadness that nothing was ever to be quite the same again, and yet her influence managed to survive.

Thus, the second reason is that she is in fashion. Over the last thirty years the Garden History Society has inspired a steady accumulation of information about her: Betty Massingham's *Miss Jekyll: Portrait of a Great Gardener* was published in 1966, most of her own books have been reprinted, and many of her garden and planting plans (rescued from destruction by the American landscape gardener Beatrix Farrand) have been revealed in the library of the College of Environmental Design on the University of California's Berkeley campus. Miss Jekyll is a satisfactory subject for interest: there is a challenge in the aura of a kindly headmistress (that deems *Miss Jekyll* so apt), and being well documented she is so much more rewarding than those of whom only hazy memories and transient flower borders remain. Hundreds of owners of quite modest gardens are now aware that they have a piece of genuine Jekyll to restore (she did 350 commissions of varying size between 1880 and 1932) and thousands of gardeners are enjoying planting their own variations on her themes.

The third, and most important, reason is that Gertrude Jekyll is the more modern equivalent of a breed that the garden historian David Jacques so nicely christens '*gentlemanly virtuosi*' of John Evelyn's kind. She must share with Evelyn the accolade of being the best qualified of gardeners to work in

Gertrude Jekyll. A rare portrait photograph of about 1880, dressed much as Edwin Lutyens later remembered her from their first meeting: 'A bunch of cloaked propriety topped by a black felt hat, turned down in front and up behind, from which sprang alert black cock's tail feathers, curving and ever prancing forwards'.

Bramley Park, near Guildford, Surrey, as it was in Gertrude Jekyll's childhood. Edward and Julia Jekyll rented Bramley Park in 1848 when Gertrude was almost five years old, and it was the family home until 1868. In her book, Children and Gardens, *Miss Jekyll wrote affectionately of Bramley Park's garden and the best shrubs and garden trees which she loved: magnolias, rhododendrons, azaleas, kalmias, pieris, the cut-leaved beech and the ailanthus, 'Tree of Heaven'. In a corner away from the house she was allowed her own garden plot where she tended with special adoration a clump of large blue cornflowers and a thornless pink climbing rose. The house was demolished in 1951.*

England, for she renewed gardening's social prestige and added enough interesting ideas to make it intellectually stimulating as well. Miss Jekyll was a hard-working, well-educated artist, a skilled practitioner of many crafts and an energetic traveller, and she allowed all her tastes and knowledge to flow freely into her gardening. In it, as seemingly in the rest of her life, she was sure of her tastes and she knew her limitations.

Her garden at Munstead Wood owed its first allegiance to its countryside. The garden was made on a high sandy heath just south of Godalming. The greensand bedrock of this part of Surrey gives it a particularly strong character; there are stretches of high heath, with small hills, some quite dramatically steep, upheld by the hard layers of a substance geologists call *chert*. Amongst these hills wind hollow lanes, worn by centuries of use and English rain. The lanes lead to the old villages, and in the Munstead area all the old villages are in the fertile valley of the river Wey; only the newcomers had to build on the high heath.

By the standards of this old countryside the Jekylls were newcomers. In 1848, when she was four and a half years old, Gertrude was rescued from a drab

Gertrude Jekyll, aged about nineteen, from a sketch by Mary Newton. From childhood, Gertrude's greatest ambition was to be a painter and she studied, sketched and copied with great enthusiasm.

London childhood of upstairs nurseries and walks in the park by her parents' decision to bring up their young family in the country. She was the second daughter and fourth surviving child (she was later to have two younger brothers) of Edward and Julia Jekyll. He came from an eminent family of lawyers and soldiers, had served in the Grenadier Guards and was a keen yachtsman, inventor and engineer with a love of classical art and architecture. Julia Jekyll was a lady of more than usual spirit and talent for music and painting. The whole family moved to a rented house, Bramley Park just south of Guildford, and they were to remain there throughout Gertrude's childhood.

She adored her country life and her first delight was the garden of Bramley Park. The big, rambling neo-classical house was surrounded with some formal bedding (which she became aware was the fashion), but the shrubs, the magnolias, rhododendrons, azaleas, kalmias and andromedas (pieris), the cut-leaved beech and the ailanthus – the Tree of Heaven – were regarded by the little girl as friendly presences to be encountered daily. Her parents, who were so infinitely sensible in many ways, and gave her a garden patch that was out of the way and in her own control where she tended beloved cornflowers, roses and ferns.

Beyond the garden at Bramley Park was the park with its woods, streams and mill ponds. As Gertrude grew older, and mainly with her brothers for company, she spent hours playing cricket, climbing trees and making expeditions to an island in the largest pond; while her brothers were away at school and her much older sister could not be bothered with her, she was left to wander with her dog and pony beyond the park and through the lanes around Bramley. She visited the cottages and workshops of Bramley village and developed her interest in the cottage economy of the countryside that was to remain with her for the rest of her life.

Despite all her leisurely wanderings she was also given a good education at home and became proficient in several languages, music and drawing. But her greatest desire was to be a painter. When she was eighteen she was sent to Henry Cole's School in South Kensington for a two-year course. She worked hard and entered the world of artists with enthusiasm. At the end of her course she was given the chance to make a long tour of the Greek islands with a friend of her father's, the eminent archaeologist Charles Newton and his wife Mary (the sister of Arthur Severn, Ruskin's friend). On this never-to-be-forgotten trip Gertrude gathered her first-hand appreciation of classical art

A corner cupboard (left), and door (right) at Munstead Wood inlaid by Gertrude Jekyll with mother-of-pearl.

and architecture that would one day make her so aware of the importance of architectural disciplines in the design of houses and their gardens.

When she returned from the Greek islands she met both John Ruskin and William Morris. She worshipped Ruskin – though that term applies advisedly to a young lady of sturdy religious faith and she devoured the volumes of *Modern Painters*, sat for hours copying Turner paintings, and sketched and studied details from nature in the way of a model pupil. With her characteristic energy she turned her attention to 'Arts and Crafts'. William Morris was nine years her senior and his passion for medieval arts and architecture, allied to his belief in the artist as craftsman, had already led to the establishment in 1861 of Morris, Marshall, Faulkner & Co, 'Fine Art Workmen in Painting, Carving, Furniture and the Metals'. Miss Jekyll would certainly not have missed the first products of the firm exhibited at the International Exhibition in London in 1862, and she came to know most of 'The Firm's' artists and supporters.

Though the social code of the time would not allow her, a lady of independent means, to set up in business, she tried her best. Over the years she amassed an impressive list of commissions: she designed and made embroideries of wreaths of flowers taken from her flower studies, including a

Drawing by Gertrude Jekyll for an embroidery design.

Wood carving by Gertrude Jekyll over the wine cellar door at Munstead Wood.

tablecloth for Lord Leighton, she painted decorations on the walls in the houses of her friends, helped with decorative schemes, made exquisite silver jewellery (with commissions from Princess Louise, Duchess of Argyll, and Sir Edward Burne-Jones) as well as lovely silver church plate. She spent hours patiently inlaying ivory and mother-of-pearl patterns into doors and tackled wood carving and wrought-iron work. Throughout her twenties and early thirties her life was frantically busy and exciting; she painted, studied, visited artists and exhibitions, spent musical evenings in London during the week, and gardened and was busy in her workshop at home at weekends or joined country house parties with her friends.

True to her faithfulness to Ruskin and Morris her favourite houses and gardens were those which still had the aura of old England about them – Montacute, Brympton d'Evercy, Haddon Hall, Packwood and Melbourne. Around these old manor houses were gardens of modest symmetry, ordered in balustraded terraces and walks, with neat parterres enclosed by yew and box. They had not been touched by Capability Brown and the English

Gertrude Jekyll's workshop showing some of her paintings, souvenirs from her travels and an example of her inlay work. Her plan chest is on the right of the photograph.

landscape style – she was never to have any love at all for Palladian mansions floating in seas of grass and felt them to be wanting in beauty. Her taste for the houses and gardens of old England was reflected in her travels; she loved most of all the gardens of the villas of Renaissance Italy, the old gardens of Spain and the south of France, with their romantic groves of scented bay, rosemary, myrtle, thyme and cistus.

All this art and activity suited her well until she began to receive the first warnings that her weak, short-sighted eyes would not stand the strain of so much close and detailed work as well as her, frankly, rackety lifestyle. Her parents had left beloved Bramley Park in 1868 to live in Berkshire, in a house her father had inherited. Gertrude never liked Berkshire – 'because it was not Surrey' – and perhaps felt she had no settled home at all. In 1876 her father died and her mother decided on an immediate return to Surrey. She had a new house built for her on Munstead Heath just south of Godalming, and they moved back in September 1878. Gertrude was thirty-four: she wrote in her diary 'To Munstead – for good'.

Over the next ten years she gradually relinquished her London life and much of her travelling, made the garden for her mother's Munstead House, and began writing about gardening for William Robinson's journal *The Garden*. She made her approach to the world of gardening with the same energy she had always had for other projects. She soon knew and admired the 'great amateurs' of the Royal Horticultural Society, Ellen Willmott, George Wilson, Canon Ellacombe and Dean Hole of Rochester. Early in the 1880s it became clear that she must have somewhere of her own and she bought a fifteen-acre plot across the road from her mother's house, which she named Munstead Wood. In gardening terms it was not a propitious purchase. Much of the plot was felled woodland, full of stumps and roots, the sandy soil was thin and all the goodness leached through with the rain; trees – especially oaks – never grew grandly and even roses required lavish feeding, and then they were all eaten by the marauding deer. But, in late 19th century gardening terms, Munstead Wood was not to be the usual garden – there would be no rose garden, no neat beds of annuals ranged across the lawn. Miss Jekyll's country childhood and her contact with William Robinson had taught her what we now call the ecological approach. This was to be enriched by her loving knowledge of the great gardens of Europe and England, and by her taste and understanding of colour and design that she had learned through her painting and embroidery. She had her new gardening friends as willing advisers, and she had that staunch band of Bramley villagers who remembered her as a child and whose families would work faithfully for her in her new venture.

Munstead Wood's plot was triangular and fell roughly into three areas. The narrow end of the triangle was a small field which was trenched and manured and made into the kitchen garden and nursery ground; the middle area, which was felled chestnut coppice, was partly open in character and this was to be for her house and flower garden. The upper and largest part of the plot, where Scots pines had been felled, was to be her woodland garden, the most personal, complex and elusive of Munstead Wood's planting schemes. The

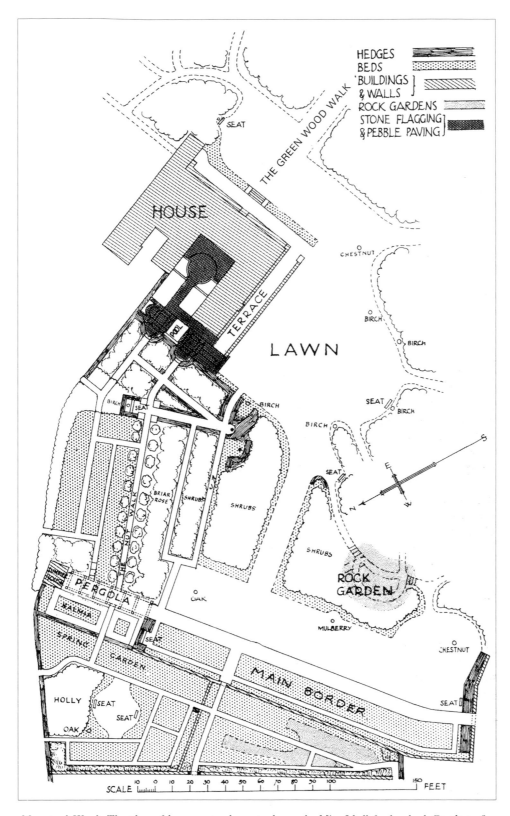

HEDGES
BEDS
BUILDINGS }
& WALLS }
ROCK GARDENS
STONE FLAGGING }
& PEBBLE PAVING }

THE GREEN WOOD WALK

SEAT

HOUSE

TERRACE

POOL

LAWN

CHESTNUT

BIRCH

BIRCH

SEAT

BIRCH

BIRCH

BIRCH

BIRCH

SEAT

SEAT

BRIAR
ROSE

SHRUBS

SHRUBS

SHRUBS

SHRUBS

ROCK
GARDEN

OAK

PERGOLA

KALMIA

SPRING

GARDEN

SEAT

MULBERRY

CHESTNUT

HOLLY

SEAT

MAIN BORDER

SEAT

SEAT

OAK

SEAT

SCALE 10 0 10 20 30 40 50 60 70 80 90 100 150 FEET

Munstead Wood. The plan of her own garden was drawn by Miss Jekyll for her book Gardens for Small Country Houses *(published by Newnes/Country Life, 1912), which she wrote with Lawrence Weaver. She shows the central portion of her plot; the woodland garden stretches farther to the south-east. The Hut with the June garden around it was south of the lawn, and the kitchen garden and nursery ground narrowed to a point at the bottom of her plan. The rock garden became surrounded by tall shrubs and was enclosed as her hidden garden.*

Munstead Wood.
The restoration policy for the
woodland areas was managed
natural regeneration (after
clearance of damage to trees in
1987 storm).

wood had been felled about fifteen years before Miss Jekyll started work and
birch, holly, oak, rowan, chestnut and seedling pine were all regenerating
naturally. By a careful, painstaking process of weeding out the poor specimens
and keeping the best, she organised her woodland. She encouraged silver
birch and holly as beautifully contrasting neighbours; a copse of oaks
progressing into one of beech and a small area of chestnut were saved.
Around the edges of the wood the Scots pines were allowed to return; their
scale was too vast for even a largish garden and they had to keep their

Munstead Wood. Miss Jekyll's 'bunch' primroses regenerating in the woodland.

distance. Her basic rule was that a single species of tree within one's view induced the required atmosphere of repose; the pleasure and delights would be added later.

On her daily strolls at every season she made the paths that revealed the woodland garden. There were originally five walks radiating from the lawn where one day her house would stand. The most precious was the wide Green Wood Walk which she made purposefully to lead off from the centre of the lawn to the Scots pine. The beginning was treated boldly, with groups of rhododendrons carefully related in their colourings – any pinks, rose and rose reds kept carefully away from the magentas – and their heavy green draped like skirts around the delicate birch stems, the birch trees supplying the required dappled shade. This walk, wide enough for two people comfortably to stroll along side by side, was also light enough for grass to grow and it was kept closely mown to emphasise its importance.

A rock path was decorated with large lumps of carefully placed sandstone, with pieris, skimmia and alpenrose planted so that glimpses of the rocks appeared entirely natural. Mostly the woodland paths were a means of revealing the 'floweiy incidents' which marked the Munstead woodland gardening year: winter aconite strewn under the outer branches of a beech; Christmas roses in a dell among hart's tongue ferns; long drifts of crocus, the purples and whites in a darker place, the yellows in the open, and never all three colours in view at the same time; daffodils in drifts, in a natural sequence of pale trumpets through to richer yellows, and the bi-colour narcissus, with nothing lovelier than a drift of poet's daffodil (*Narcissus poeticus*), pheasant's eye narcissus, were set to catch the light through a break in the branches; yellow and white primroses were planted to turn translucent in the greenish light of young oak leaves; cream, orange and gold azaleas were set to bloom against the russet carpet of dead chestnut leaves; holly was laced with honeysuckle; a patch of white foxgloves or lilies was planted at the hem of a dark rhododendron skirt; a clearing was full of pink and white cistus, and, a surprise, a clump of lupins stood majestically at the dark wood's edge.

On and on throughout the year the surprises kept coming, though carefully contrived. In fact, so carefully that it all appeared utterly natural, for the plants were merely displaying natural glories that so often go unremarked, confused and unseen. Miss Jekyll's magical woodland was ever changing for the amusement of her friends and visitors – whatever the weather a walk

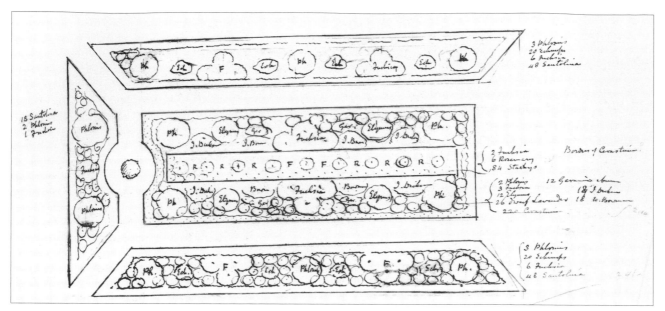

Chinthurst Hill, Wonersh, Surrey, the grey garden plan. The house was built by Lutyens for a friend of Miss Jekyll, Miss Aemillia Guthrie, in 1893. Miss Jekyll made her 'first tentative suggestions' about this garden and it was the beginning of her long partnership with Edwin Lutyens. It was one of the first one-colour gardens she designed for any client, with thick edgings of Stachys lanata, *its felty leaves complemented by the ferny textures of lavender, santolina and rosemary; for further contrast she used echinops, phlomis (Jerusalem sage), lyme grass (elymus) and fuchsias,* F. riccartonii *with purple and pink flowers and* F. magellanica gracilis *with scarlet/violet flowers. She would have ordained that the yellow flowers of the santolina were clipped as they were of unsuitable colour, and she preferred stachys flowers clipped to retain the bushy character of the clumps.*

through the woodland was her gift and without it a visit to Munstead was no visit at all. She designed the framework of woodland gardens, or wildernesses, with paths winding through trees and clumps of shrubs, for several of her clients, but she would have always pointed out that they must add the flowery incidents to suit themselves.

It was six years after she had started making her garden that Miss Jekyll, in her mid-forties, met Edwin Lutyens, then just twenty, who had set himself up in his chosen profession as an architect. The first house Lutyens designed for her was a traditional Surrey cottage in her Munstead Wood grounds. Called The Hut, it was finished in 1894 so that she could live in her garden. Around The Hut she planted her version of a cottage garden, at its best in June, with masses of flowers inside box-edged beds divided by narrow sandy paths. The flowers grew in what was to become the usual Munstead profusion – that is they spilled out of their allotted spaces with the luxuriance and splendour of a Dutch flower painting, engulfing the visitor in clouds of scent and showers of scented rain. The fountain sprays of Miss Jekyll's favourite rose, the hybrid musk rose 'The Garland', arched over the paths; a large bed was crammed with dusky pink roses on looped ropes, with ferns, white columbines, pink and white peonies, white foxgloves and creamy snapdragons at their feet. The colours were warm and soft, the whites always creamy, the pinks pale and salmony, with splashes of orange lilies and always the solid green backdrop of holly and yew somewhere in the picture. The border outside her studio bay window was a miniature version of the mixed border with colours in graduated sweeps for which Munstead Wood was to become so famous; from her window she saw London pride, *Iris pallida* and lupins in creams and pinks backed by waving fronds of meadowsweet, with *Campanula lactiflora* and pink

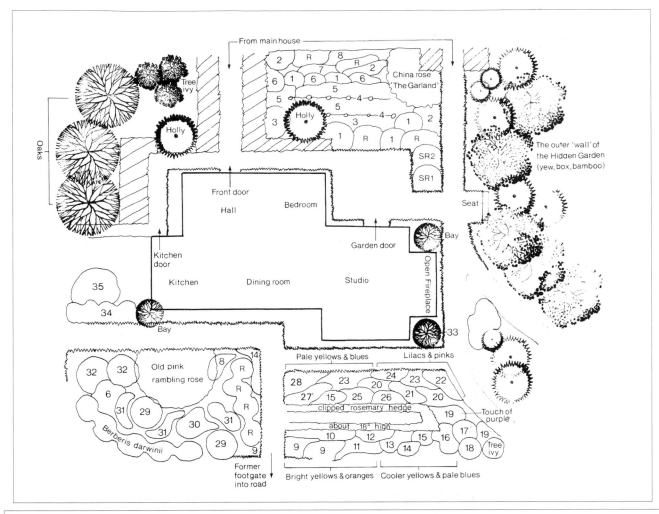

The following labels appear on the garden plan:

From main house
Tree ivy
Holly
China rose 'The Garland'
Oaks
The outer 'wall' of the Hidden Garden (yew, box, bamboo)
Front door
Hall
Bedroom
Seat
Kitchen door
Bay
Garden door
Open Fireplace
Kitchen
Dining room
Studio
Bay
Old pink rambling rose
Berberis darwinii
Pale yellows & blues
Lilacs & pinks
clipped rosemary hedge
about 18" high
Touch of purple
Tree ivy
Former footgate into road
Bright yellows & oranges
Cooler yellows & pale blues
SR2 SR1

R	Old shrub roses, mainly R. damascena 'Celsiana' and R. centifolia	17	Olearia phlogopappa (gunniana) *(Tasmanian daisy-bush)*
SR	Standard roses: 1 'Celeste'; 2 'Madame Plantier'	18	Kerria japonica
1	Paeonia officinalis *(pink and white)*	19	*Pale yellow iris (Dutch hybrid)*
2	Snapdragons *(pink and cream)*	20	*Lupins (creamy, bluish lilac and a few purple)*
3	*Underplanting of orange lilies, ferns and white foxgloves*	21	Paeonia lactiflora *(flesh pink)*
4	*Roses on hoops -* R. moschata *and* R. chinensis	22	Iris pallida dalmatica
5	*Underplanting of male fern,* Myrrhis odorata *and white aquilegias*	23	Saxifraga umbrosa *(London pride)*
6	*White foxgloves*	24	Iris pallida *(pinky lilac variety)*
7	Penstemon barbatus *(these and the snapdragons to carry on flowering)*	25	Nepeta mussinii *(faassenii) (catmint)*
8	Bergenia cordifolia	26	Campanula lactiflora
9	Papaver orientalis *(apricot and oranges)*	27	*Creamy lupins*
10	*Deep orange lilies*	28	Geranium ibericum *(purple blue cranesbill) with pale yellow and white Spanish iris*
11	*Warm yellow iris*	29	Crataegus monogyna *(whitethorn)*
12	*Yellow tree lupin*	30	Verbascum bombyciferum
13	*Cream foxgloves*	31	Heracleum giganteum (mantegazzianum)
14	*Clear yellow iris and white lupins*	32	Thuya occidentalis
15	Aruncus sylvester *(meadowsweet)*	33	Viburnum tinus
16	*Pale blue anchusa*	34	Berberis darwinii
		35	Prunus lusitanica

Munstead Wood. The June cottage garden around The Hut, a small house built by Edwin Lutyens in 1894 as his first commission for Miss Jekyll. She lived in it whilst her bigger house was being built and afterwards she used it as a retreat, a studio, a pot-pourri 'factory', or she let it to friends. This garden plan is based on one she drew herself with additions from her own writings. The overwhelming characteristic of the June garden was abundance and almost all the plants blossomed beyond these allotted spaces.

Munstead Wood. The Green Wood Walk opposite the south garden door, from a Country Life *photograph of the early 1900s. The layering, from mown grass to rough grass, to shrubs and trees was a vital part of the Munstead harmony. These rhododendrons are in shades of pink; the one at the back on the left of the picture is possibly the dappled pink and white hybrid raised by Harry Mangles at Littleworth Cross and named 'Gertrude Jekyll'.*

peonies. Another sequence was of pale yellows and blues, iris and anchusas, with warmer yellow iris and lupins leading to orange and apricot oriental poppies and deep orange lilies. The far corner of The Hut's garden was for old but not forgotten friends – old roses, a much loved whitethorn, *Verbascum bombyciferum* and a companion giant (the bane of modern gardeners but much loved by ecologists) the gigantic hogweed, *Heracleum mantegazzianum.*

The Hut was her retreat to the simple life. Miss Jekyll used it when she felt in need of economy or quiet; her housekeeper slept in a tiny room upstairs while her own bedroom was by the front door, next to her studio, and convenient for making sure that the workmen turned up on time when they were building her 'big' house. Lutyens's Munstead Wood was finished in 1897. It was fitted so carefully into the garden that awaited it and built of such mellow Bargate stone by the superb craftsmen of Thomas Underwood, the builders from Dunsfold (who did have a very exacting overseer) that it seemed to have been there forever. This rightness was to become the ultimate test of a good Arts and Crafts house and, oddly, because it was so superbly crafted, at roughly one hundred years old it has hardly aged at all and looks brand new.

With the coming of the house the garden could be finished. Munstead Wood is really a series of garden rooms, but they are disposed according to soil, shelter and purpose, rather than to fit the geometry of a building. The harmony of house and garden depends on the siting of the house and its only piece of formal design, the North Court. This small courtyard, sheltered on three sides by the house, is paved in precious water-marked sandstone, surrounded with box-edged borders of shade-loving greenery brightened with the addition of pots of lilies or hydrangeas in season. From the court the principal path was the thirteen-foot wide Nut Walk, a double avenue of *Corylus maxima* underplanted with red, crimson and brownish polyanthus. For later seasons there are other, parallel, walks through shrubs and roses, and – for September and October – through Michaelmas daisies in purple and pinkish masses.

From the Nut Walk the path of desire led beneath the pergola to a door in the wall and the enclosed Spring garden. The spring flowers overflowed from borders around a tiny lawn, with sheltered seats placed to catch the sun.

Heracleum mantegazzianum

'In Munstead Wood Garden' by Helen Allingham RWS.

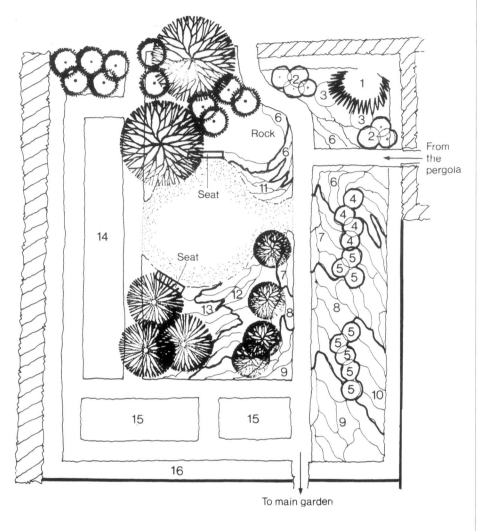

Munstead Wood, the Spring garden.

The larger trees were oaks, the smaller ones hollies and hazels (Corylus maxima)*. The choice of paths through the garden revealed its twin characters, the first spring flowers being beside the right hand path, with beds of tree peonies undercarpeted with silver foliage for later effect beside the other paths. The bold* Yucca gloriosa *(1) and* Acanthus spinosus *(2) were for later effect, but* Euphorbia wulfenii *(3),* Myrrhis odorata *(4) and* Veratrum nigrum *(5) were the heart of groups of base planting, with* Bergenia cordifolia *and* Helleborus niger*. At 6 were the most vivid colours – red and scarlet tulips, orange Crown Imperials and brown wallflowers; at 7 the colours toned down to rose pink tulips,* Dicentra eximia *with drifts of white arabis, white primroses and white daffodils leading to and mixing with 8, the yellows - tulips, wallflowers, daffodils, doronicum and Crown Imperials. The palest colours were in drifts in groups (9) - all pale lemons and whites: tulips, aubretias, wallflowers, pale yellow iris, pale daffodils,* Tiarella cordifolia*, a dreamy and luminous green, and pale primroses with a dash of palest lilac aubretia. The final group, behind the veratrum and mingling with it, were the purple wallflowers and dull red tulips (10). Opposite the path from the pergola a large rock was embedded for height, and was almost covered with carpets of iberis and lithospermum with white tulips; at 11 the colours changed to blues - forget-me-not, blue iris and* Phlox divaricata*. At 12, beneath garlands of* Clematis montana *strung on ropes beneath the nut trees, grey antennaria and* Stachys lanata *merged with pink aubretias and* Phlox amoena *into honesty and purple wallflowers (13). At 14 were yellow tree peonies with* Stachys lanata *and white tulips,* Hebe brachysiphon, Ruta graveolens *and* Leycesteria formosa*; at 15 pink tree peonies with* Stachys lanata *and white tulips, with R. 'Mme Alfred Carrière' on arches. At 16 were red polyanthus with* Heuchera richardsonii.

Because Miss Jekyll felt it was in the nature of spring flowers to be ephemeral they needed a good firm basic background – and she gave them clumps of myrrhis, veratrum and *Euphorbia wulfenii*. Rocks were added to give short flowers height. Drifts of pale yellow primroses, *Tiarella cordifolia*, pale yellow daffodils and iris, double white arabis, candytuft, white anemones and pale lilac aubretias were backed by strong colours of dull red wallflowers, double purple tulips and the veratrum. The pale swathes progressed into stronger yellows – doronicums and Crown Imperials to a climax of colour with orange Crown Imperials, orange tulips and browny wallflowers. Around the little lawn the sun filtered through young oak and hazel leaves and the carefully placed rocks were tumbled with candytuft, aubretias, Alpine phlox, with spires of small white tulips and blue iris. Around and beneath one seat was a scheme of pinks and purples with grey antennaria, pink aubretas, darker pink phlox and pink honesty.

Munstead Wood. The exuberance of planting. Olearia gunniana (phlogopappa) *with hostas, ferns and bergenias in the edging of a shrub border.*

The Spring garden was of interest until early May, then, at the busiest season of work for her army of gardeners and garden boys, there was her hidden garden, surrounded by yew, ilex and holly and with no very obvious entrance to the curious eye. Here she retreated to write. In keeping with the atmosphere the flowers were in subdued and quiet colours – though they sound no less delicious for that – with good contrasts in textures and shapes. Roses – 'Paul's Carmine Pillar' and R. *brunonii*, the heavily scented Himalayan musk rose with white flowers – were encouraged to climb into the hollies. The hidden garden was a passing fancy – its surrounding shrubs soon shaded out the possibilities of growing anything but ferns – but it was a delicious fancy and a romantic concept; how delicious and romantic sound pale lilac pansies surrounded with catmint (a retreat for the beloved Munstead cats) and London pride with white St Bruno's lilies (the best plant relationship she ever

The Munstead cats.
Far left: Tabby *in the catmint.*
Left: Tabby *and the photograph basket.*
From Children and Gardens.

Helen Allingham shows more of Gertrude Jekyll's abundant flower experiments with the massings of colour in her book In a Surrey Garden. *In* Wood and Garden *Gertrude Jekyll wrote of her wish to raise white and blood-crimson hollyhocks of the 'Pink Beauty' strain she had found in a cottage garden, and they are seen in this painting.*

found, wrote Miss Jekyll), followed by pale lilac iris and hart's tongue ferns with clouds of iberis falling from the rocks above. What nostalgia is there in the sound of *Anemone sylvestris* floating amongst stonecrop, catmint, plume hyacinth, fern and asphodel?

And so Munstead Wood comes into high summer – the period from July onwards, when by dint of careful planning and constant attention Miss Jekyll disproved the convention that no English garden was worth looking at and it was best to decamp to the Highlands. Her means of doing this was her herbaceous border. Two hundred feet long and fourteen wide, it was backed by a high sandstone wall covered with shrubs carefully chosen to complement each section of the border. As this border was constantly changing, my plan (pp.32/33), adapted from Miss Jekyll's own plan, shows one version of the planting. Writing in the 1920s she described a variation that was equally faithful to the rules of colour, form and texture, and also involved some of the practical tricks she had learned. She had also refined her use of colour: 'There is one thing to be noted, that whereas all the strong warm

*Munstead Wood, Surrey.
Part of the main flower border
painted in 1900 by Helen
Allingham from her* Happy
England, *originally published
in 1903. In the book Mrs
Allingham gives a detailed
description of the border: 'The
orange red flowers hanging
over the wall are those of the*
Bignonia grandiflora; *the
bushes on either side of the
archway with white flowers are
choisyas, and the adjoining
ones are red and yellow
dahlias, flanked by tritomas
(red hot pokers); the oranges in
front are African marigolds
(hardly reproduced sufficiently
brightly), with white
marguerites; the grey-leaved
plant to the left is the*
Cineraria maritima. *Miss
Jekyll does not entirely keep to
her arrangement of masses of
colour; whilst, as an artist, she
affects rich masses of colour,
she is not above experimenting
by breaking in varieties'.*

colours, deep yellow, orange, scarlet, crimson and any deeper kinds of rich colouring, are best suited for a gradual progression of intermingling shades, the cool colours, and pure blue especially, demand a contrast'.*

At the blue end the border begins with delphiniums and anchusas in true blue, the vivid blue *Commelina coelestis* with *Salvia patens* 'dropped in for the summer'. This was the first practical hint – patches can be temporarily and summarily filled with potted plants. The second hint followed quickly – a strong *Clematis flammula* grown on supports behind the delphiniums can be trained over the tall stalks when the delphinium seed pods have been cut away. The border continues with white dahlias, creamy spiraeas and tall snapdragons of palest yellow: 'pure pale yellow snapdragons are delightful with blue flowers'. At the front of these is a long drift of *Mentha rotundifolia* with leaves variegated with warm white, and the striped grass *Glyceria maxima*. This foliage links to the pure yellows: 'the fine old pure canary yellow' *Calceolaria amplexicaulis*, yellow hollyhocks and dahlias, tall yellow *Thalictrum flavum*, and even a bush of the brightly gold variegated Privet is not out of

* *Colour Planning of the Garden*, Tinley, Humphries and Irving, 1929, introduction by G. Jekyll.

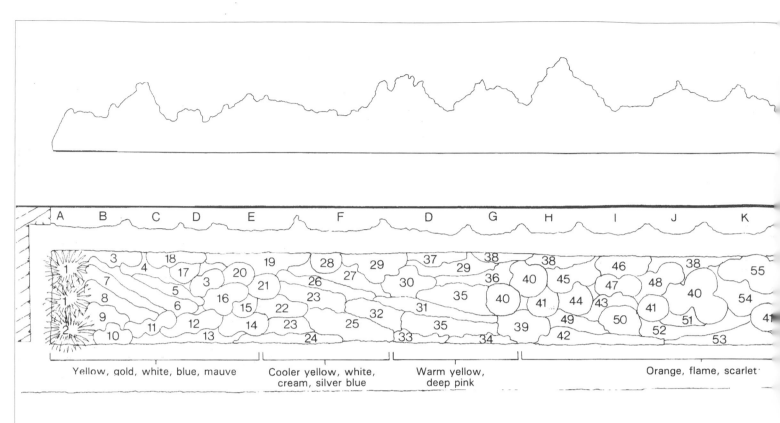

Munstead Wood: the main flower border was Miss Jekyll's masterpiece, the pride of a lady who felt that the best place to be in July and August was at home.

A	*Crimson rambling rose*	8	Campanula lactiflora
B	Robinia hispida	9	Lilium longiflorum
C	Viburnum tinus	10	Crambe maritima
D	Nandina domestica	11	Clematis davidiana (heracleifolia)
E	Abutilon vitifolium	12	Iris pallida dalmatica
F	Eriobotrya japonica	13	Iberis sempervirens
G	Laurus nobilis	14	Ruta graveolens
H	Punica granatum	15	*White lily*
I	Ligustrum japonicum	16	Salvia officinalis
J	Pyrus (*hybrid* P. salicifolia)	17	Ligustrum ovalifolium *'Aureum'*
K	Chimonanthus praecox	18	Verbascum olympicum
L	Fuchsia magellanica gracilis	19	Thalictrum angustifolium *and* Rudbeckia speciosa *'Golden Glow'*
M	Vitis coignetiae	20	Miscanthus sinensis *'Zebrinus'*
N	Magnolia conspicua	21	Aruncus sylvester
O	Choisya ternata	22	Iris orientalis
P	Cistus ciprius	23	*Yellow snapdragon*
Q	Piptanthus laburnifolius	24	Bergenia cordifolia
R	Carpentaria californica	25	Tagetes erecta (*primrose yellow African marigold*)
1	Yucca recurvifolia	26	Filipendula ulmaria *floro plena*
2	Yucca filamentosa	27	Digitalis ambigua (*yellow or white*) *and* Verbascum olympicum
3	*White everlasting pea*	28	*Tall yellow dahlia*
4	*Blue delphinium*	29	Helianthus multiflorus
5	*Pale pink astilbe*	30	Achillea eupatorium
6	Elymus arenarius		
7	*White snapdragon*		

Diagram labels — top row: A B C D E F D G H I J K

Border section labels: Yellow, gold, white, blue, mauve / Cooler yellow, white, cream, silver blue / Warm yellow, deep pink / Orange, flame, scarlet

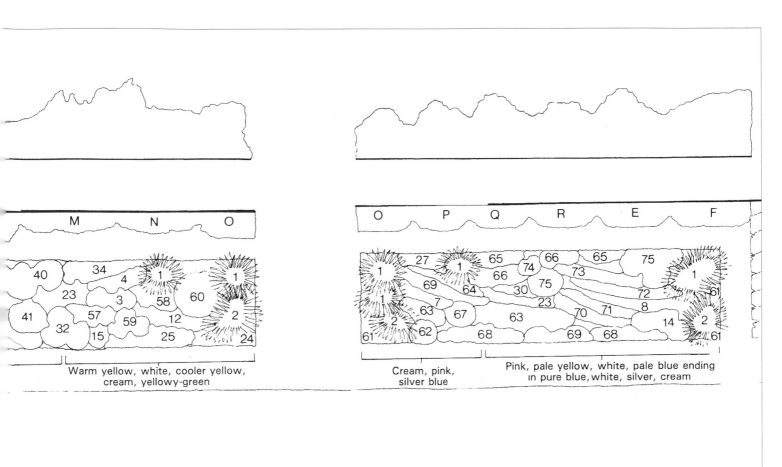

Warm yellow, white, cooler yellow, cream, yellowy-green

Cream, pink, silver blue

Pink, pale yellow, white, pale blue ending in pure blue, white, silver, cream

31	Monarda didyma *(scarlet)* and ligularia *(yellow flowered variety)*	
32	Eryngium oliverianum	
33	Helenium pumilum magnificum	
34	Rudbeckia speciosa newmanii	
35	Coreopsis lanceolata	
36	Helenium striatum	
37	Helianthus *(tall single hybrid)*	
38	*Dark red hollyhock*	
39	Kniphofia galpinii *(dwarf variety)*	
40	Kniphofia uvaria	
41	Gypsophila paniculata	
42	Salvia superba	
43	Lilium tigrinum	
44	Canna indica *(scarlet)*	
45	Dahlia *'Cochineal'*	
46	Dahlia *'Lady Ardilaun'*	
47	Dahlia *Fire King*	
48	Dahlia *'Orange Fire King'*	
49	Lychnis chalcedonica	
50	*Orange hemerocallis*	
51	Phlox paniculata *'Coquilot'*	
52	Gladiolus brenchleyensis	
53	Celosia thomsonii *(red)*	
54	Tagetes erecta *(orange African marigold)*	

55	Canna indica *(tall red)*
56	Tropaeolum majus *(dwarf yellow variety)*
57	Eryngium giganteum
60	Euphorbia wulfenii
61	Stachys lanata
62	Crambe maritima
63	*Blue hydrangeas*
64	Saponaria officinalis
65	*Suphur yellow hollyhock*
66	Echinops ritro
67	Dictamnus (fraxinella)
68	Cineraria maritima
69	Santolina chamaecyparissus
70	Geranium ibericum
71	Aster acris (sedifolius) *(blue)*
72	Aster shortii *(pale mauve)*
73	Aster umbellatus *(tall cream)*
74	Clematis jackmanii
75	*White dahlia*

Munstead Wood. Looking through the gate in the long wall towards the house, with restored planting.

place'. The yellows get even stronger with *Helenium pumilum* (in a large, important drift), oenotheras, and then orange helianthus and *Coreopsis lanceolata*, and deep orange African marigolds. In front are orange pot marigolds, orange and rust tropaeolums and gazanias, with her favourite tritomas in the centre and a backing of dahlias of deep oranges and scarlet.

The climax of the border comes in scarlet and rich blood-red dahlias and hollyhocks softened with the annual *Atriplex hortensis rubra*, red mountain spinach, *Prunus pissardii* (pruned hard annually to keep the shoots red), and *Ricinus communis gibsonii*, the red-leaved castor oil plant. She also uses scarlet phloxes, penstemons and gladioli, and in front 'the grand bedding geranium' 'Paul Crampel'. A blackish-crimson dahlia and deep claret tinted hollyhock are the darkest flowers before the border retreats down the scale, through oranges, warm yellows to white and palest green foliage. The massings of white, the dahlias, the everlasting sweet peas, and the striped maize, make the required break to the pink flowers – hollyhocks and lupins, and grey leaves (*Cineraria maritima*, stachys and santolina – with the flower heads always

Munstead Wood. The restored beds framing the west side of the house, with a glimpse of the workroom door.

clipped off) accompany the pinks through to mauves and purples. Echinops and erigeron are grouped with white *Chrysanthemum maxima*, pink and white gladioli, purple asters, white dahlias and hollyhocks, and creamy Michaelmas daisy, *Aster umbellatus*. As the finale, the sentinel yuccas, stemmed and bush varieties, show their abundant creamy spikes of flowers.

The surprising thing is that, with such a planting scheme, Miss Jekyll proved also how beautiful bedding out could be, if done in her way. So many of the plants she used herself and recommended to her garden clients over and over again were just those beloved of Victorian park keepers, which are still to be found crowding the stagings of English garden centres. It was by judicial, artistic use of sweeps of African marigolds, lobelias and their fellows that her

Munstead Wood. The North Court, set within the 'arms' of the house and forming the focus of the link with the garden. The seat was designed by Lutyens and behind it plaques are set in the wall naming the client, architect and builder (T. Underwood of Dunsfold) for the house. The paving is of watermarked sandstone, specially saved by Miss Jekyll for this court. The enormous hosta leaves, ferns and white lilies were set out in pots; hydrangeas were used later in the season. This was the most formal and special part of the garden; the timbered overhang is the famous Munstead Wood long gallery.

amazing effects were obtained. After all, as she wrote, it was not the fault of the geraniums, lobelias and calceolarias that they were badly used; if they were properly employed they were important and valuable plants.

Miss Jekyll's presence looms over 20th century gardening because she was firm in her allegiance to the irrefutable rules of nature, she used nature as her ally, and she used her artist's judgement to transform discredited planting ideas into delicious pictures. She has been criticised for not actually painting the pictures that would have enshrined her garden artistry, as Claude Monet did, but she did bring integrity and good taste back to English gardening, and some of her influence, however subtle, infiltrates the gardens and garden designs subsequently described in this book. The lady herself settled into her new home and her 'second' gardening life just before the 20th century arrived. The years that followed, up until the outbreak of war in 1914, were as busy as any in her long life. She immediately wrote two books about Munstead Wood: *Wood and Garden* was published in 1899 and *Home and Garden* in 1900. The rest of her important books, eight in number, on roses, lilies, wall and water gardens, flower decorations for the house, her ideas on children's gardens, her colour theories, *Gardens for Small Country Houses* (with Lawrence

Munstead Wood. The contrasting textures of planting – begonias, bergenias and yuccas. Miss Jekyll did not despise bedding plants but used them in her own way: 'The setting of the more solid leaves gives the begonias a better appearance and makes their bright bloom tell more vividly' she wrote in Colour Schemes for the Flower Garden. *Begonias were also planted in colour sequence: yellow, white, palest pink, full pink to deep rose, orange scarlet to orange.*

Weaver) and her book on traditions of *Old West Surrey*, were also published during this period. Her last important book, *Garden Ornament*, was published in 1918, and she continued to contribute to many other books during the rest of her life. In the period before the war she was also writing regularly for *The Garden* (to which she made her first contribution in 1881) and *Country Life* and frequently for *The Guardian*, *The Ladies' Field* and *Gardening Illustrated*.

Munstead Wood was the basis for all her writing and she prided herself that she never recommended any idea that she had not tried first; it was also a nursery business, employing about a dozen gardeners and garden boys, supplying some plants for almost all her clients, as well as selling 'the best hardy plants' and herbs that she listed in her printed catalogue.

And then there were her garden design commissions. At first they had come from friends, mostly in Surrey, and this circle widened as she established herself at Munstead Wood; then Surrey was filling up with a particular brand of rich Edwardian society members who had artistic tastes and patronised the coming architects. She found herself advising on the gardens for two of Robert Lorimer's houses at Hascombe, just up the road from Munstead Wood (Whinfold in 1897 and High Barn in 1901), and when Sir Algernon and Lady

Methuen asked for her help at New Place, Haslemere, in 1901 she encountered a house by Charles Voysey for the first time. Her Arts and Crafts connections continue right through her garden-designing career; she did two gardens for M.H. Baillie-Scott (Greenways at Sunningdale, 1907, and Garden Court, Guildford, 1915), she designed and planted the garden at the Old Manor House, Upton Grey in Hampshire for Charles Holme, the Editor of *The Studio* (1908), she worked at Durbins, the Guildford home of Roger Fry in 1910, and for the eccentric architect Robert Weir Schultz at Tylney Hall, Hampshire, in 1906. Her commissions were endlessly variable: from a small water garden in a dell at Vann, Hambledon, for the architect W.D. Caroe in 1911 to an enormous and complex commission for the hospital gardens of the King Edward VII Sanatorium at Midhurst.

In the years before the war she averaged six of her own commissions a year and may well have been working on six for Lutyens as well. 1906 is an example: she was doing Tylney Hall, Highcroft in Burley, New Forest, which would lead directly to two other Burley gardens and eventually a fourth, as well as gardens in Lincolnshire (her family's native county), at Hindhead and Wimbledon.

The Manor House, Upton Grey, Hampshire. A garden originally designed and planted for Charles Holme, editor of The Studio *in 1908, and painstakingly and brilliantly restored to its Jekyll plans by John and Ros Wallinger.*

Above: the flower terrace, with stone 'mounts' for displaying the best flowers.
Opposite, top: the border of warm colours.
Opposite, below: a yucca detail.

	EACH.	DOZ.
Tritonia aurea Nearly allied to Montbretia, orange and red flowers ; very free-flowering, 2 feet 6 inches ...	3d.	2/6
Uvularia grandiflora A graceful, North-American wood-plant, in habit like a small Solomon's Seal, with drooping yellow flowers	9d.	
Valeriana Phu aurea ; golden foliage in spring	6d.	
Valerian, *see* Centranthus.		
Veratrum nigrum Remarkably handsome foliage developed early in the season, followed by tall spikes of chocolate-coloured flower, 5 to 6 feet	1/6	
Verbascum olympicum (*Mullein*). Pale-grey, downy leaves of large size, and large branching spikes of yellow flowers, 6 to 8 feet	9d.	
,, **phlomoides** This and the preceding are the two best of the tall garden Mulleins, yellow, 6 to 8 feet	6d.	
Veronica Traversii Extremely neat small shrubs with abundant spikes of white bloom	1/-	
,, **buxifolia** A low shrub of the same character ...	9d. & 1/-	
Vinca minor (*Periwinkle*). A small white, of very neat habit collected in Italy	6d.	5/-
,, ,, Red-purple, half double		
,, **acutiflora** A beautiful periwinkle of the larger size flowers bluish-white very late in autumn ; a little known but highly desirable plant	9d.	

Yucca gloriosa — 10/-
Y. recurva — 7/6
Y. filamentosa — 2/-

A page from Miss Jekyll's catalogue of 'Some of the Best Hardy Plants for Border, Shrub and Rock Garden', printed by Craddocks of Godalming. These are the last entries and she has added the yuccas in her own hand.

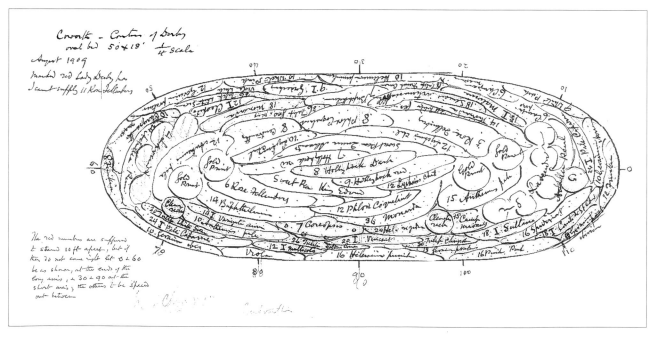

Munstead Wood. The south garden front, photographed by Country Life *in the early 1900s. Miss Jekyll believed, as did Vita Sackville-West after her, that rosemary was the best plant to brush against and run through the fingers as she passed in and out of the garden door. A loose hedge of briar roses runs parallel with the house both sides of the steps; all the paths in the garden were of rolled sand and the borders edged with hard pieces of sandstone called chert, as in this picture.*

Opposite: Coworth Park, Sunningdale, Berkshire. Island bed for the Countess of Derby, 1909. Many of Miss Jekyll's commissions were for a single garden feature such as this. The fifty-foot long bed was intended for high summer – the social high summer of July. The peak of the flower bed is achieved with massed hollyhocks, dark red and red, with the colours graded downwards to the centres of the long sides, ending with warm yellows and pinks. The oval shape of the bed is emphasised with strong patches of golden privet and lavender with Achillea *'The Pearl' calming to hostas and hardy geraniums; these plantings provided the visual punctuation to the whole scheme in terms of colour, shape, texture and the overall form of the bed.*

Hestercombe, Somerset. Four photographs of the grandeur and the details of the restoration of the great set-piece of Lutyens-Jekyll design. Now in the care of the Hestercombe Garden Trust and open all year round.

For Lutyens she was doing the planting plans for their most flamboyant garden, Hestercombe in Somerset, working on a complete set of more intimate plantings for Barton St Mary near East Grinstead, designing flower borders for the Dormy House at Walton Heath, Surrey (later illustrated in *Gardens for Small Country Houses*), discussing the overall layout of New Place at Shedfield by letter with Lutyens, and still overseeing their speculation in good design of a small house and garden, Millmead in Snowdenham Lane, Bramley. It was a typical year.

Miss Jekyll's partnership with Edwin Lutyens affected her life most in the pre-war decade. Legend has it that she made her first suggestion about a planting scheme for the small formal grey garden for Chinthurst Hill, a house Lutyens built across the Wey valley from Munstead in 1893. As many of his early clients were her friends and neighbours, and she introduced him to his most influential patron, Edward Hudson, the owner of *Country Life* magazine, it must be admitted that she was a tremendous help to his career in purely practical terms. However, it was her sureness of taste that was her greatest gift to Lutyens who, though he possessed a prodigal talent and great determination to build beautiful houses, was naïve in his understanding of what his well-to-do clients would want. She educated him as to how his houses should relate to their gardens and how the gardens should be used, all in the traditions of her experience of such things. In turn she had the deepest respect for the brilliant geometrical inventiveness of his talent, which could not be brought into play until the houses had been set properly, according to the advantages and limitations of their sites. It is the basic integrity of houses and gardens within their settings that makes the work of their partnership unique: it was an integrity Miss Jekyll shouldered from her happy childhood in an idyllic landscape – she found Lutyens a receptive pupil, with enough spirit to amuse her – and once this basis was established the details of design fell naturally into place.

Their gardens, full of outdoor rooms, cool vistas of yew, majestic pergolas, circular steps and pools, flower-filled rills, sunbursting arches and quiet courts, correctly dressed in her planting, became an Edwardian craze. Of just over one hundred gardens they worked on together, eighty were done before 1913. Their most famous houses and gardens belong to these years: The Deanery at Sonning, Marsh Court at Stockbridge and Folly Farm, Sulhamstead, in Berkshire.

Lutyens received his great commission to design the Imperial New Delhi in 1912, and this and the war parted them. The war put an end to Lutyens's country house practice but only, it seems, enhanced people's desires to find comfort in their gardens; during the war Miss Jekyll was busy with as many as twelve commissions a year of her own. Towards the end of the war Lutyens asked her to help him with the planting of the War Graves' Commission Cemeteries, which she did, but after that the secluded, flower-filled world of Munstead Wood and the frantic, stressful, peripatetic life of the famous architect drew further and further apart. They remained friends, and in 1928 they worked together for Edward Hudson's last house, Plumpton Place in Sussex, and she made great efforts to please Lutyens's daughter Ursula, who had married Lord Ridley and wanted flowers to warm up her cold Northumberland home. Miss Jekyll died quietly at Munstead Wood in December 1932.

'Aunt Bumps' was Edwin Lutyens's nickname for his angelic fairy godmother.

Selected reading

Gertrude Jekyll's books were popular in her day and many editions were printed: good copies of *Home and Garden, Wood and Garden* and *Colour Schemes for the Flower Garden,* the three best can be found at around £50 from book dealers. These three titles and some others are reprinted in paperbacks, but the best selection, reprinted in the original hardback format at £14.95 each is available from The Antique Collectors' Club; there are eight titles, the three above, plus *Children and Gardens; Roses for English Gardens; Lilies for English Gardens; Wall, Water and Woodland Gardens;* and *A Gardener's Testament.* The Antique Collectors' Club also has Jekyll and Weaver's *Gardens for Small Country Houses,* reprinted as *Arts and Crafts Gardens,* and the spectacular *Garden Ornament;* these were both originally large-format Country Life Books and are very expensive in original editions.

Miss Jekyll has now attracted three biographers: her nephew, Francis Jekyll, wrote his Memoir using all her surviving papers after her death and it was published in 1934: these papers were subsequently scattered or destroyed so Betty Massingham's *Miss Jekyll, Portrait of a Great Gardener* (1966) had to rely on the reminiscences of those who knew her. Sally Festing's *Gertrude Jekyll* (1991) is more substantial and in the exhaustive modern style of biography; she has made effective use of letters, diaries, plans, drawings and paintings which have gradually emerged from hiding places. Not strictly a biography but of immense value and interest is *Gertrude Jekyll: Essays on the life of a working amateur* (Michaelmas Books, 1995) by Miss Jekyll's great niece, Primrose Arnander, and Michael Tooley, a Jekyll scholar of long standing.

Amongst the many other Jekyll-inspired offerings I suggest the following: the best book to analyse her planting design is Richard Bisgrove's *The Gardens of Gertrude Jekyll* (1992). A large collection of Miss Jekyll's black and white photographs has been revealed in *Gertrude Jekyll: A Vision of Garden and Wood* by Judith B. Tankard and Michael R. van Valkenburgh (1990) and Judith Tankard, an American historian who has been researching Gertrude Jekyll with great dedication for many years, has also published *Gertrude Jekyll at Munstead Wood,* 1997. My own, *Gardens of a Golden Afternoon,* telling the story of the Lutyens and Jekyll partnership, first published in 1982, was reissued in a new edition in 1995.

Apart from books, there is an increasing amount of Jekyll-inspired gardening to be seen: her own Munstead Wood has been spectacularly restored in the 1990s and is open for the National Gardens Scheme. Two great Somerset gardens display her planting, Barrington Court (National Trust, open as advertised) has restored 'garden rooms' to her planting plans, and Hestercombe, north of Taunton, (open every day) has her planting for Lutyens's formal garden magnificently maintained, at its best May to September. Other Jekyll gardens will be discovered by good detective work in the annual 'Yellow Book' of *Gardens Open for Charity,* especially in Surrey, Sussex, Berkshire and Hampshire, but gardens cannot be static, and the gardens that are open do vary. Finally, Godalming Museum (01483 426510) in Surrey has a permanent Jekyll exhibit and books and information on its local heroine.

Compton End, near Winchester. G.H. Kitchin's own garden, made before the First World War. Kitchin was an architect and antiquarian, and, like many fellow architects, he found satisfaction in designing and making his own garden of 'rooms'.

New Place, Haslemere. The romantic remains of a kitchen garden designed by Charles Voysey, c.1899.

TWO
The Arts and Crafts Garden

The first definable garden fashion of the 20th century has now come into perspective as the 'Arts and Crafts' garden: this is essentially the mix of formal design with luxuriant planting. It revolved around Gertrude Jekyll, and its heyday coincided with her gardening eminence, from about 1890 to 1914, with some nostalgic late blooming in the 'twenties. These gardens accompany the exodus from stiff and stuffy Victorian drawing rooms into the bright but brief sunlight of Edward VII's nine glorious years, 1901 to 1910. They form part of our image of Edwardian England, of long hot summers which were just right for white dresses drifting over paved terraces, for interminable teas beneath rosy arbours, for crunching along well-rolled gravel paths, twirling a lily in the fingers on the way to long, dreamy conversations in the summer house.

But just as Victorian England bequeathed the wealth and innocence to a large middle class of people who could own and enjoy these gardens, so the gardens themselves were spawned in a long genesis through the 19th century. Garden history is only green cultural history, and the Arts and Crafts gardens were the product of the romantic socialism of Ruskin and Morris, of Philip Webb and William Lethaby, as much as they were demonstrations of fine craftsmanship and a love of nature and of hardy native plants.

Typical of the age, and called by his contemporaries 'the most successful landscape gardener' of his time, was Robert Marnock (1800-80). Marnock specialised in garden settings for exotic tropical and subtropical plants. He was the first curator of the Royal Botanic Society's garden in Regent's Park which he planted with a geographical arrangement; true to Victorian ideals it was not only a garden to delight but also one which would instruct. Marnock

William Robinson in his garden at Gravetye Manor, Sussex.

retired in 1862 to practise privately as a landscape gardener but, in the year before his retirement, he made a decision that changed the course of gardening history. With all the attention being given to the foreign plants he thought it would be wise also to give a place to native English plants. He gave the task of researching and planting the English garden to a young man from Ireland called William Robinson.

William Robinson (1838-1935) made the most of his chance. He had already taken an intense dislike to plants being treated like troops on a parade ground, and his new job allowed him to study plants in their natural settings and to gather good natural gardening ideas from all over Britain and Europe. He soon began to write about what he liked in *The Times* and the gardening papers; by 1870 he was ready to conform to what was almost an obligatory practice for Victorian gardeners and started his own magazine *The Garden*; his book *The Wild Garden* was published in the same year.

Thirteen years before Gertrude Jekyll began her Munstead woodland, Robinson explained the term 'wild garden'; he cited winter aconite flowering in a grove of native trees, lupins staining an islet in a Scottish river purple, a blue carpet of *Anemone apennina* in an English wood; he included more delicious ideas for flower-draped hedges, a meadow of violets, fritillaries, crocus, tulips and narcissi, walls sprouting Cheddar pinks, ferns and saxifrages. He included a list of hardy plants (many of which had once been foreign) and their uses. *The Wild Garden* reads like a good cookery book, mouthwatering in its earnestness, spiced with Robinson's brusqueness.

With his most important book, *The English Flower Garden*, first published in November 1883 (at the moment Miss Jekyll was buying Munstead Wood) Robinson established himself as the Mrs Beeton of the gardening world. He attacked and effectively destroyed the most precious gods of Victorian gardening; he hated the 'crude colours of carpet bedding', and the 'ugly monstrosities' of the topiarist were only fit for a comic journal. Beloved rustic pergolas and palisades were reviled for being complex and ugly, their only merit being that they soon fell down. It is rare to see a garden seat that 'is not an eyesore' was one of his parting quips. Robinson also objected to every part of garden design that was, or had been, the province of the architect; he scourged Paxton's landscape setting for the Crystal Palace at Sydenham and Charles Barry's formal garden at Shrubland in Suffolk, a place Robinson particularly loved. And he brought in his reinforcements. Only a small part – the explosive part – of *The English Flower Garden* was written by Robinson himself; the rest was made up of contributions from the leading gardening writers of the day, including Gertrude Jekyll and her friends, as well as the

Cheddar pink, saxifrage and ferns on a cottage wall from Robinson's The Wild Garden.

The Crystal Palace at Sydenham. A bird's-eye view by James Duffield Harding as exhibited at the Royal Academy in 1854. Sir Joseph Paxton's setting for his Crystal Palace on its permanent site enraged William Robinson, who thought it a prime example of a beautiful landscape made ugly; his particular bête noire *was the 'mosaiculture', the carpet bedding, of the large area nearest the Palace.*

authorities W.J. Bean, then foreman of the arboretum at Kew and later renowned for his definitive *Trees and Shrubs Hardy in the British Isles*, and Peter Barr the great cultivator of daffodils.

For all Robinson's brusqueness and bad temper, which deterred a lot of would-be followers in his day (but only makes him the more alluring in ours), he did galvanise the gardening world into thinking about the welfare and talents of plants, and he published the best of other people's ideas (even if he did sometimes infer they were his own). He was a visionary, with wide interests in every part of landscape design and management, and he loved England deeply, especially that part of it, a thousand acres, which he came to own at Gravetye in Sussex. 'I am the happy owner of the source of the Medway', he wrote to Vita Sackville-West in 1928, when he was ninety years old, and he invited her to visit his garden and woods; but he was also the happy owner of a delightful parterre of flower beds outside his garden door! Privately he admitted that there *was* a place for formal design in the garden, but he had taken his stand, and there were naturally to be consequences.

Seven years after the first edition of *The English Flower Garden*, a civil engineer and fellow of the Linnaean Society, Henry Ernest Milner, published in 1890 a rather different book, *The Art and Practice of Landscape Gardening*. Milner felt himself to be the natural successor to Capability Brown and Humphry Repton, and he was right in thinking that Repton's reputation had been discredited for the wrong reasons: that vast ornamental parks, nullifying hundreds of acres of otherwise good agricultural soil, were neither desirable nor practical in an early 19th century landscape of recurring agricultural depression. But that did not mean that his theories were wrong; on the contrary, Repton's analysis of the underlying reasons for the beauty of the English landscape were more than ever valid for the creation of landscapes and gardens. In the hands of architects, wrote Milner, and even under the influence of artists, nature was in fetters. The

Nature seldom presents a straight line in any of her forms, unless in the seeming regularity of an oceanic horizon, or the smaller line of water surface. A straight line is the product of art, for even the apparently upright line of the Parthenon columns results from a delicate curve. Nature presents in her broad effects and graduated detail, an infinity of curvilinear features.

There is beauty in contrast of form.

Lines or objects placed in a direction going from the line of vision, make the space so marked appear longer, whilst lines running across it, make the space appear less distant.

Grass clothing the ground surface has an expression of stability and repose; in colour it illustrates the tint of foliage to which it forms a base and background. A calculated shadow on a lawn is a resource of value for the artistic use of natural effect.

Trees and shrubs, by the contrast of foliage, give variety, and a gradation of colours may promote the idea of distance. They should clothe the hilltops and slopes in masses of irregular outline. A skyline of trees should not be continuous, but should be broken. A valley appears deeper by not being planted, as a hill appears higher than it really is by being planted to its summit. Single trees emphasise falling ground, and they, like the shadowy regions of a wood, conduce to a sensation of mystery, subtly stimulating imagination. They induce an idea of possible shelter that bestows pleasurable sensations.

Falling ground appears shorter, whilst level ground at the base of a hill, as also rising ground, seems longer than it in reality is. The idea of spaciousness can be artificially promoted, particularly by the breaking of continuous lines and hard boundary lines, and by providing various objects for the eye to count, just outside the direct line of sight.

Vision invariably travels down a hollow, or depression, or through any opening. Thus the idea of distance may be created, and the eye be conducted to realise what is desired.

Trees especially serve to frame a particular view.

In every situation a beyond implies discovery, and affects the imagination.

The beauty of water, in motion or still, is of universal acceptance. The created character of a water-feature must be consonant with the surrounding land; for fitness to surrounding conditions is a measure of beauty to both. A lake expresses spaciousness; but much of its charm is due to its outline. A river expresses action.

Trees or high banks on the edge of water diminish its extent and make it dull. An opening in the trees, or the lowering of a high bank, make a gleam of light, and the length in that direction appears greater.

Words from Ernest Milner's The Art and Practice of Landscape Gardening, *1890, outlining the essence of his 'litany' of beauty in landscape terms carried down from Humphry Repton.*

landscape architect was her only true champion. The term 'landscape architect' implying a much wider role than that of mere gardener, was in common use in America but hardly ever heard in England at this time. Milner's book contained a litany of beauty in landscape terms which calmly, even blandly, set out the virtues of the serpentine line, the visual quality of rising and falling ground, of lines and groups, the colours, textures, forms of trees, and the effects of water. It was a litany of beauties that were so natural that everyone took them for granted so did not *see* them.

Milner was doing for the landscape exactly what Robinson and Jekyll did for flowers – advocating appreciation. And he seemed such a quiet man, content with little rustic boathouses and bridges, and with conservatories and terraces as perfectly allowable conventions so long as they were sited according to the sacred rules handed down from the paintings of the landscape masters Poussin and Claude. But quiet Mr Milner brought the world of gardening down about his ears. The combination of William Robinson's wild flowers and Milner's lakes 'expressing their natural outline' was just too much for the architects.

At first it was a battle joined in velvet gloves. Some people influence by bombast, some by caress. John Dando Sedding (1838-91) was of the latter kind.

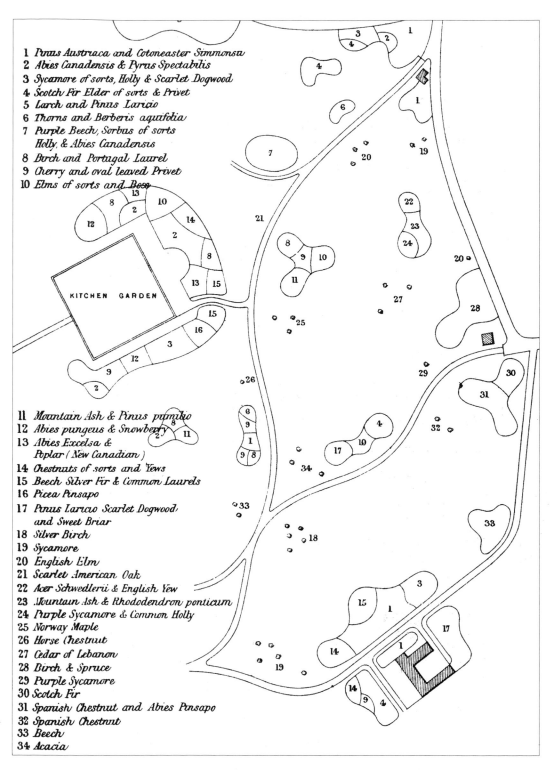

1 *Pinus Austraca and Cotoneaster Simmonsii*
2 *Abies Canadensis & Pyrus Spectabilis*
3 *Sycamore of sorts, Holly & Scarlet Dogwood*
4 *Scotch Fir Elder of sorts & Privet*
5 *Larch and Pinus Laricio*
6 *Thorns and Berberis aquifolia*
7 *Purple Beech, Sorbus of sorts*
    Holly, & Abies Canadensis
8 *Birch and Portugal Laurel*
9 *Cherry and oval leaved Privet*
10 *Elms of sorts and Box*

KITCHEN GARDEN

11 *Mountain Ash & Pinus pumilio*
12 *Abies pungeus & Snowberry*
13 *Abies Excelsa &*
    Poplar (New Canadian)
14 *Chestnuts of sorts and Yews*
15 *Beech Silver Fir & Common Laurels*
16 *Picea Pinsapo*
17 *Pinus Laricio Scarlet Dogwood*
    and Sweet Briar
18 *Silver Birch*
19 *Sycamore*
20 *English Elm*
21 *Scarlet American Oak*
22 *Acer Schwedlerii & English Yew*
23 *Mountain Ash & Rhododendron ponticum*
24 *Purple Sycamore & Common Holly*
25 *Norway Maple*
26 *Horse Chestnut*
27 *Cedar of Lebanon*
28 *Birch & Spruce*
29 *Purple Sycamore*
30 *Scotch Fir*
31 *Spanish Chestnut and Abies Pinsapo*
32 *Spanish Chestnut*
33 *Beech*
34 *Acacia*

Plan of layout and planting around a country house from Milner's The Art and Practice of Landscape Gardening. *J.D. Sedding's attack on the landscape school as having little art, using paths that represented tortured horseshoes and planting trees in a happy-go-lucky way, was addressed to William Robinson but clearly aimed at this kind of work.*

J.D. Sedding's design for the decoration of a fireplace, with owls, poppies, woody nightshade, moths and a stag beetle, is typical of his work inspired by a deep love of nature.

His book, *Garden Craft Old and New,* was published by his friends shortly after his death. Sedding was a most sincere artist-craftsman, with a love of fun, a hearty laugh and a zest for life which endeared him to everyone around him. With these characteristics he was one of the most inspiring 'fathers' of the Arts and Crafts Movement in architecture; a founder member of the Art Workers' Guild, he was also enthusiastically religious as well as having a deep love of nature. He had 'discovered' gardening while working in his own garden at West Wickham in Kent, and in pursuing his discovery he found his love for the garden pleasances of the days of the Tudors and Stuarts. He assumed that Loudon, in calling the irregular, modern or natural style 'English', implied that the English had had no style until Brown and Repton. Those two 'heaven-directed geniuses', who purported to have discovered an 'English' style, had actually swept away comforting gardens that we already possessed. Sedding was therefore, in his good-natured way, the first champion of the old, formal gardens. He criticised Robinson for not allowing any art into the garden and conceding everything to nature, and he implied a criticism of Milner and the landscape school by saying that they used 'so little art' that there was nothing for nature to destroy.

The Formal Garden in England by Reginald Blomfield, another mentor of Arts and Crafts architects, was published the year after Sedding's book. This, in its original editions, is a delightful book to handle, beautifully printed with alluring line drawings by the architect F. Inigo Thomas. In its time it was rather like a gift-wrapped stick of gelignite. It was Blomfield who crystallised the feelings for 17th century gardens. They were gardens of their time, 'when tradition was active' and all the arts were aware of each other. Garden design took its place in the 'great art of architecture', resulting in a well-ordered harmony that was characteristic of the house and garden in England down to the middle of the 18th century. Blomfield, like Sedding, plumps wholeheartedly for Haddon Hall, Melbourne, Montacute, Avebury, Brympton d'Evercy and Pitmedden, gardens of regular courts, stately terraces, herb-filled knots, parterres of coloured gravels, rectangular ponds, arbours, palisades, groves, dovecots and sundials *ad infinitum.*

Robinson prolonged the battle of words with a reply called *Garden Design and Architects' Gardens,* published quickly in 1892. But his serious difference, it was only too clear now, was not so much with the architects as with the landscape architects 'in his own camp'. He sneered at 'worrying Nature into a resemblance to Claude' and claimed the English landscape to be more beautiful in reality than anything that was *ever* painted. He had 'never seen a

George Samuel Elgood (1851-1943), 'Melbourne', from Some English Gardens *by George S. Elgood and Gertrude Jekyll, 1904. One of the old gardens beloved by Arts and Crafts' architects.*

painted landscape to compare with the view of the Suffolk countryside from the Chestnut Walk at Shrubland', he cried, diverting the attack to Charles Barry for his formal garden there. But it turns out that Barry's chief crime was in allowing coloured gravels in the beds and along the house walls, and once Robinson had been allowed to fill the terrace beds and clothe the house walls with real plants the architect's design was perfectly allowable!

It really was a battle of words, and Blomfield had the last say in the preface to the third edition of *The Formal Garden in England*, published in 1901. He acknowledged the 'acrid controversy' that had raged because architects said gardeners knew nothing about design, and gardeners said that architects knew nothing about gardening. He admitted that formal design was not always correct for a place and it must not be produced blindly but, equally, 'that favourite device of the landscape gardener, who cannot resist the manufacture of a hummock in order that he may wind his path all round it, is not so good either'. Blomfield falls on some of Robinson's more picturesque phrases, but sadly his real difference is clearly with the landscape architects, whom he accuses of having little theory, no art and precious little to show. They did not realise it themselves but Robinson and Blomfield were united in their arguments against the new breed of landscapists, the 'landscape architects'; sadly these differences opened a rift which has not been healed to this day.

Blomfield and Sedding were interested in gardens as an intrinsic part of their Arts and Crafts philosophy, a cult which began among architects in the 1880s. It was inspired by William Morris and the Society for the Protection of Ancient Buildings which he founded in accord with his passion for the old building traditions and

Three line drawings by F. Inigo Thomas from Blomfield's The Formal Garden in England: *they are,clockwise, the terrace at Brympton d'Evercy, Somerset, the garden with terraces at Montacute, Somerset and the garden gate at Avebury, Wiltshire.*

virtues of hand craftsmanship. A strong love of England and all things English was a mark of the movement. Just as Morris had started his 'anti-scrape' crusade with churches, so church restoration and architecture formed the background for a whole group of architects who were to make their mark with Edwardian country houses. All architects could not but become aware of 'gardens' during 'the formal versus natural' controversy, and their holistic philosophy happily embraced the surroundings of their houses, decreeing that the garden and its every detail should be as honestly beautiful and free from pretension as the house and its every content. That such a highly individual philosophy welded itself into a movement is due solely to the office apprenticeship system of training architects that prevailed in late Victorian England. The young would-be architect was influenced by both the personality and the work of his 'master', and found himself rubbing shoulders with as many as a dozen other young men with enthusiasms and ambitions. It is not at all surprising that the good-natured Sedding, with his deep love of hand craft-work, turned out Ernest Gimson and Ernest Barnsley who migrated to the remote Cotswolds to hand-build furniture and houses. (Rodmarton Manor and its garden, the greatest fulfilment of their beliefs, is the subject of my next chapter.) Blomfield seems to have been a much smoother character, able to enthuse and write at will; he recovered from his Arts and Crafts phase to become very grand, and his garden at Mellerstain for Lord Binning is a beautifully crafted set piece that typifies his work. His fellows W.R. Lethaby and Ernest Newton were also uninterested in the earthier aspects of gardens. Lethaby's Avon Tyrell in the New Forest, much admired by Miss Jekyll, had flower motifs indoors and architect-drawn details for garden steps and walls, but there the gardening connection ceased; while Newton seemed happy with gardens as formal but attractive settings for his comfortable neo-Georgian houses.

Among this clannishness there was one extreme individual, Charles Francis Annesley Voysey (1857-1941). Voysey's houses have a distinctive severity that makes them unmistakable but often less appealing than the more romantic

Reginald Blomfield's garden layout for Mellerstain, Berwickshire, for Lord Binning, 1910 (drawn by Adrian Berrington). This was one of Blomfield's most ambitious schemes and has all the elements of architectural tradition that he championed in The Formal Garden in England.

'*Perspective of Fouracres, West Green, Hampshire*', drawn by Thomas Hamilton Crawford, 1902. Ernest Newton, was not greatly interested in gardens, but he typifies the attitude of architects of comfortable country houses, in that he wished his houses to have organised and flowery settings. This watercolour shows exactly the kind of controlled luxuriance, albeit in vague and unidentifiable plants, that the Arts and Crafts mainstream expected.

work of Lutyens. The severity is softened, on closer encounter, by Voysey's devotion to drawing every detail of the design, cutting his heart motif into the smallest cupboard doors, adding a bird or flower to a metal air vent, designing a bird bath and pigeon cote as well as garden furniture and summerhouses. But his perfectionism also worked in the opposite direction and he was the most humble of architects in his subservience to his sites. He used his building design vocabulary – long bands of windows, sloping buttresses against soft rough-cast walls, precisely pointed gables and sweeping roofs, if and where individual features harmonised with their setting. This is demonstrated at Oakhurst in Sussex, and at Greyfriars, the house he built for Julian Sturgis in 1896 on the south-facing slope of the Hog's Back near Guildford.

The Hog's Back is so named because it is an elongated ridge of chalk that forms a bridge between the north Hampshire downland and the North Downs in Surrey. Greyfriars, too, is elongated, dominated by the horizontals of its window bands with a long grey roof that originally swept almost to the ground at the garden end. A narrow terrace crosses the south-facing front forming a natural balcony, guarded with a retaining wall, before the land falls away to Puttenham Heath below. The view across this balcony is of a vast expanse of southern England; the only garden necessary is a small formal room, also elongated, leading west from the gable end. From Puttenham Heath Greyfriars appears like some exquisite geological stratum revealed amongst the trees that hang on the chalk slope.

In contrast, on a more softly sloping site, Voysey built Oakhurst, at Fernhurst in Sussex for Mrs E.F. Chester in 1901. The house nestles in its slope surrounded by wild flowers, orderly hedges and garden walls, with strong planting at their feet – Voysey's favourite device for linking his houses to their gardens. His use of this device is fresco-like, and when he painted his delightful watercolours of his houses the flowers do tend to look like the borders on a plate. He loved the visual qualities of flowers but clearly did not understand the science too well.

In another garden, New Place at Haslemere, where the design motifs of the house are repeated all over the garden in summerhouses, gates and walls, Voysey wanted borders full of rue, undoubtedly for its romantic bluish haze but also, perhaps, because its young leaves are heart-shaped. Lady Methuen, for whom

C.F.A. Voysey's drawing of Greyfriars, Surrey. Voysey's love of nature went one step further into faithfulness to his landscape setting. Greyfriars' elongated bands of windows and long roof reflect the shape of its cliffside site – painted white with a grey roof it harmonises with the chalk ridge of the Hog's Back. The house appears like some exquisite geological stratum revealed amongst the trees, with a long terrace on the garden front and a formal garden to one side.

C.F.A. Voysey's design for a house called Oakhurst in Ropes Lane, Fernhurst, Sussex, 1901. Watercolour perspective painted by the architect. The house, built of brick and rough cast, with local stone used for garden walls and terraces, is carefully fitted into a sloping site. The gentle mix of wild meadow leading to a formal garden with old-fashioned flowers, illustrates the sense of well-being that Voysey's integrity imparted to his work.

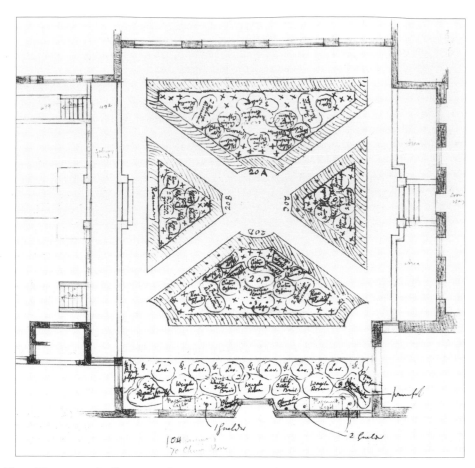

King Edward VII Sanitorium. Gertrude Jekyll's planting plan for the West Rosemary Garden.

New Place was built, was adamant: no rue, she could not stand the smell. She resorted to Miss Jekyll, who placed flowering shrubs on Voysey's walls and decreed a rose garden. It was divided into four beds, each bed containing four half-standards ('Viscountess Folkestone', 'Madame Lambard', 'Madame Abel Chatenay' and 'Grace Darling') standing among dwarf bushes of 'Marquise de Salisbury', 'Little White Pet', 'Camoëns' and 'Grüss an Teplitz' respectively. The walls were clothed with jasmines, choisya, clematis and *Robinia hispida*, mixed with noisette climbing roses 'Céline Forestier', 'Gloire de Dijon', 'Alister Stella Gray' and 'Maréchal Niel'.

A drawing from Gardens and their Form and Design *by Frances Garnet, Viscountess Wolseley, who shared Gertrude Jekyll's interests in domestic architecture and 'cottage economy', and who founded the Glynde School for Lady Gardeners which did the planting work at the King Edward VII Sanatorium.*

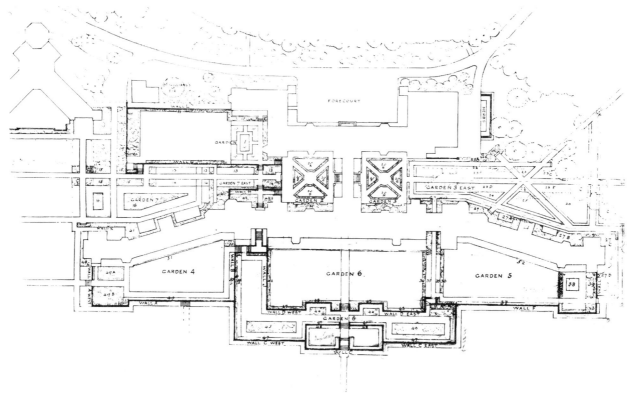

H. Percy Adams's and Charles Holden's plan for the King Edward VII Sanatorium, Midhurst, Sussex, 1908. Gertrude Jekyll provided planting plans for seven separate gardens (see detail opposite) for the patients within the framework of this plan, and subsidiary planting schemes for the rest of the site and the Medical Superintendent's House.

Maybe if she had not been so monopolised by Lutyens, Miss Jekyll would have been able to help Voysey bring more life to his gardens. The problem was mostly a simple matter of work-load, there being one Miss Jekyll and at least twenty architects whom she knew and was in sympathy with. She knew Lutyens's office fellows Herbert Baker and Robert Weir Schultz; some remaining shreds of her voluminous correspondence show that she did help Baker with ideas for Groote Schurr, his house for Cecil Rhodes, but – probably because of the sad Baker/Lutyens feud over New Delhi – her only formal work for Baker was to plant Winchester College's Memorial Cloister in 1923. Weir Schultz turned to her in desperation with his vast commission for work at Lionel Phillips's Tylney Hall in Hampshire; he could clearly manage the formal gardens and garden buildings but a wilderness was required. A picture remains of the bearded Schultz, who had a tendency to wear Arab clothes, standing in a wet copse at Tylney painstakingly marking every bush and tree in order to send Miss Jekyll a survey drawing; in return she rearranged the woodland with a series of delectably curving paths to produce a wilderness.

On rare occasions, her work was equal in importance to that of the architect. H. Percy Adams, and particularly his assistant Charles Holden, carried Arts and Crafts philosophies into the building of hospitals, and in 1908 Miss Jekyll was asked for help with the garden plans for the King Edward VII Sanatorium at Midhurst, which was being built specifically for the treatment of consumptive diseases on a ridge five hundred feet high overlooking the Rother valley. The Sanatorium was spread along the ridge site to embrace a series of small courts and gardens so that every patient had access to sheltered and scented air. Miss

Deanery Garden, Sonning, Berkshire. Designed by Lutyens for Sir Edward Hudson, 1901. The garden front of the house with the mock bridge is seen here from across the terrace lawn.

Jekyll prepared plans for seven small gardens – mostly little rooms of knot garden character – which she planted with variations of scented flowers and herbs, using rosemary as a hedge plant for border edges. She was helped in this commission by Frances Garnet, Viscountess Wolseley (1872-1936), whose Glynde School for Lady Gardeners did the planting at the hospital.

In 1900 William Robinson had sold his interest in *The Garden* to Edward Hudson, who had started his magazine *Country Life* in 1897. This latter magazine has assumed such a gloss that it is difficult for us now to realise just how important the word 'country' was then; the word, and the magazine, symbolised and supported the Arts and Crafts lifestyle in every aspect, and captured the growing importance of gardens to a society that would pay for the work of all the architects already mentioned, and especially for Lutyens. Edward Hudson was a very private, sombre and inarticulate man who vented his passions through his publications. He loved the English countryside (especially its ancient castles and 17th century manor houses and their gardens), Jacobean oak furniture, 17th century Dutch interiors and romantic flowers. He had an enormous respect for Miss Jekyll and, in their different ways, they believed in the young architect Lutyens. It seems almost that these two solid characters willed their own integrity into his brilliantly inventive work; but the love of life and the joy of architecture were Lutyens's very own, and with them, and Miss Jekyll, he brought the Arts and Crafts garden to life.

At first it was a logical, environmental process. The Surrey sandstone houses

The garden side of Deanery Garden viewed through the trees of the orchard. The original orchard was retained when the house was built and turned by Miss Jekyll into a wild garden of mown paths through rough grass sprinkled with spring meadow flowers.

stood on sandstone terraces with sandstone paths leading beneath oak pergolas to small seats surrounded by yews. The seats, pergola piers, and paths would enjoy the same decoration in layers of tiles that was used on the house walls. The naturally thin sandy soil suited the grey-leaved sunlovers, santolinas, lavenders and *Stachys lanata*, as well as the old shrub roses, honeysuckles and vines on the pergolas. The dry-stone terrace walls provided happy niches for rock plants – candytufts, aubretias, rock roses, pinks and valerian.

One of the best of these early Surrey gardens was Orchards, not far from Munstead Wood, for the sculptress Julia Chance, who was also a keen gardener. Orchards's site has a wonderful view over the Thorncombe valley which the design takes fully into account, and the garden is laid across the slope below eye level, with sheltered rooms, walks and a large and useful *jardin potager* for vegetables and flowers.

But with Deanery Garden at Sonning near Reading, the first house for Edward Hudson, which was finished in 1901, came the culmination of all the Surrey lessons learned so well, together with an added touch of brilliance. Deanery Garden captured the feeling of old England. Hudson wrote: 'So naturally has the house been planned that it seems to have grown out of the landscape rather than to have been fitted into it.' It is a remarkable performance. It is also a remarkably apt symbol of all the Arts and Crafts Movement represented with that Movement's, and Hudson's, aesthetic puritanism taken to a pitch. In a landscape and village that devote themselves to the grandly flowing Thames, where everyone, but everyone, built lavish villas with lawns floating down to the river, this house, the finest of them all, takes no notice of the river whatsoever. It could not, for Hudson had found himself an old orchard site, completely enclosed by the village streets and lanes, with no outlook. When Lutyens first surveyed it he carefully noted the positions of the orchard trees so that most of them could be left undisturbed. He fitted the house logically to the side of the main street, and used less than half the orchard for formal garden with the rest left wild. The fruit trees were underplanted with a succession of spring and summer flowers and paths mown to emphasise the vistas.

The garden front of The Deanery is gloriously asymmetrical, with a splendid oriel window balanced by concentric recessing around the garden door and a massive chimney sweeping skywards beside it. From the door a mock bridge, really a device for changing levels, leads to an imposing set of circular steps into the orchard grass. This main axis is slightly off centre. On the left and higher level as one emerges from the garden door are the detailed parterre gardens; on the right, and lower down, is a long level lawn cut by a stone-edged iris rill – Miss Jekyll's device for bringing the wild water plants that she loved (yellow water iris, arrowhead, water forget-me-not, flowering rush) into the formal garden setting. The borders of this lawn were planted in delicate colours and an old-fashioned mixture of herbs and scented flowers absolutely in keeping with the faintly Elizabethan glories of the house. There was, after all, a way of restoring the old gardens of England to life again.

Though most of Lutyens's country houses were of a moderate size according to Edwardian standards (and seem large to us today) Miss Jekyll was anxious that they should set an example of good design in terms of a small house and

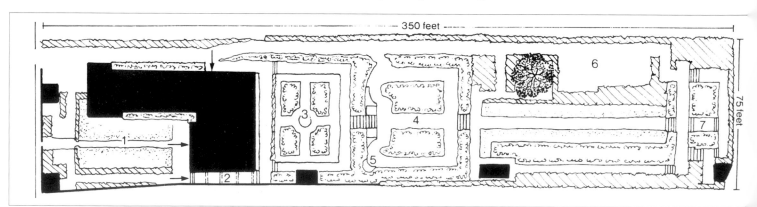

Layout plan for the garden at Millmead, Bramley, Surrey. The rectangular plot was completely bounded by other properties on the east and west. The foot entrance from the road (Snowdenham Lane) enters the court (1), through which a central path leads to the front door, with a secondary access to the garden via the pergola (2). On the garden front, the rose garden (3) consisted of four beds of hybrid tea roses of toning colours, a single variety in each bed (or they may have been divided with lavender into different varieties, with surrounding borders of varied greens, good textures and pale flowers). The second level of the garden (4) had a small dipping well in the corner (5); the third level is the longest with a large old pear tree and the compost and rubbish areas (6) concealed behind hedges. The final level (7) has a third summerhouse, a sundial and another dipping well, and overlooks the woods of Bramley Park. The linear layout belies the softness of this garden – produced by luxuriant planting which spilled out from its allotted spaces. All the paths were of natural rolled sand and there were no harsh edges.

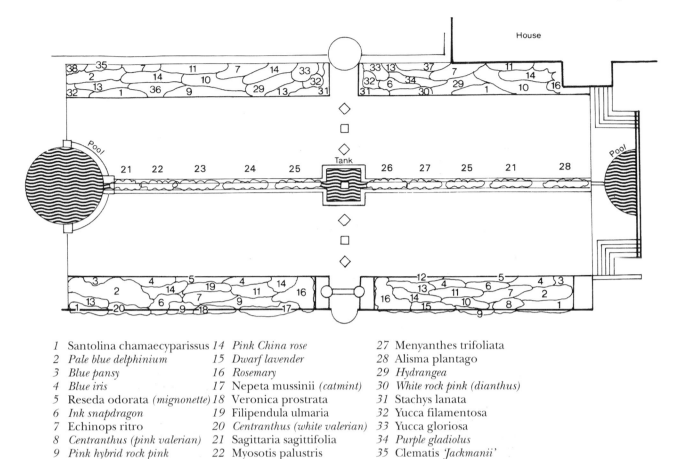

1 Santolina chamaecyparissus	*14 Pink China rose*	27 Menyanthes trifoliata
2 Pale blue delphinium	*15 Dwarf lavender*	28 Alisma plantago
3 Blue pansy	*16 Rosemary*	29 Hydrangea
4 Blue iris	*17 Nepeta mussinii (catmint)*	30 White rock pink (dianthus)
5 Reseda odorata (mignonette) *18 Veronica prostrata*		31 Stachys lanata
6 Ink snapdragon	*19 Filipendula ulmaria*	32 Yucca filamentosa
7 Echinops ritro	*20 Centranthus (white valerian)*	33 Yucca gloriosa
8 Centranthus (pink valerian)	21 Sagittaria sagittifolia	34 Purple gladiolus
9 Pink hybrid rock pink	22 Myosotis palustris	35 Clematis 'Jackmanii'
10 Lavender	23 Sparganium ramosum	36 Chrysanthemum maximum
11 Pink hollyhock	24 Iris laevigata	37 Clematis flammula
12 Lilac pansy	25 Butomus umbellatus	38 Hamamelis mollis
13 White snapdragon	26 Iris pseudacorus	

Gertrude Jekyll's planting plan for the borders of the terrace at Deanery Garden typifies the delicate, refined, old-fashioned planting that was so appropriate for this garden – with touches of sophistication provided by the yuccas, iris and gladioli. The colours are kept to the delicate pinks, pale blues and silver, with occasional touches of purple; the plants on the south wall – santolina (1), pink snapdragon (6), pink centranthus (8), rock pink (9), rosemary (16), catmint (17) and Veronica prostrata *(18) – would hang over the retaining terrace wall. 21-28 are flowering water plants in the iris canal – cream, rose and purple flowers with a touch of yellow from the* Iris pseudacorus *(26).*

garden. The result was Millmead, built in 1905-6 on a long thin plot beside a lane in Bramley, which overlooked her childhood home, Bramley Park. Millmead is L-shaped, in early Georgian style and 'reminiscent of some of the small houses of good type built in England under Dutch influence in the early years of the 18th century', as Miss Jekyll described it. It is set behind a high stone wall, with a quiet entrance court; on the garden side, the garden – long and thin – was terraced in flowery sequence down to a seat overlooking Bramley Park woodlands.

Deanery Garden and Millmead were each honoured with a chapter to themselves in Miss Jekyll's book of the Arts and Crafts return to Englishness, *Gardens for Small Country Houses*, first published in 1912. She worked on the book with Lawrence Weaver, then Architectural Editor of *Country Life*, and it portrays exactly the world they shared. Page after page of Charles Latham's pictures of flowers scrambling up to deep gables, of lilies and lavender against yew walls, of little conical-roofed gazebos, rose-wreathed pergolas, steps, statues, pools and

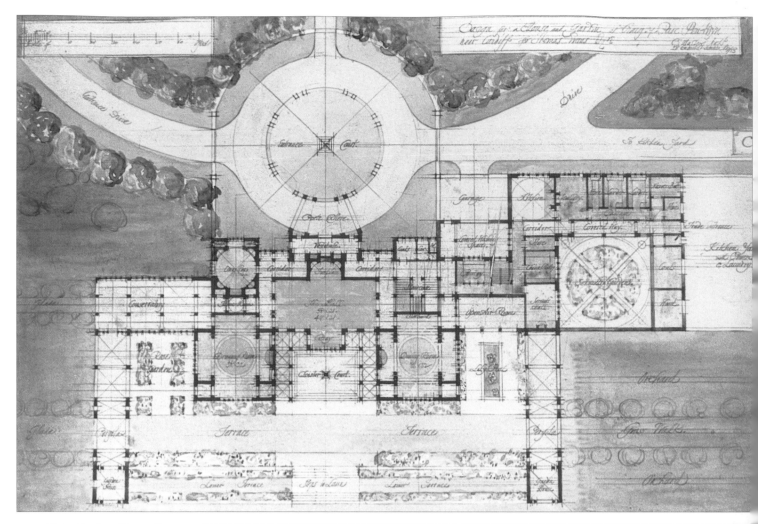

Top: Craig y Parc, Gwent, house and garden by Charles Mallows 1913-14, one of the first layouts to signify the arrival of the motor car in the garden.

Castle Tor, Torquay. An Arts and Crafts garden which still exhibits ornaments such as the dolphin head, illustrated by Gertrude Jekyll in Gardens for Small Country Houses.

C.E. Mallows's design for a house and garden near Sherborne, Dorset, 1907. Mallows was one of the lesser-known architects whose work was illustrated in Gardens for Small Country Houses. *He wrote his own series of articles on architectural gardening in* The Studio, *1908-10, and all his work is in this very formal manner.*

seats, all given the accolade of good design, of approved Englishness. Everyone had a mention: Blomfield, Detmar Blow, Walter Cave (who was in Sir Arthur Blomfield's office with Reginald Blomfield), Gimson, L. Rome Guthrie, Lethaby, Lorimer, C.E. Mallows, Thomas Mawson, Harold Peto, Baillie-Scott, Unsworth and Triggs and Voysey and – over and over again – Mr Lutyens. It seemed a perfect world, but there were, included in the book, the seeds of discord.

M.H. Baillie-Scott was a young architect from the Isle of Man who did not come from the London office system. Nor did he attract a stream of rich clients – just enough to start him off – and then his most valuable work was done on comparatively small houses and gardens. He published his philosophy in his book *Houses and Gardens*, published by Hudson's friend and partner George Newnes, in 1906. In the book, along with the 'bluebell' bedstead (with a stylised bluebell on head, foot and bedcover) and the 'daffodil' dresser (with a single daffodil painted on each door), he attended to the design of a garden for the smaller house owner: 'On sunny hills, where the purple heather grows, purple heather shall be the dominant note in his garden scheme; or by the sea, the thrift which blooms on the cliff shall be invited to lend its pink blossoms to edge his paths'. Baillie-Scott went back to Robinson's wild gardens, unmown orchards with spring flowers and paths for traffic lines, water let out of its formal pool to became a stream running back into the wild wood. He advocated the cottage gardener's good sense in mixing vegetables and flowers, function and beauty. And there's the rub – that word, function. In all the gorgeous pages of *Gardens for Small Country Houses* it was ornament and beauty that were important, not function and use. Edwardian gardens were for pleasure and to provide a decorative background for beautiful people; Baillie-Scott slated 'this modern conception of

M.H. Baillie-Scott, Houses and Gardens, *1906. Design for a pergola for Rose Court.*

Opposite above: Heather Cottage, Sunningdale, Surrey (now demolished).
Opposite below: 48 Storey's Way, Cambridge. House and garden 1912-13, both restored by the architect Diane Haigh.

Garden plan for Burton House, Longburton, Dorset, also from Houses and Gardens, *1906. It illustrates Baillie-Scott's ideal: 'A garden of average size may include a lawn for tennis, croquet or bowls, an orchard, a kitchen garden, and a flower garden in two main divisions – one a rose garden which may be square or nearly square in form, and the other, which may be long and narrow, devoted to perennial flowers'. All the 'outdoor apartments' were to be connected with straight walls bordered with perennial flowers.*

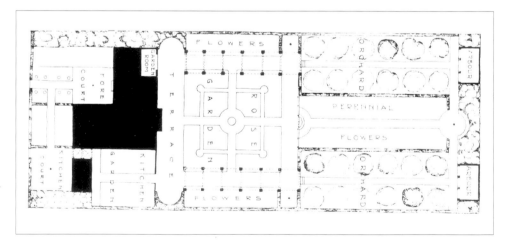

beauty, allied solely to uselessness'. His suburban garden of average size would include a lawn for tennis, croquet or bowls, an orchard, a kitchen garden, a place for sitting, for walking, for cut flowers, for roses. He has started us on the slippery road that crams ever more differing uses – swimming pools, children's playgrounds – into an ever smaller space. The quality of repose in the Edwardian English garden is in danger of being lost forever.

And then there was the old professional jealousy that would not die. In 1908 Lutyens was confident enough as an architect of gardens to take on his major rival Thomas Mawson. The encounter had more than a touch of David and Goliath. Mawson, like Edward Milner, imagined himself Repton's successor and he was successful. He was born in a small Lancashire village, had studied drawing at the Lancaster Mechanics' Institute and, by sheer hard work, had made a successful business, Lakeland Nurseries at Windermere, with his brothers. From this base he built up a garden design practice which he extended to public landscape projects all over England. Lakeland Nurseries attracted many rich clients, including Lord Leverhulme and Thomas Bibby, and Mawson worked extremely hard. He became the first President of the Institute of Landscape Architects, President of the Town Planning Institute and the first holder of the Chair of Civic Design at Liverpool University. In 1908, when he and Lutyens met, most of this was still in the future, but Mawson called himself a landscape architect, he did have influential clients, and he had published in 1900 his very successful book *The Art and Craft of Garden Making*. It was Mawson who said that the art of garden design was in a distressful state: 'For too long [it has been] the prey of spurious dilettantism which, by its vagaries, its sham ruins, its miniature alps and impossible vistas, has reduced it to utter absurdity'. So much for the Picturesque, the Sublime, the Victorians and the English landscape style. It was Brown, said Mawson, who began the decadence: 'By turning his back on creative design to caricature Nature' he 'destroyed the very root-foundations of his art'. This had led, Mawson continued, to 'a happy field for *laissez-faire*' with too many trying to instruct Nature in 'her own unapproachable sphere'.

The solution he put forward was to make landscape architecture mistress of the liberal professions and to install the landscape architect, who had had a catholic education in classical arts, forestry, horticulture, engineering and a smattering of other sciences, as overall co-ordinator and mastermind of every large scheme. In 1908 this was a staggering suggestion, especially to an architect; Mawson was advocating turning history upside down: putting Henry Wise in charge of Hampton Court instead of Sir Christopher Wren.

The joust was staged at the Architectural Association in April 1908. Mawson had formidable presence, and though the thirty-nine year old Lutyens was at the peak of his country house reputation and the name on everybody's lips, he was no public performer. He was terrified and nervous: 'Last night was horrible – my hand shook', he wrote to his wife Emily the next day, 9 April, when he sent her the notes for his contribution to the debate. His notes had been prepared on a visit to Miss Jekyll the previous weekend and they have survived as the only detailed statement on garden design that he ever made. He started his defence of his profession by reference to the quality of artistic conception, saying that all problems could be solved with enough ingenuity.

Drawings of gates from Mawson's The Art and Craft of Garden Making.

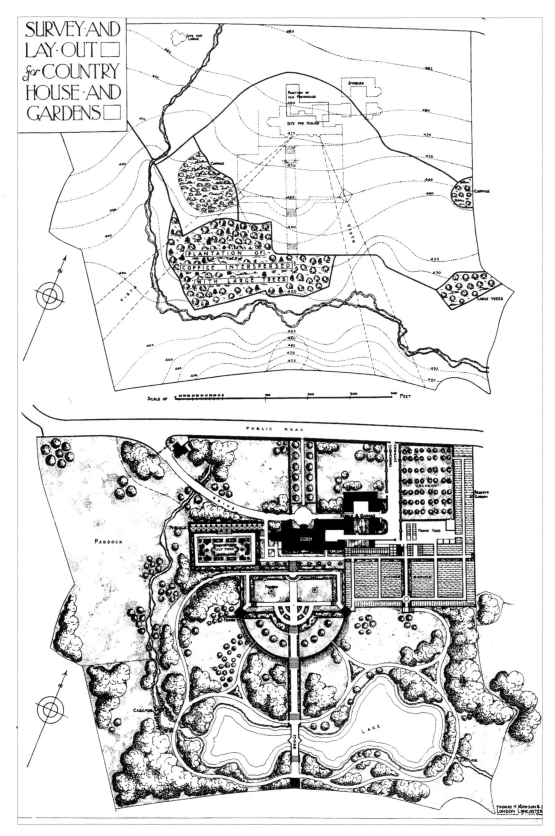

A survey and layout of a particular site by Thomas Mawson from his book The Art and Craft of Garden Making, *first published in 1900. The thoroughness and skill of these drawings and the information they convey aptly illustrate the knowledge of surveying, forestry, horticulture, engineering and artistic design that Mawson felt were correctly the province of the 'landscape architect'.*

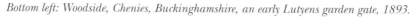

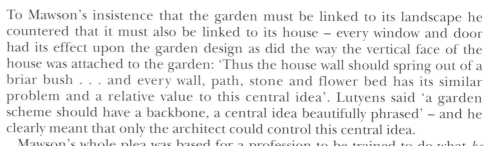

The Hoo, Willingdon, Sussex, 1902. The domed pool with the sparkle of the water reflected on the smooth brickwork; this device, inspired by Italian gardens (and probably suggested to Lutyens by Miss Jekyll), was first used at Deanery Garden in 1901 and followed in many other guises in many other gardens. It was Miss Jekyll's belief that the correct planting for all formal pools was the water lily.

Bottom left: Woodside, Chenies, Buckinghamshire, an early Lutyens garden gate, 1893.

To Mawson's insistence that the garden must be linked to its landscape he countered that it must also be linked to its house – every window and door had its effect upon the garden design as did the way the vertical face of the house was attached to the garden: 'Thus the house wall should spring out of a briar bush . . . and every wall, path, stone and flower bed has its similar problem and a relative value to this central idea'. Lutyens said 'a garden scheme should have a backbone, a central idea beautifully phrased' – and he clearly meant that only the architect could control this central idea.

Mawson's whole plea was based for a profession to be trained to do what *he* could do, with his talent and enormous hard work. Lutyens's defence (a weak one in political terms, but then he never was a politician) was that it was all up to the individual. And it was all very well for him – he had his own landscape consultant of the highest skills and experience secluded down at Munstead Wood anyway. His real answer was in his work.

Deanery Garden was followed by other great houses with gardens: Grey Walls on the Firth of Forth at Gullane for Alfred Lyttelton in 1900; Little

The Hoo, Willingdon, Sussex. Designed by Lutyens in 1902 for Alexander Wedderburn, KC. One of a pair of garden gazebos set to guard the garden steps in 17th century fashion and surrounded with lush planting.

Thakeham at Storrington, Sussex for Ernest Blackburn, 1902; Marshcourt at Stockbridge, Hampshire for Herbert Johnson, 1904; Heathcote at Ilkley in Yorkshire for J.T. Hemingway, 1905; and Folly Farm, Sulhamstead in Berkshire. There were also many smaller and perhaps less ingenious houses, like The Hoo, at Willingdon in Sussex, 1902, which were given lovely gardens and garden features.

Folly Farm was originally a long Georgian house sideways on to the road, on a bend in the middle of Sulhamstead, a small village in the lush valley of the Kennet south-west of Reading. In front of the house was a large black barn. In 1906 Lutyens added a symmetrical, double-fronted 'Dutch' extension to the end of the farmhouse, facing south towards where the garden would be.

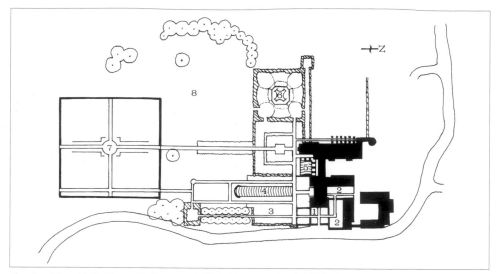

Garden plan, Folly Farm, Sulhamstead, Berkshire, completed 1915. The Entrance Court (1) leads on the right to the Barn Court (2) and on the left to the Lime Walk (3). In the Canal Garden (4) Lutyens used a formal sweep of water on a large scale. The tank (5) is edged with steps – a Lutyens characteristic.
The Sunken Rose Garden (6) is surrounded by the original yew hedges and is one of Lutyens's most elaborate garden rooms. The kitchen garden (7) is a walled area of almost an acre. After the intensity and brilliance of Folly Farm's formal gardens comes the calm sweep of the lawn (8).

The Dutch extension has the charm of a doll's house – it is built with bricks 'the colour of a ripe (blue) plum with the bloom on it', trimmed with russets. It contains a double-height central hall which Lutyens decorated with black walls and a white ceiling with bright red interior balconies in a post-Chinese Chippendale pattern. It was enchanting, at the expense of being practical – a failing many of his clients forgave him, for there were only two small rooms each side of the hall and two very low bedrooms above them. The courts now formed between the L-shaped house and the barn were walled, and had arched doorways and brick herring-bone paths flanked by small flower borders. The treatments of both courts – the Barn Court and the Entrance Court (with its green footgate as the main entrance off the village street) – were kept small scale and cottagey in character with borders of columbines, poppies, gypsophila, *Iris foetida* and white campanulas against a background of cistus, jasmine, clematis, laurustinus and hardy fuchsias, with roses 'Aimée Vibert', 'Dorothy Perkins' and 'The Garland' against the walls. The borders in the Entrance Court were edged in box, four squares filling the square court. The 'front' door opposite the footgate enters a strange curved passage – Lutyens's means of placing the front door in keeping with the symmetry of the court even though tricks had to be played with the interior. This was what he meant by the range of the artist's ingenuity, and by every door having its effect on the garden design – or vice versa.

This was the first stage of Folly Farm's development. The garden on the south front was simply divided into tennis and croquet lawns, separated by double herbaceous borders with a rose pergola over the grass path. The road wall was bordered with a rhododendron walk with beds of Michaelmas daisies, these early borders having been planned by Miss Jekyll.

At the end of 1911 Folly Farm was bought by Zachary Merton who, understandably, felt he required a dining room and decent-sized bedrooms. Lutyens, equally understandably, did not want to spoil the symmetry of his Dutch front, and he built on in the only direction he could with such bold

Folly Farm. The Tank Court and the 1912 extension to the house, from a Country Life *photograph taken soon after the building was completed. This picture clearly shows the drama of Lutyens's design and the crispness, even harshness, of the craftsmanship that needed to be complemented by strong and generous planting.*

asymmetry that it takes the breath away. The 1912 wing of Folly Farm doubled the size of the house and was built parallel to the old house to the west. To link the hall to the new dining room (with a master bedroom above with its own sleeping balcony) Lutyens devised a corridor which is all roof and massive brick-supporting buttresses. Now the garden design could really take off. The Dutch front was given a suitable formal long canal, and in the recess formed by the linking corridor Lutyens fitted a rectangular tank. Here the still dark water creates a perfect foil for the curtain roof and the swelling pillars and doubles the visual drama of these features by reflecting them. Then Miss Jekyll came along and tut-tutted about the danger of the tank, so it was fitted with steps down into the water which deterred over-adventurous children. Mary Lutyens, the architect's youngest daughter, remembers how she sat on these steps and fished for golden carp with a piece of string.

On the axis of the new west wing, outside the dining-room window, Miss Jekyll and Lutyens added a flower parterre which gave way to an avenue of fruit trees out to the lawn. And beyond the west wing, the final delight: the Sunken Rose Garden, the most wonderful garden room of the whole partnership, is walled in yew, carpeted with swirling brick and stone paths and ornamented with a pool and beds of roses and lavenders. Sadly, almost at the moment of completion, Zachary Merton, the rich and kind benefactor of Great Ormond Street Hospital for Children and so many other charities, died. In the year after his death, 1916, Mrs Merton lent her home to the Lutyens family. That was when Mary Lutyens did her fishing, while her father enjoyed one of his own houses at last and played long games of croquet, always dressed in his London clothes. Miss Jekyll was persuaded away from Munstead Wood and enjoyed playing Mrs Merton's pianola; the garden was a haven of peace away from London and the war.

Above: Folly Farm, Sulhamstead, Berkshire. Lutyens's 1906 extension to the house with 'Dutch' formal pool added c.1912.

Opposite, above: the final Lutyens addition of a dining room and master bedroom, c.1912 for Mr & Mrs Zachary Merton.

Opposite, below: architecture softened by flowers, as originally intended and maintained at Folly Farm.

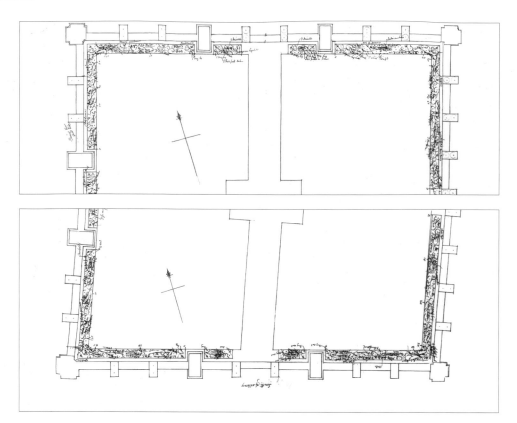

Herbert Baker's plan for the War Memorial at Winchester College, Hampshire, 1923. The planting was by Gertrude Jekyll.

The partnership between Sir Edwin Lutyens and Miss Jekyll which had so pleased the beau monde now ministered to its downfall. While young architects like Oliver Hill went off to the war, Lutyens became one of the Principal Architects (with Reginald Blomfield and Herbert Baker) of the Imperial (now Commonwealth) War Graves' Commission and designed as many war cemeteries as he had done gardens, together with great memorials, including the Cenotaph in Whitehall. In his report to the Commission he noted that while it was important 'to secure the qualities of repose and dignity', there was 'no need for the cemeteries to be gloomy or even sad-looking places'. As always, Miss Jekyll filled in the planting details on his plans. The planting plans that have survived vary slightly in details, but in general her recommendations were for surrounding a cemetery with a holly or yew hedge, with native trees planted for shelter, while the fastigiate oak or Lombardy poplar were chosen as symbolic trees for focus planting. Borders and spare pieces of land were planted with shrubs, the workaday shrubs of the English country lanes – blackthorn, whitethorn, hazel, guelder rose and honeysuckle. The ground was scattered with spring flowers – daffodils, Lenten roses, fritillaries, forget-me-nots – and the borders where the headstones stood were to contain the most familiar flowers of English gardens – foxgloves, columbines, London pride, bergenias, nepeta and plenty of roses.

It has become something of a cliché to leave the brightest and the best of English life on those foreign fields, but certainly the ideals of the Arts and Crafts Movement never survived the war. Nor, I think, did an innocent pride in Englishness as a creative force in art, architecture and gardening, or as a motive for a lifestyle. After 1918 it was somehow not quite right to indulge in serene tradition and purposeless beauty, for living was now a more serious and desperate matter. After all, why was it necessary to plagiarise the delicious Elgar melody that is 'Pomp and Circumstance No.1', into the jingoism of 'Land of Hope and Glory', if not because the hope and the glory had slipped away?

Oliver Hill's perspective of the gardens at Moor Close, Binfield, for C. Birch Crisp, 1914. Hill was the link between Miss Jekyll, whom he knew, and the world that came after the Great War; he was also the link between the Englishness of the Arts and Crafts Movement and the Modernism of the 'thirties. Moor Close is one of his most lavish designs in the former style.

Selected Reading

William Robinson's *The Wild Garden* (1870) and Reginald Blomfield's *The Formal Garden in England* (1892), both essential reading, are both available in reprint.

The whole period has now been lavishly covered in David Ottewill's *The Edwardian Garden* (1989) and in Wendy Hitchmough's *Arts & Crafts Gardens* (1997). Margaret Richardson's *Architects of the Arts and Crafts Movement* (1983) is based on the marvellous drawings in the Royal Institute of British Architects' Drawings Collection (the British Architectural Library) and Roderick Gradidge's *Dream Houses: The Edwardian Ideal* (1980) gives a wonderful insight into this architectural world. *The Catalogue of the Lutyens Exhibition* at the Hayward Gallery (1981) edited by Colin Amery and Margaret Richardson gives the richest summary of Lutyens's work; Mary Lutyens's Memoir of her father (1980) is poignant and revealing of his private life. I decided that Lutyens's clients deserved some attention, so my *Lutyens & The Edwardians* (1996) is now in paperback; but he is not yet finished, with a biography from his great-grand-daughter, Jane Ridley, to come.

Other architects and the Arts and Crafts Movement in general are the subjects of a slow but steady revival. Diane Haigh's *Baillie Scott, The Artistic House* (1995) includes his gardens, and Baillie Scott's own *Houses and Gardens* (1906) has been reprinted in small format by The Antique Collectors' Club. Peter Davey's *Architecture of the Arts and Crafts Movement* (1980) is now in a 2nd edition (1995) and Isabelle Anscombe's *Arts and Crafts Style* (1991) and Fiona MacCarthy's biography of *William Morris: A life for our time* (1994) all contribute gloriously to this glorious period. Perhaps I should have mentioned before that Brent Elliott's *Victorian Gardens* (1986) catalogues the achievements of Victorian gardeners, and applies the balm of wisdom to all that ignited the Arts and Crafts revolution in the first place.

THREE
Rodmarton Manor

Above: looking through the pleached limes at the corner of the Chapel, at the Troughery.

The ideals of Arts and Crafts attracted extremes of personalities. There was the boyish, high-flying Lutyens, who never had a country house of his own and always wore black city clothes; there was the sociable Oliver Hill who made his own envelopes; there were others who wore tweeds to their smart West End offices but felt suburbia as near to nature as they wanted to go. And then there were the purists, retiring and unworldly people, who needed to live out their philosophy to the full.

Into the last category came Ernest Gimson and the brothers Ernest and Sidney Barnsley. They were the pioneers of the craft workshop economy of the Cotswolds that survives and thrives to this day, and in Rodmarton Manor they created the purest symbol of the Arts and Crafts Movement. Rodmarton Manor has a garden which is a series of outdoor rooms, not a large garden, not a great set piece like Blomfield's Mellerstain, nor full of Lutyens-like geometrical games. It is a garden of sanity, sobriety, and modest comfortable logic – all those staid English virtues, and it is lovingly crafted and deeply rooted in its countryside.

Opposite: the Leisure Garden.

79

Ernest Gimson was born in Leicester in 1864, the son of a successful iron founder and engineer of profound socialist principles. His philosophy meant that Gimson father took Gimson son to hear William Morris speak in Leicester, and it was on Morris's advice that Ernest Gimson was eventually accepted into J.D. Sedding's office at 447 Oxford Street, next to Morris & Co's showrooms, as an apprentice architect. The Barnsleys (Ernest, born 1863 and Sidney, born 1865) came from a similar Midlands background and, as there was no place for them in the family's Birmingham building business, they too set out for London to train as architects in the Royal Academy Schools. Ernest Barnsley then went to Sedding's office, and Sidney to Richard Norman Shaw, the master who had built baronial Cragside in Northumberland and the candy-striped New Scotland Yard by the Thames. All three were given thorough apprenticeships. Then they set out into the world in different directions: Ernest Barnsley went home to Birmingham to be an architect, Sidney stayed to build a church at Lower Kingswood in Surrey and Ernest Gimson concentrated on his furniture designs and plasterwork. He had endured the messy process of teaching himself to model friezes and ceiling ribbings, using flowers and fruits as his design inspiration.

The approach front at Rodmarton Manor around a simple green. The house was built in stages between 1909 and 1929.

In the early 1890s Gimson and Sidney Barnsley joined others from the Shaw office (including Blomfield and Lethaby) in a partnership to supply furniture of good design and craftsmanship. Most of the partners really wanted to be architects so the company, Kenton & Co, was disbanded after about eighteen months, no one having lost a great deal and Gimson and Barnsley certainly benefiting from the exhibition of their work. It was at this point, in 1892, that

Ernest Burnsley's house and garden in Sapperton village.

The workroom at Rodmarton Manor. All the furniture in the house was designed by the Barnsleys and made, as were the roof timbers and floors, by local carpenters and joiners.

The luxury of yew 'walls' as a frame for flowers.

The Leisure Garden was paved from the first to lessen the mowing!

Gimson and Sidney Barnsley decided to search for a place to live and work where the 'natural beauty gave them physical satisfaction'. Ernest Barnsley, who was not over-successful in Birmingham, was persuaded to join them. After considerable thought the three of them, together with Ernest's wife and two small daughters, arrived at Ewen, a straggle of cottages in rather flat Gloucestershire just south-west of Cirencester. From here they set out to look for workshops going north to the more interesting edge of the Cotswolds. They found their first base at Pinbury Park, just north of Sapperton, in the dramatic tree-clad valley of the river Frome. For several years they were very happy in the Elizabethan house and its surrounding farm buildings. In June 1901 Sidney Barnsley wrote to Philip Webb: 'The gardens are looking most beautiful now after the rains, with roses in masses, hanging over grey stone walls and climbing up in the cottages, but fruit we have none save gooseberries and currants'. They did have a thousand gallons of cider in the cellar though, and were enjoying the pleasures of splitting big logs, storing them and then watching them burn. While they were at Pinbury, Sidney married Lucy Morley, a farmer's daughter from Lincolnshire and Gimson's cousin, and Gimson himself married Emily Thompson, a vicar's daughter

The Long Border Walk viewed from the Summerhouse.

The garden front has paved and sheltered enclosures for variable directions of wind and sun.

The Leisure Garden, paved to reduce labour and with beds filled with roses and silver-leaved plants.

from Yorkshire, who also loved sketching from nature and was a great help to him. They were a certain sure and strong little community, to whom their old friends from London paid many joyous visits.

The Pinbury idyll continued until 1901. By then all three had built houses for themselves in Sapperton and the workshops were moved to the barns of the medieval stone manor house, Daneway, which sits on the opposite side of the Frome valley from Sapperton village. The workshops were thriving and a sound workforce of craftsmen had been established. Daneway itself was used as a showroom for finished furniture – rush-seated traditional chairs, wooden settles, majestic tall bookcases, tables and chests, some hand-crafted in fine oak, and other pieces of ebony or walnut veneer, decorated with gesso, inlaid with coral and mother-of-pearl. Gimson, who was not physically strong, 'lived like Wordsworth' in the adored countryside; he took cold morning baths and long daily walks, and out of his observations came inlaid decorations of snowdrops, hares and swans and swirling leaves and flowers in plaster and ironwork designs. The Barnsleys continued as architects and sprinkled their work over the area, the mark of their buildings being that it is impossible to tell them from the really old ones. From about 1905 the formal business relationship was dissolved, but the three of them were held by sterner bonds and could not but continue to be close. Then, in 1909, came the commission for Rodmarton Manor.

Rodmarton is a cluster of a village between Sapperton and Ewen; it is an old village and had a manor house, though this was largely demolished at the end of the 18th century. The Rodmarton estate had been given to the Hon. Claud

The Long Border Walk with a vista to Ernest Barnsley's summerhouse. The long double border is laid out parallel to the kitchen garden wall.

Biddulph by his father in 1894, but it was not until 1909 that he began to make plans for his retirement from the family city bank to live in the country. His idea was to spend £5,000 a year for several years, starting with a cottage to which he would add gradually. Claud Biddulph got on well with Ernest Barnsley, who was a much more jovial and robust character than his two partners, with a great interest in cooking and eating good food. Ernest Barnsley was to be the chief architect of Rodmarton. He was given almost a free hand, and worked his way in well, so that what began as a 'cottage in the country' ended up twenty years later as 'the last great house built in England'. Of course it was neither a cottage nor a great house, rather a series of cottages set around a green. Nor was it for the isolation of a lord, but it was, as it still is, a centre for the life of the surrounding community. Rodmarton Manor was built as a direct rebuff to the general belief that the life of the English countryside was dying for want of employment or inspiration; Goldsmith's lines from *The Deserted Village* were its *raison d'être* and its inscription:

> Ill fares the land, to hastening ills a prey,
> Where wealth accumulates, and men decay;
> Princes and lords may flourish, or may fade;
> A breath can make them, as a breath has made;
> But a bold peasantry, their country's pride,
> When once destroy'd, can never be supplied.

Rodmarton Manor. The long borders. These borders were, and still are, planted in the Jekyll tradition with generous sweeps and intervening spires of the more traditional English garden flowers, including delphiniums, hollyhocks, columbines and lilies. The conversion of 'cottage gardening' to this grander scale was in keeping with Arts and Crafts loyalties to rural traditions and applied a patina of permanence and maturity to their buildings.

Rodmarton Manor. The garden door with attendant hydrangeas, expressing perfectly the unity of house and garden, of craftsmanship and flowers, at the vital point of passage from house into garden. This was the elevation of the idea of pinks or London pride at the cottager's step, the kind of device that convinced the Arts and Crafts idealists that they were part of a rural tradition.

Rodmarton grew, piece by piece, in no hurry, out of its own land. All the stone and slate was locally quarried, delivered by farm carts, and cut, shaped and laid by local masons. The oak for roof timbers and floors was chosen, felled and seasoned on the estate before it was worked by local carpenters and joiners. Furniture, such as the benches and trestles of the dining hall, was designed by Ernest and Sidney Barnsley, but made by those same estate carpenters and joiners. More elaborate furniture was made by Sidney Barnsley in his workshop, and Ernest Gimson did the plasterwork in the house. The local blacksmith made all the window and door fastenings. The care that went into every detail was just as Miss Jekyll had exercised over her own home at Munstead Wood in the 1890s. But who would carry this integrity into Rodmarton's garden?

In the Cotswold version of self-reliance this did not really seem to be a problem. Ernest Barnsley was perfectly able to arrange the garden, traditionally, in a series of rooms and walks around the house and a large walled kitchen garden, as his old mentor Sedding and his former colleague, Blomfield, would have approved. Furthermore, the Barnsleys had a great

Opposite: the Long Border vista as it is today, showing how the borders have widened, compared to the Country Life *photograph c.1930.*

87

The garden front of Rodmarton Manor consists of a series of paved enclosures for sitting and eating out of doors. Photograph c.1930.

respect for Miss Jekyll and her books; in 1925, when Rodmarton's garden was growing, she was writing to Sidney Barnsley about the garden for Combend Manor not far away, and it is definitely her spirit that rules at Rodmarton. The maker of the garden though, was a local man, William Scrubey, who actually supervised the layout, was the first Head Gardener and knew perfectly well what would grow. Visiting Rodmarton Manor today is like stepping back in time; now into its third generation as a Biddulph family home, the house and garden atmosphere has been perfectly maintained. It is not a showy garden, nor a horticultural masterpiece, nor even a great or important design, but it is 'all of a piece', a marvellous unwinding of a reel of images, with memories of William Morris, of *The Formal Garden in England*, of Lutyens and Miss Jekyll, even William Robinson, all brought to life.

The main garden room, overlooked by the sleeping balconies, so that the scents could creep upwards on balmy nights, is the Leisure Garden. It is paved, in a pattern reminiscent of the Dutch Garden at Orchards by Lutyens, but on a larger scale, with beds of roses and silver-leaved plants set directly in the paving. The word 'leisure' was taken seriously: there are no fussy little edges of grass to be trimmed, a fact which adds to the serene enjoyment of the scents and colours of the flowers. From the Leisure Garden the path leads underneath the pleached limes which shield the chapel windows, and thence to the Troughery, a collection of discarded sinks and drinking troughs that have found new purposes filled with plants. Treasuring outdated farm and kitchen utensils in this way is exactly in keeping with Rodmarton as the centre of an agricultural estate that may change but does not forget.

The Lower Garden Walk with its borders of predominantly white flowers.

The pleached lime arbour and the Troughery.

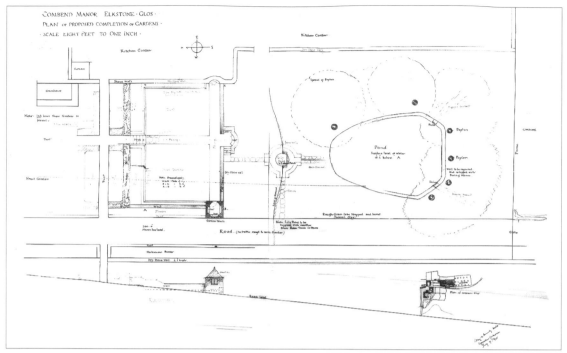

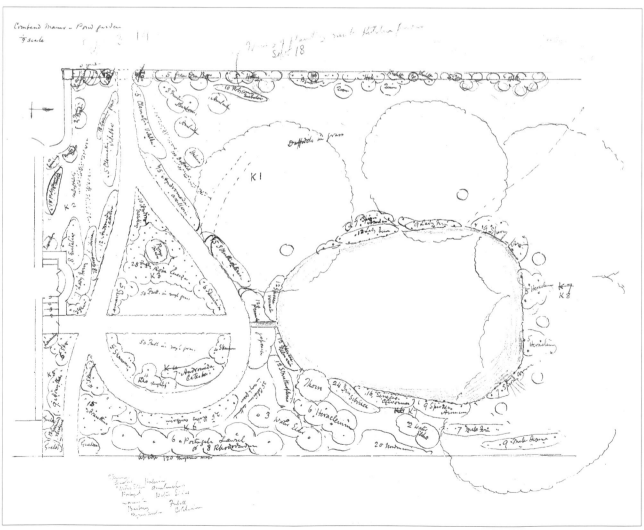

Rodmarton Manor. Lilies and the summerhouse, a picture that sums up the Arts & Crafts ideal.

Opposite: Combend Manor, Elkstone, Gloucestershire.
Sidney Barnsley was working for a client, Asa Lingard, when he sent the plan of the layout for this garden to Miss Jekyll in the summer of 1925. Dated 17 July, 1925, Barnsley drew the walls, levels and existing trees around the pond for Miss Jekyll's information. Additional notes on soil, the amount of shelter and the client's wishes were put in a letter. Miss Jekyll never visited the garden except, of course, in her imagination; at the time she was aged eighty-two, almost blind and confined to Munstead Wood.

Miss Jekyll's scaled-off plan for Combend Manor which she has dated 3 September, showing how she has transformed the Pond Garden into a romantic wilderness. On the bottom of the drawing she has noted a little aide-mémoire *of the chief shrubs she recommends – skimmias, guelder rose, water elder, Portugal laurel, laurustinus, berberis, with pears and cherries, and fritillaries and colchicums beneath them. She has also planted drifts of acanthus, ferns, daffodils, primulas, Rosa lucida and the giant heracleum – for which she had a great affection towards the end of her life. It was this wild gardening that seemed to please her most when she was old, though she also did flower borders for Combend Manor.*

The garden front of the house faces south and provides a habitat for myrtles, abutilons and pittosporum as well as gigantic hydrangeas. The south terraces are arranged into compartments within yew walls, with seats in the Barnsley tradition (a similar design also appears at Hidcote Manor) and decorative pots of pelargoniums. Below the terrace is the Lower Garden Walk, a long walk between borders that are predominantly of white flowers. Entirely in keeping with its working tradition, the garden also has its full complement of working areas – kitchen garden and potting sheds and greenhouses. Alongside the kitchen garden wall Ernest Barnsley laid out long double borders with a central walk leading to his little summerhouse. These double borders of the Long Border Walk have always been planted in the Jekyll tradition, with masses of phlox, hemerocallis, astrantias, peonies, old roses and hardy fuchsias, clumps of Jerusalem sage and white lilies. In the wilder parts of the garden, especially beneath the hornbeam avenue, the elegant giant hogweed *Heracleum mantegazzianum*, which Miss Jekyll also planted at Combend Manor, has been allowed to survive. Ernest Barnsley died in January 1926, just before Rodmarton was quite finished. For a time Sidney Barnsley took charge, and this was when he was working on Combend Manor with Miss Jekyll's help. The giant heracleum, may well signify at Rodmarton's garden the path of influence of the lady herself.

The last word on Rodmarton comes from Mary Comino's book on Gimson and the Barnsleys, which is subtitled 'wonderful furniture of a commonplace kind': 'Rodmarton Manor remains largely unaltered today, and, furnished as it is with the work of two generations of Barnsleys, Peter Waals, and contemporary craftsmen working in the same tradition, provides an impressive monument to the fine design and craftsmanship of the Cotswold School'. Perhaps Rodmarton has a commonplace garden too, but conserved as it is within the safe bounds of these traditions, the garden is also an impressive monument to a movement which at least realised that the art of living was not entirely contained within the house walls.

Selected reading

Mary Comino's book on *Gimson and the Barnsleys* (1980) is now in a 1991 edition, and under her married name, Mary Greensted: she has also written and edited additional essays for The Arts and Crafts Movement in the Cotswolds (1993). Mary Greensted is on the staff of Cheltenham Museum and Art Gallery, a mecca for those interested in the period.

Rodmarton Manor is located off the A433 between Cirencester and Tetbury. Both house and garden are open by prior written appointment to Simon Biddulph, Rodmarton Manor, Cirencester, Glos. GL7 6PF. The garden is open on Saturday afternoons in summer; details will be found in the up-to-date *Yellow Book* and *Hudson's Guide*.

Opposite: the hornbeam avenue in the Wild Garden. The giant hogweed in the foreground can also be found in Gertrude Jekyll's planting plan for nearby Combend Manor, as well as in her garden at Munstead Wood, and, since Sidney Barnsley was working with Miss Jekyll on Combend Manor while Rodmarton was in the final stages of completion, it is fair to assume that the Barnsleys were influenced by her plantings.

Portmeirion, Penrhyndeudraeth, Gwynedd. The Italian dream of a brilliant and flamboyant Welshman, Clough Williams-Ellis. It was as a result of his discovery of the derelict Aber Ia estate on the Dwyryd Estuary near his Welsh home, and his success as an architect, that Williams-Ellis could indulge his passion for Portmeirion. By the summer of 1926 he was proving that a beautiful landscape could be developed and remain beautiful. His wife, Amabel Williams-Ellis, in her book All Stracheys are Cousins, *has described his joy in the opportunity: 'Not the least of his delights at Portmeirion was not having a client. Clough could be the sole arbiter, for there were also, then, no Building Regulations, no Town and Country Planning Act, no regulations about Historic Buildings and, though he thought there ought to be all these things (and he said so repeatedly), privately, secretly, he relished their absence'.*

94

FOUR
An Italian Affair

Few English gardens of the 20th century can escape the influence of the villa gardens of Renaissance Italy. Any brief foray into precedent finds their names – Lante, d'Este, Gamberaia, Marlia, Garzoni, Medici at Fiesole – swathing the taste of western garden design like a magnificent cloak of brocade lined with rose velvet. The Italian influence can be a delicious suffocation which allows only weak imitations; it has also been, in this century, the source of great garden inspiration. This chapter is concerned with imitations and the gardens of inspiration before the point came, as it did with all ideas gleaned from abroad and from that other country, the past, when the scales were tipped and a modern gardener introduced enough of him or herself to make something new.

The seeming paradox of both suffocation and inspiration in the gift of the Italian villa gardens was pointed out by Edith Wharton in her book *Italian Villas and Their Gardens*, first published in 1904. Despite Mrs Wharton's formidable reputation, it might have gone unnoticed among an elegant spate of similar works, were it not for two small beams of highly distinctive light which shone from its pages. First, it was no use copying in the letter but not the spirit – 'a marble sarcophagus and a dozen twisted columns will not make an Italian garden' – but a plot planned and planted in accordance with the principles of the 'old garden-craft', while not producing an Italian garden in the literal sense, will produce 'what is far better, a garden as well adapted to its surroundings as were the models which inspired it'. Secondly, she pointed out, 'The Italian garden does not exist for its flowers: its flowers exist for it; they are a late and infrequent adjunct to its beauties, a parenthetical grace'. She was aware that this was

Above: the cover of the first edition of Edith Wharton's Italian Villas and their Gardens, *published in 1904.*

shocking: 'It is hard to explain to the modern garden lover, whose sole conception of the charm of gardens is formed of successive pictures of flower loveliness, how this effect of enchantment can be produced by anything so dull and monotonous as a mere combination of clipped green and stonework'.

Mrs Wharton's book was not the first of the turn-of-the-century craze, but it was the only one to earn Sir George Sitwell's approval for these hints of her valuable perception. Almost out of duty there was a book from the *Country Life* stable, *The Gardens of Italy*, photographed by Hudson's brilliant photographer Charles Latham, and published in 1905. There were also H. Inigo Triggs's *The Art of Garden Design in Italy*, 1906, and Sir George Sitwell's *On the Making of Gardens*, 1909. Triggs was an architect. His book could hardly fail to be noticed, it was large, expensively produced, profusely illustrated, and is now only found in collectors' folio cases. Sitwell's book is small, just a few essays really, and not a notable success on publication; but now no self-respecting gardener would be without it; it is much loved and much quoted. Triggs pursued his academic, pedestrian journey, counting terraces, calculating areas, through every detail of the most famous villas and their gardens: 'In this villa the student of garden-craft may often return to find fresh material for study . . . The masterly management of the varying levels and terraces, the contrast of light and shade between the plane woods of the upper garden and the brilliance of the parterre in the lower, the superlative genius displayed in the management of the water, and the beauty of the architecture . . . combine to produce a result surpassing any of the old garden schemes remaining in Italy'. This was Triggs making even the Villa Lante sound boring.

Sir George Reresby Sitwell, on the other hand, sounds enchanting: 'A tall, distinguished-looking Englishman with a high-bridged nose, and with fair, fine hair and a slightly darker golden moustache, flourished upwards a little in the manner of the Kaiser, seated on a bench, regarding his surroundings with analytic attention. Probably he would be sitting on an air-cushion, and would be wearing a grey suit and a wide, grey hat, while beside him, for he was careful to sit in the shade, was a sun-umbrella lined with green'.* Accompanied by the faithful Henry Moat, Sitwell spent a long convalescence in Italy recovering from a nervous breakdown. It was perhaps the vulnerability of his mind that gave his book its outstanding value and made it a lovable indulgence. It was the culmination of twenty years spent drifting through the morals, motives, scents, sounds and dreams of two hundred gardens, large and small. He cites Ruskin endlessly and Herbert Spencer frequently. One extract from Triggs is enough, but from Sitwell the quotes are irresistible. On the Giusti garden at Verona: 'Across the bridge along a dull and dusty street' the heavy entrance doors are swung back . . . 'an enchanted vista holds the traveller spell-bound – the deep, refreshing green of an avenue of cypresses . . . leading to a precipice crowned by the foliage of a higher garden. For pure sensation there is nothing in Italy equal to this first glimpse through the Giusti gateway'. On Isola Bella: 'Not a garden, but a mirage in a lake of dreams...a great galleon with flower-laden terraces' anchored here. On Caprarola with its giant guard of sylvan divinities 'playing, quarrelling, laughing the long centuries away'.

And finally, Sitwell on Lante, where he has climbed up through the park to find the source of the stream 'upon which pool, cascade, and water-temple are

* G. Sitwell, *On the Making of Gardens*, 1959 edition, introduction by Osbert Sitwell.

96

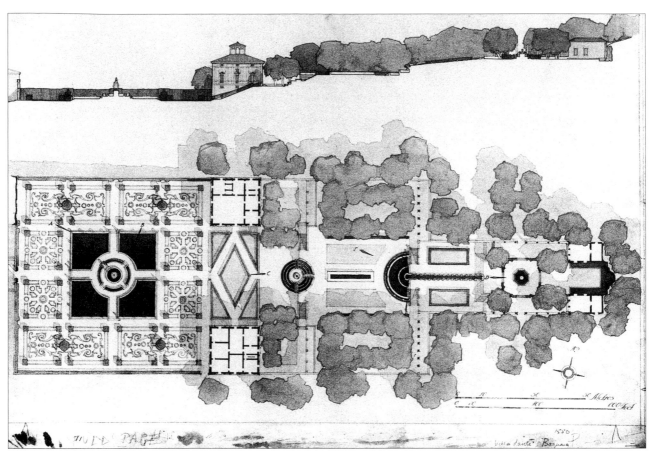

Villa Lante. Plan and elevation by Geoffrey Jellicoe of a garden whose legacy to English Italian gardens was considerable.

threaded like pearls upon a string'. Lante's stream rises in a fountain, disappears underground to emerge in the centre of a flight of steps 'between the claws of a gigantic crab' (the maker of the garden was Cardinal Gambara whose cognisance was the crab), then races down a scalloped trough and drops over the edge of a small basin between two colossal river gods, into a pool below. 'The fall to the next level gives us a half-recessed *temple d'eau*, with innumerable jets and runlets pouring from basin to basin; and here, flanked by stately plane trees and by the two pavilions which make up the casino, is a grass-plot commanding the loveliest view of the garden. Before us lies a square enclosure jutting out into the vale below, with high green hedges, sweet *broderies* of box bordered by flowers, and in the midst a broad water garden leading by balustraded crossways to an island fountain which rises like a mount to four great figures of sombre-tinted stone. Water gushes from the points of the star which the naked athletes uplift, from the mouths of the lions by their side, from the masks on the balustrade, from the tiny galleys in which vagrant cupids are afloat upon the pools. It is a colour harmony of cool refreshing green and brighter flowers, of darkest bronze, blue pools and golden light'. The magic and 'strange elusive charm' may come from the visions that can be shifted at will from the garden to the misty distant hills or orange-lichened roofs of near buildings, 'but the soul of the garden is in the blue pools which, by some strange wizardry of the artist to stair and terrace and window, throw back the undimmed azure of the Italian sky'.

Our legacy from these Italian villa gardens is so rich that we are apt to forget that the personality of that Duke of Lante and that Crab Cardinal must have had

Gateway to Giusti garden in Verona. 'For pure sensation there is nothing in Italy equal to this first glimpse through the Giusti gateway.' (Sir George Sitwell – see page 96)

considerable effect on their creations; perhaps we are now too far away in time ever to know the full story. With the gardens made from Italian passions conceived in this century the personalities are still shining bright and their influence is inescapable. The Italian garden at Hever Castle in Kent is made up of the collection of statuary and ornaments made by the fabulously wealthy William Waldorf Astor whilst he was American Minister in Rome. It is exactly what Mrs Wharton meant by 'a dozen twisted columns' and a lot more, but it is a wonderful garden for two reasons. First, the surprise of finding such a garden attached to the Boleyn's old castle which Astor found in 1903 and converted almost overnight into the most lavishly accoutred of English Edwardian estates disguised as a Tudor village. Wisely realising the incongruity of his classical collection he put it out of sight of the castle, and it is the very unexpectedness of the garden that makes it so memorable – along with the surprising quality of the statues and ornaments, for Astor only collected the best. Here is the most exquisite gathering of ghosts from a past civilisation – beautiful white marble bodies without arms, pensive or cruel faces peering sightless from bowers of roses and vines, a grinning lion's mask, luscious patternings of stone fruits and leaves, real leaves and flowers, all along an endless walk, beneath princely pergolas. In these days when the ugliness of reproductions of garden ornaments knows no bounds, Hever's garden offers a

The Italian Garden, Hever Castle, Kent. The essential beauty of Lord Astor's collection of antique art set amidst bowers of blossoms.

revelation of the quality of the arts involved in the gardens of Italy, but it has none of the spirit of Italian gardens. Harold Peto (1854-1933) was also a collector, but on a more modest scale than Astor and an architect as well. He was in partnership with one of the fathers of the Arts and Crafts Movement, Ernest George, from 1876, but in the 1890s he gave up architecture to concentrate on garden design. In 1899 he bought Iford Manor, a small Palladian building facing a 14th century bridge over the river Frome in a steep-sided valley in the Wiltshire countryside. The manor had been there since before Domesday in various guises and there were the remnants of many old buildings on the site, to which Peto added his own collection from Italy. His collection may be less beautiful than Hever's, but it is

The Fernery in the Italian garden at Hever Castle.

more amusing – abundant animals in lead and stone, scowling Caesars and their sarcophagi, Romulus and Remus and their she-wolf, lions in red Verona marble, with pavilions, loggias, pools, walls, urns and vases. Iford's garden is crammed with architectural bric-à-brac, it has the strength of tiers of rugged walls, a glorious marching colonnade (made for Peto by the masons of Westwood, the neighbouring village) and miniature villas and temples, but it has equal strength in its landscape setting, the tree-hung slope of the Wiltshire hill.

Harold Peto's skill was the arranging of this marriage between his Italian tastes and his English home, and the delight of his garden is in the changing levels that answer the contours of the hill and produce surprise at every turn, and in the ever-changing effects of English light and rain, of the sun shining through young spring leaves or on the autumn carpets of gold, of banks of lavenders, roses and wistarias tumbling over the stones, and of delicately coloured heads of flowers nodding against a rough wall. In his way Peto taught the most important lesson to those English who would make Italian gardens at

The Italian garden at Iford Manor, the home of the collector and architect Harold Peto. Peto's skill was in arranging the marriage between his Italian tastes and his English garden set in the tree-hung slope of a Wiltshire hill.

home – that with love, attention to detail and due regard to nature, the garden could convey the satisfaction of all the arts in harmony, of man reflecting the glory of his Maker, even though the aura of undimmed azure had to be exchanged for silver grey.

Iford Manor with its garden is still a much-loved and well-tended family home; there is no sense of a lost dream; the garden embodies one man's dream very carefully perpetuated and enjoyed into our time. But nostalgia, that sense of loss, is such a powerful notion in a garden that it can now convey romance where none existed before. This is especially true of the garden at Port Lympne, designed before the First War by Philip Tilden for Sir Philip Sassoon, who already owned a lavish garden at Trent Park in Middlesex. Port Lympne, near Hythe in Kent, was not a labour of love nor of sensitive harmony with nature; it was the flamboyant imposition of one man's wealth and pride upon a hillside overlooking Pevensey Levels, merely for the convenience of a holiday home in August, and during that month in the 1920s the garden was maintained in flower show condition by at least

Iford Manor, Wiltshire. A view of Harold Peto's own garden.

Opposite: Garinish Island, Glengariff, Co. Cork. The Italian garden by Harold Peto.

The view from the top of the Great Stair at Port Lympne across the Water Garden court to the distant sea.

thirty gardeners. And yet, such is that elusive spirit of gardens, the best place in England to find a substitute for d'Este or Garzoni may well be Port Lympne. Here one is in the presence of titantic ghosts – Clemenceau, Churchill, the Windsors, Lloyd George, Beaverbrook, Lawrence of Arabia and Charlie Chaplin, as well as the intangible Sassoon himself – in a garden that could match the superlatives they encountered everywhere else. The flowers that the magic of money crowded into August merely scented and sweetened the intrigues and wars of the world.

The approach to Port Lympne is along a mile-long drive which ends in the gravel-circled east court. The first impression is comforting, one of welcome and prettiness. The 'pretty' house was built by Herbert Baker during the First War in his Cape Dutch style developed at Groote Schurr for Cecil Rhodes and rooted in the curly gable Dutch 17th century tradition. The 'prettiness' is enhanced by richly detailed brickwork, extended to all the garden features as well, using the special four-and-a-half inch French bricks with traditional Kentish tiling. A marble floored corridor stretches from the east entrance door through to the west garden door, and on right and left are the delights that money could buy from the best artists of the period. First Rex Whistler's Tent Room, a gold and blue striped canopy offering glimpses of an 18th century world; opposite Michel Sert's African elephants rest their feet on the chimney piece of the Exhibition Room; then Glyn Philpot's Egyptian murals in the dining room and finally the pink Moorish courtyard with white columns and green marble pools.

The south garden front at Port Lympne seen from the Striped Garden. The pergolas, balustrades and their PS motifs, for the owner Philip Sassoon, can be seen above the young yew hedge of the dahlia enclosure.

After all this the garden needed some impact of its own. Out of the garden door on the west is a Water Garden from which rises the staggering 135-step Great Stair of Cumberland stone. The Stair is of heroic proportions and presents the first intimation of like sentiments to come. Further west are tiered Magnolia Walks, an upper and lower, and terraces, the Dahlia and Aster Terraces and the Bowling Green, where the marquees were set up for parties. On the south front of the house, between twin curving lodges, is the elaborately crafted main terrace, with its balustrades twisted with the initials PS. At one end it overlooks the Chess Garden, enclosed in yew, chequer- boarded with annuals, and at the other, also enclosed in yew, the Striped Garden, planted in stripes of dahlias. The centre of the terrace overlooks the Pool Lawn and the swimming pool which was flanked by side pools with their own raised terraces where Sir Philip and his guests could drip dry and survey the end of England and the English Channel. The rest of the garden falls away down the slope – two tennis courts, one for morning, one for evening, a vineyard, a figyard, and a long double herbaceous border – and finally melts into the Virgin Forest. This hillside garden has never been taken quite seriously in English gardening terms, and yet it is worth suggesting that Sassoon and the Medici princes had much in common in terms of desires and resources, as well as immensely high standards and a taste for the best of their own time. Port Lympne, which is rather appropriately now part of John Aspinall's Howletts and Port Lympne Estate and Zoo Park, is the nearest England can come to the Italian villa gardens in aesthetic terms.

Port Lympne, Kent. The cartouche of the garden plan painted on the wall of the Tent Room by Rex Whistler.

Dumbarton Oaks, Washington, DC, USA, the great garden created for Robert and Mildred Woods Bliss by Beatrix Farrand, and now the property of Harvard University. Beatrix Farrand (1872-1959) was Edith Wharton's niece and she became a prolific landscape architect whose understanding of Italian gardens was instinctive rather than imitatory. She worked in England at Dartington Hall, but Dumbarton Oaks is the garden which continues to inspire both English and American designers.

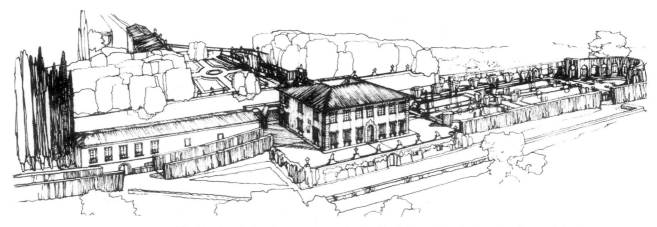

Villa Gamberaia, Settignano, drawn by Geoffrey Jellicoe, from Italian Gardens of the Renaissance. *The gardens which he saw in Italy, and especially Gamberaia, impressed the young Jellicoe so much that he was to feel their subconscious presence throughout his long and creative life.*

Yet there were other and more elusive charms than azure pools and exquisite artistry. The villas needed their beautiful Italian landscapes, their creamy grey, lichen-dressed statuary, immaculately clipped evergreens, tumbling waters, but they needed their man-made geometry as well. The geometry was truly discovered and presented as important by two young architects on a Rome scholarship who spent a summer pacing, sketching, measuring and making notes in all the important gardens. The result, *Italian Gardens of the Renaissance*, a book mainly of drawings by Geoffrey Jellicoe and J.C. Shepherd, was published by Ernest Benn in 1925. Again this is a small book, but it has become infinitely precious to all who are interested in the best kind of garden design. Shepherd's misty watercolours of plans and elevations and Jellicoe's comfortingly hand-drawn bird's-eye views divined the secrets of proportion in layout and fixed the elements

Gordon Russell's garden at Kingcombe, Gloucestershire. The garden steps drawn by Robert Micklewright. Jellicoe and Russell discussed this garden only once but it was a discussion of instinctive sympathies. When Gordon Russell built his garden, including these steps with their flanking cascades in the Italian manner, he was expressing his own understanding of all the domestic arts in harmony in a true Renaissance manner.

Villa Gamberaia. A garden salon 'flooded with light and air', qualities which have ensnared the hearts of generations of garden designers from chillier climes.

of visual design. As they paced and drew the elevations they realised how lovingly the villas and their gardens clung to their landscapes – of the Italian Medici princes Jellicoe wrote: 'Their first duty lay in being sympathetic to the country in which they had planted themselves'. As they measured and sketched and sat in the sun of endless afternoons they realised the quality of the gardens as 'outdoor rooms' and 'salons flooded with light and air', but with great differences from the indoor rooms – for a garden belonged as much to the countryside as it did to the house and 'it was the mutual ground on which the two met and absorbed each other's views'. Jellicoe especially found in these gardens immense inspiration, an inkling that the human mind could reach out to the gods; he later acknowledged that it was not a conscious inspiration at the time, but the villa gardens, and especially Gamberaia, had embedded their beauty into Jellicoe's soul, and his subsequent teachings and work would become a kind of

Villa Gamberaia. The change in perspective from the picture on page 109, showing how the garden clings lovingly to the landscape.

holy grail, requiring a 20th century quest.

The two immediate outcomes of *Italian Gardens of the Renaissance* were, on the face of it, rather prosaic – a small garden and a large one to be done at home, but in the hands of Jellicoe and the particular clients they became symbolic. Gordon Russell – 'a rather tall man with a new hat' – came straight out of the Cotswold furniture-making community. In 1924 he and his wife Toni built Kingcombe at Broadway in the direct tradition of the Barnsleys' cottages of rough stone tucked into their sloping sites. But Russell had read Robinson, Miss Jekyll *and* Edith Wharton and yearned for something 'Italian'. He asked Jellicoe down to the Cotswolds for a day, a summer day and lunch in the garden and a long talk. After this lovely day out Jellicoe remembers returning to London on the train, with the satisfaction of knowing that his client had got what he wanted, but unaware that he had done anything at all. And he had been paid well. Gordon Russell, on the other hand, spent happy years creating his own version of an Italian garden and always gave credit for the inspiration to Jellicoe. They remained friends but no plan nor plant list passed between them; the meeting of two minds that understood craft and design had been enough for the experienced and intuitive Russell to find out all he wanted. This little story introduces another element into 20th century gardens – the relationship between the right designer and the right client, a relationship that like a love affair can produce something greater than the sum of its parts.

Ditchley Park, Oxfordshire. The great terrace, three hundred yards long, reinstated by Geoffrey Jellicoe.

The second outcome was just as much a meeting of minds, but the object involved was that much bigger. Ronald Tree was a rich, very rich, American with the tastes and lifestyles of an English gentleman. He and his wife Nancy had found the great classical mansion house of the Dillons, Ditchley Park built by James Gibbs, sleeping amongst its hayfields in Oxfordshire in the summer of 1933. They fell in love with it. In London they lived opposite Edward Hudson, and at Hudson's recommendation they asked the young Jellicoe to step from his little house on Highgate Hill and his work attic in Bloomsbury to their great house and park, to see what he could do. Tree, Jellicoe has written, 'was a true Palladian with a purist instinct for the grandeur of geometrical proportion',* whilst his wife Nancy was a perfectionist for detail; they were immensely vital and gregarious and Ditchley was to resound to some of the greatest parties of the 'thirties.

First, however, it had to be restored; in garden terms both Ronald Tree and Jellicoe were happy to examine James Gibbs's original ideas and reasons for the siting of his house. In Gibbs's plan of 1726 his intention was clear – the house should be balanced by a circular entrance court, and on the opposite side a long terrace across the garden front. It is interesting that before the house was finished such classical inspirations were discarded – Lord Burlington and his fellows had seen the Italian landscape paintings, and Palladian mansions must now float in their seas of grass as decreed by the English landscape style. Ditchley had so floated

* G. Jellicoe, 'Ronald Tree and the Gardens of Ditchley Park: The Human Face of History', *Garden History*, vol 10, no 1, 1982.

Ditchley Park. The formal garden in 1936 with the parterre from Wrest Park and the closing curtain of water.

This photograph of the garden loggia at Ditchley Park gives an idea of the elegance that did not survive the Second World War.

for one hundred and fifty years. Jellicoe, immersed in his London life, in the day-to-day world of the 'thirties and the Modern Movement, found himself transported back in time, and set to work according to classical rules he knew so well but had never actually handled; after much earth heaving the great terrace was 'restored'. Ronald Tree wrote in his autobiography, *When the Moon was High*, of Jellicoe's 'great achievement': 'Three hundred yards in length, it ran north and south on the west side of the house, overlooking the lake. At the south end, elevated to dominate the long terrace, was a temple we had found hidden away'. Besides the terrace Jellicoe created formal gardens for Nancy Tree. The terrace was separated from the formal garden by a beech hedge cut with 'scallops' which each held a statue. The statues came from Wrest Park, Lord Cowper's great classical garden of the 18th and 19th centuries, and were of a quality that the Trees required. The stone framework of a parterre also came from Wrest (it has since been returned) and this was set out between hornbeam alleys and ended in a fountain curtain of water falling into a semi-circular pool.

The splendours of Ditchley were short-lived; the Trees' parties of the immediate pre-war years are remembered by many with deepest nostalgia as the end of another era, but after the war Ronald Tree no longer felt able to live in England and Ditchley was sold. Nancy did, there was a divorce, she became Nancy Lancaster and discovered Haseley Court in 1954 which she restored to her own immaculate taste with the help of the interior designer John Fowler. She also made a glorious garden, with another Jellicoe terrace and plenty of her favoured formal plantings in soft greys and muted greens of good form which Edith Wharton would have loved. The Italian-villa-inspired garden of good form and foliage plantings, where flowers were 'a parenthetical grace', was on its way back into fashion, but that is a later story.

Ditchley Park. The formal garden view through the water curtain towards the house. Jellicoe here used imitations of the Villa Gamberaia for Ronald Tree – a client he felt to be a 'true Palladian'.

Above: Plas Brondanw, Gwynedd. Clough-Williams-Ellis's own garden.
Below: Anglesey Abbey, Cambridgeshire. Two 20th century gardens of Italian inspiration, albeit not quite seriously in the first, nor compatibly in the flat fen edge landscape of the second.

Dartington Hall. Spring flowering walks and sunny glades, the late 20th century maturity of Beatrix Farrand's and Percy Cane's designs.

The essential influence of the Renaissance villa gardens found only one more true expression in an English garden, and in a way it brings the 20th century's Italian affair full circle. The garden is Dartington Hall in Devon, which Leonard and Dorothy Elmhirst came to in 1925; he was English, she was American. Dartington was to become the setting for the ideal community of their liberal dreams, and the heart of the community, and their home was the romantic ramble of buildings around a 14th century Great Hall set in a naturally spectacular small park. Both the buildings and their setting had been neglected when the Elmhirsts arrived. Dorothy Elmhirst came out of the élite East Coast world of Edith Wharton; she was born a Whitney, and her first husband had been the banker Willard Straight, who had died in 1918. The gardens for the Straight Estate at Old Westbury on Long Island had been planned for Willard and Dorothy by Beatrix Farrand, Mrs Wharton's niece, who had travelled with and learned from her aunt and had become the first really effective woman landscape architect (though she preferred to call herself a landscape gardener). She had been a founder member of the American Association of Landscape Architects in 1899, and had worked for Mrs Woodrow Wilson at the White House, at Vassar, Harvard and Yale and for a long string of American society clients; she worked on well over a hundred large and complex commissions from 1891 (when she was nineteen) to 1949 (when she was seventy-seven). It was only natural that Dorothy Elmhirst, despairing of finding an English designer who understood her, asked Beatrix Farrand to come to Dartington.

The staircase down the Heath Bank to the Tiltyard Lawn at Dartington Hall, designed and planted by Percy Cane.

What Beatrix Farrand did, between 1933 and 1939, can either be dismissed in prosaic terms: 'landscaped the north court, created the formal design around the Hall and planted the woodland walks', or it can be seen as much more. Even before she arrived she had inspired Dorothy Elmhirst to talk of making Dartington into an English version of Dumbarton Oaks, Farrand's undoubted masterpiece, made for the Robert Woods Blisses between 1921 and 1947, and now proudly owned by Harvard University. The thought is enough to make us regard Dartington with eyes of hope. On her first visit Mrs Farrand was her usual self – regal, energetic, formidable and hard working – and for two weeks she examined every corner and angle, took notes, put up measuring stakes and paced about them, 'planning every hour of the day and night'. She had learned her garden craft out of doors and firmly believed that that was where the planning of vistas and planting of borders should be done; she possessed (what the myopic mind of Gertrude Jekyll so desperately lacked) an expansive vision of formality, a deep sense of restraint and that vital landscape quality, a sense of aptness. She respected Dartington's age, accepted that the Tiltyard Lawn surrounded by grass terraces (which it was thought had been made by champion jouster John Holand, Duke of Exeter in the 14th century) must be the centrepiece of the garden and realised that the garden had enough strength of form – 'simple nobility of line and long human association' – for it to be treated gracefully and not confused with too many flowers. She would only allow native plants to be used in the strong base planting that is the backbone of any serene landscape, and she added her experience of designing for cloistered calm (done so successfully at Yale and Harvard); she balanced the Great Hall with a great oval of green and a path around the perimeter, rather in the way she did the Harkness Memorial Cloister at Yale. So Dartington has, from Beatrix Farrand, the

*Dartington Hall. The entrance courtyard to the old house and hall which was part of Beatrix
Farrand's contribution to the setting of Dartington.*

Right: Dartington, the courtyard as it is today.

Anglesey Abbey. A rare corner of human scale design in this 100-acre garden.

Anglesey Abbey, Cambridgeshire. The Temple Lawn in Lord Fairhaven's 20th century Italian garden in England, now owned by the National Trust. The garden was made to hold a collection of classical ornaments.

serene setting of grass, paving and good shrubs for the Hall, the restrained logic of the borders around the house buildings – and in contrast, the magic of the woodland walks that drift so pleasingly through glades of camellias, magnolias and rhododendrons, with an endless cavalcade of wild flowers. After the war Mrs Farrand could not come to Dartington, so the Elmhirsts found Percy Cane. Not that Cane was difficult to find – he was the leading garden designer who had stayed outside the profession of landscape architecture when it was organised in England in 1929. Cane (1881-1975) had studied art and horticulture, started work as a gardening journalist and set up in practice as a designer in 1919. He had not joined the profession because he had not needed to; he was very successful and could illustrate his successes in his own books. His first book, *Garden Design of Today*, published in 1934, showed the beauty of much of his early work: a lavender-lined terrace and lovely rock garden slope at Hascombe Court in Surrey (where he followed Miss Jekyll), lakes, lawns and drives of 18th century elegance at Stoneleigh Abbey in Warwickshire and West Woodhay House in Berkshire, and – one of his best gardens – Boden's Ride at Ascot. Here the full Cane treatment of formal terraces and paved flower gardens led to lovely woods and, his favourite device of all, a mown glade curving through carefully planted shrubs and trees. The terrace, indeed the sloping site, was Cane's first love from his knowledge of the gardens of southern France and Italy; at Dartington his best legacy is the wonderful staircase flight down the Heath Bank, through magnolias, heathers and maples into the Tiltyard Lawn. His other legacy to Dartington is a wonderful example of his second love – the Glade – mown grass winding through curving beds of flowering cherries, liquidambar, laburnum, rhus, viburnums, hydrangeas, enormous old roses and ceanothus, all planted in drifts of yellows, golds, ambers and russets, with purples, smoke-pinks and bronze. His philosophy for the glade was that a certain amount of formal control in terms of vista and curving line allowed each plant the right conditions to give of its best and so create an exquisite whole. But it was essentially control of the shapes and textures of leaves and flowering branches, the beginning of the non-flower flowering garden.

Cane also had a definite architectural talent and could add the perfect formal touch to a beautifully planted setting; his book, which the Elmhirsts must have perused before they contacted him, showed his serene, plainly paved paths curving through borders or making definite aim for the statue at the end of a vista. They must have noticed the similarity between his taste and Mrs Farrand's; the sad thing is that Cane apparently never appreciated the great designer that he followed. Granted the war years must have blurred Beatrix Farrand's growing vision of her garden, but Cane only recorded that there was 'much to be desired' in the harmony of Dartington's setting. At Dartington, where the Elmhirsts have been succeeded by a devoted Gardens' Committee and good gardeners, this lack of appreciation did not matter, for the work of both Farrand and Cane is conserved and the garden is cherished. But, what I suppose must be called professional jealousy does turn out to be one of the curses on 20th century gardens!

With Cane's staircase at Dartington finished in 1947, and Henry Moore's figure of a reclining woman placed in the Glade the same year, we have the last inspiration of the Renaissance Italian villa gardens played out in England. From now on that inspiration is the motif of one designer, Geoffrey Jellicoe, and he will make of it something of his very own. In his Selwyn Brinton Lecture to the Royal Society of Arts in 1952 Jellicoe summarised the inspiration as based on four essential elements: first the geometry, the elusive link between the mind of man and the order of the universe (Cane's staircase reverberates back to Port Lympne's, Ditchley's parterre echoes Gamberaia's, Mrs Farrand's courtyard at Dartington finds echoes in Oxford quadrangles and Palladio's sketchbooks); second, 'A feeling for the beauty of form of the human nude' which breathed emotion into the gardens with sculptures, and curving mouldings and balustrades; this is the reason for the continuing desire for a classical statue in an arbour of yew or stone niche – but at Dartington Henry Moore turned the old feeling into something new: 'I wanted the figure to have a quiet stillness and a sense of permanence', he wrote in 1947, 'as though it could stay there for ever to have strength and seriousness in its effect and yet be serene and happy and resolved, as though it had come to terms with the world, and could get over the largest cares and losses'.* Moore was Jellicoe's friend and inspiration for fifty years; they made a formidable partnership and their shared philosophy and its effect is the great hope for gardens and our surroundings of the latter half of this century. But more of that later.

Jellicoe's third element from the Renaissance mind is that of movement, without which nothing we create can be in harmony with our universe; movement is achieved by repetition, whether it be of stone vases along a walk or repeated textures of plants along a border. And finally, and most formidably, rightness, aptness of design to its site, love of the place, understanding of the

* Dartington Hall Gardens guidebook.

genius loci. And this is why we have to leave Italian gardens behind, for the essence of this last element is that the *place* comes first – all right for a Medici prince who knew what he wanted and commanded it to be done, all right for Geoffrey Jellicoe when he found Ronald Tree's true Palladian taste coincided perfectly with what Ditchley required, all right for the Elmhirsts because Beatrix Farrand loved her English step-child and saw in it the rebirth of her beloved Dumbarton Oaks. But how many love affairs can a professional designer have? From now on gardens of any size that could echo the true Italian ideals had to be made by owners who loved them, such as the patriot architect Clough Williams-Ellis at Portmeirion and Lord Fairhaven at Anglesey Abbey, and it can almost be said that the more a place is loved the better the garden that is made. And with Sissinghurst Castle, Hidcote Manor, Tintinhull House – gardens which contain all the elements of Italian Renaissance design – the love of an English place tipped the balance once again into something new.

Finally, and sadly, we have reached the point where the garden owner will no longer be at one with his or her professional designer, so whether the designer loves or no, the design will no longer always be of the purest. Even Percy Cane's *Garden Design of Today* showed a disturbing propensity for crazed paving, thatched summerhouses and overly-complicated patterns of grass and pavings; as the 20th century garden got smaller and smaller disaster could only be avoided by practice of great restraint or the unfolding of a completely new philosophy.

Selected reading

Georgina Masson's *Italian Gardens* is now the classic on the subject and there are several editions around; there always seem to be spectacular books about Italianate gardens on the shelves, but still, so far as I know, no book dedicated to the outbreak of the Italianate in English gardens. Of the gardens mentioned and illustrated here, Hever Castle, Harold Peto's Iford Manor, Port Lympne, Portmeirion, Ditchley Park, Dartington Hall and Anglesey Abbey are all open to visitors to varying degrees and details will be found in the annual guides to houses and gardens. My biography, *Beatrix, The Gardening Life of Beatrix Jones Farrand 1872-1959* (1995) puts Dartington Hall and Dumbarton Oaks into the context of her career. George Plumptre's *Great Gardens, Great Designers* (1994) fits Peto, Farrand, Jellicoe, Russell Page, Mawson and Lutyens and Jekyll into an Anglo-American gardening scene. Percy Cane has not found a champion, but his autobiography, *The Earth is My Canvas* (1956) reveals an under-appreciated designer and his gardens.

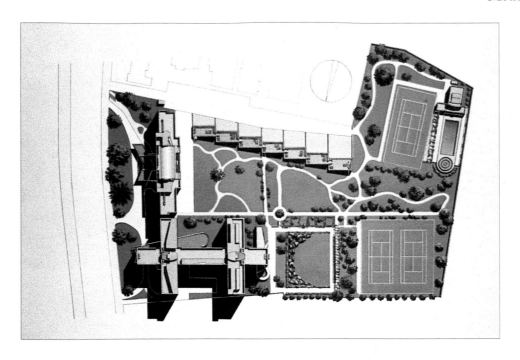

FIVE
Modern Movement Gardens

The word 'modern' was the talisman of the later 1920s, and the obligatory password to the 1930s in terms of house, garden and interior design. The winter number of *The Studio* for 1926-7 was devoted to 'modern gardens', but showed only the merest glimpses of the effect of serene white rectangles and clean white paving on garden atmosphere; the 'Modern' (with a capital M) architects Peter Behrens and Tony Garnier were mentioned, but Behrens's early small white house of concrete in Northampton still sported rustic dry-stone terrace walls and circular steps in true Arts and Crafts English style. *Country Life's* contribution, *The Modern Garden*, published in 1935, pictures the houses and gardens that follow here in its introduction, but then concentrates on over two hundred pages of pictures of Englishness and Italian inspiration as have gone before. At the other end of the scale the rows of semi-detached cottages with curved Crittall windows and sun-burst front doors that spread down the new arterial roads were still given recherché crazy paving and rustic sundials among little beds of roses. The influence of the International Modern Movement in architecture upon gardens in Britain was brief, late and inconsistent, but it was as vivid as the blaze of the sun on the white painted concrete houses, and has both vitally influenced and deeply confused garden designers ever since.

Above: Highpoint One and Two. Plan for the gardens, 1938, by the Tecton partnership.

Left: High and Over, Amersham, 1934. Two recent views of the garden with the ghosts of modern ideals. (Top) The white steel-framed structure of the house extended to make 'frames' for pictures of the garden. (Below) The concrete steps and circular pool as the main features of the garden.

At the 1928 International Exhibition of Garden Design, Lakeland Nurseries Limited, Thomas Mawson's Company, was a prominent exhibitor with gardens such as Keen Ground, Hawkshead in Lancashire.

The prelude to the 'thirties was an exhibition called the International Exhibition of Garden Design held at the Royal Horticultural Society for a week in October 1928. This exhibition illustrated the quandaries of contemporary books and magazines, and demonstrated completely the confusion of English and Italian traditions that were crowding into ever smaller and smaller gardens. The explanation of why there was a need for new thinking in garden design terms became very clear.

The exhibition was divided into five sections. The first was a lavish retrospective to 1850 made up of *Country Life's* photographs of Hampton Court, Wrest Park, Penshurst, Stowe, Canons Ashby, Bramham Park, Badminton, Castle Ashby and Kew. It was arranged by the patrician architectural editor of the magazine, H. Avray Tipping, whose monumental three-volume *Gardens Old and New* (new?) had just been published, and who (even in *Country Life's* Lutyens-designed offices) was felt to be 'a distinguished visitant from another and more cloistered world'. Tipping's own garden at Mathern Court near Chepstow was much praised at the time and he was to give early advice at Dartington Hall before Beatrix Farrand.

The second and largest section, 'Garden Planning for Town and Country', was contributed by a committee chaired by Mark Fenwick, the owner of Abbotswood in Gloucestershire. Prominent in this section was the work of Percy Cane (Boden's Ride, Ascot, Little Paddocks, Sunninghill and Abbey Chase, Chertsey), Lutyens (Hestercombe and the Mogul Garden in Delhi), Mawson's Lakeland Nurseries, Clough Williams-Ellis (Portmeirion), Reginald Blomfield (Mellerstain and Apethorpe) and the architects Darcy Braddell and

Mathern Court, Chepstow. The garden of the doyen of Country Life *writers, H. Avray Tipping, an organiser of the 1928 Exhibition.*

Craft Cottage, Norfolk. The architects were Deane & Braddell and the design was exhibited in the 1928 Exhibition as the epitome of a small owner's taste in the inter-war years.

Humphry Deane. Darcy Braddell exhibited a rather lovely but old-fashioned water garden at Melchett Court, Romsey (which was a repository for avant-garde sculpture by Carl Milles and Charles Sargent Jagger), and the amazing folklorish Craft Cottage at Paston, Norfolk (see above). There was a third, small section on public work, mostly municipal post-Victorian but also showing the work of Madeleine Agar, the first woman landscape designer in the public sector in England, with her management scheme and memorial garden for Wimbledon Common Conservators.

Reaction to the exhibition was prompt and portentous. The obvious 'lack of unity', illustrated even in the most 'up-market' journals such as *The Studio* annuals and in the work of English designers, prompted two of them, Stanley V. Hart and Richard Sudell (author of popular gardening books including *The Town Garden*), to call a meeting in February 1929 at which it was resolved to form some kind of professional association. It was advertised that all who were interested should gather at an arranged spot at the Chelsea Flower Show on 23 May. Brenda Colvin remembered standing among a group of thirty to forty to hear Sudell's plans, and that Percy Cane 'prowled around' listening but taking no part. The result was the British Association of Garden Architects, with Sudell as Chairman and Hart as Honorary Secretary. Fairly speedy amendments to the original ideas followed: the BAGA was to be a strictly professional body and garden contractors 'who had done sterling work' were only allowed in as Honorary Associates. The name was soon

The architect who links Miss Jekyll and the Arts and Crafts Movement with the Modern Movement was Oliver Hill, who designed Marylands, Hurtwood, Surrey. The pool court shows the beginning of Hill's transition to modern design.

changed to the Institute of Landscape Architects.

An early and important boost to the new profession was given with the arrival within its ranks of four architects – Oliver Hill, Geoffrey Jellicoe, Gilbert Jenkins and Barry Parker. Parker (1867-1947) was a good catch; he was at the height of his reputation as the architect of Letchworth Garden City, his partnership with Raymond Unwin having been dissolved in 1914 when Unwin became a government adviser, and now Parker worked on his own from his Letchworth home. With his international reputation he had to spend hours on large schemes, like the new plan for Oporto in 1915, but his heart was really in improved designs for worker housing and gardens, and in 1927 he had been commissioned to plan a garden suburb for 100,000 people at Wythenshawe near Manchester. He represented the public ambitions of the new profession. In many ways the unsettled state of garden design was typified by the architect Oliver Hill (1887-1968). Hill had been trained before the First War, come through it with a Military Cross and then found he had to work in the ever-changing atmosphere of the 'twenties and 'thirties. He was brilliant by any standards, but his ability to design in any style – he designed a picturesque thatched and timbered house, Woodhouse Copse in Holmbury St. Mary, Surrey, in 1925 for which Miss Jekyll did the garden – could also be called a neurosis, the reaction of a sensitive man to the turmoil of the post-war years.

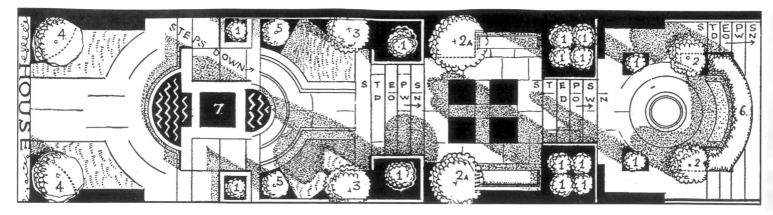

Charles G. Holme, editor of The Studio, *included this plan
(bird's eye view below) among ten he recommended for smaller
gardens in 1936. In all of them the aim seemed to be to
include as many points of 'interest' derived from as
many gardening traditions as possible. Illustrated
here is 'Garden Number Four' – an Anglo-Italianate
affair that seems to offer only a sense of claustrophobia
and confusion.*

1   Irish yews or Lombardy poplars
2   Horse chestnuts (red)
3   Horse chestnuts (white)
4   Catalpa
5   Clipped standard bay trees
6   English yew or *Cupressus macrocarpa*
7   *Cotoneaster horizontalis*

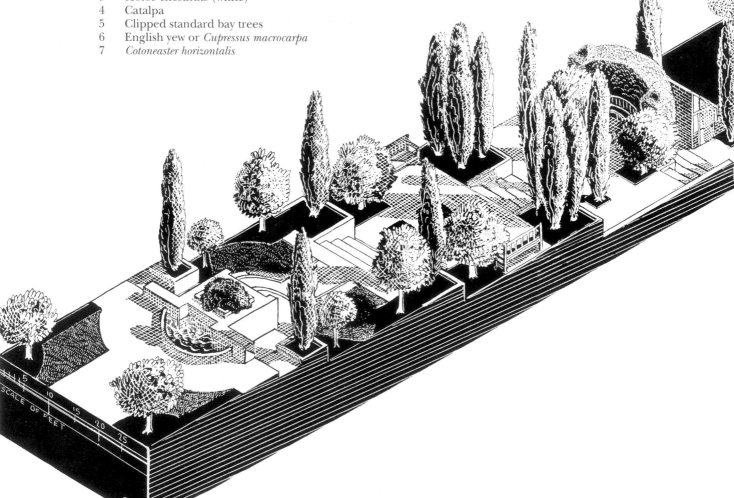

'Garden Number Ten' recommended by Holme for a smaller garden, was to be Anglo-Japanese. The first half of the garden is intended to give the impression of a quiet country bridle path; it leads to an 'Eastern' garden with water, willows, small bridges and a tool shed thatched with Norfolk reed .

A   Garden house, Norfolk reed thatched
B   Flight of three steps down to moraine
C   Tool shed, white plaster walls and
    Norfolk reed thatch
D   Group of boulders among which is a
    supplementary supply of water for
    pond
E   Stone flag bridges
F   Small gate to kitchen garden
G   Field gate under group of trees
H   Curved seat

1 Collection of bamboos	6 Myrtle	12 *Cydonia japonica*	18 *Lonicera nitida*
2 Collection of trollius	7 *Meconopsis wallichii*	13 *Virburnum plicatum*	19 Red chestnut
3 Pernettya	8 Weeping willow	14 *Berberis thunbergii*	20 Crataegus (red)
4 Pyrus malus.	9 Judas tree	15 *Berberis darwinii*	21 Collection of iris in moraine
'Niedwetzkyana'	10 *Cotoneaster horizontalis*	16 Veronica (blue)	22 Shrubby spirea
5 *Arbutus unedo*	11 Bay tree	17 Berberis	23 Collection of primulas

Joldywynds. The steps down to the bathing pool from the terrace.

Hill set the pattern of the Modern Movement in English house and garden terms with another house at Holmbury St Mary, for the barrister Wilfred Greene in 1925. Joldwynds was built on a spectacular hillside site, facing south across the Weald with, on clear days, a glimpse of the sea through Shoreham Gap. The house was placed into the matured garden of a former house (the important early Arts and Crafts house by Philip Webb, unfortunately destroyed). Hill's curvaceous white Joldwynds was set into the slope of its garden to make maximum use of the backdrop of dark trees; it had a simple and direct entrance drive with an unadorned, but beautifully correct, turning circle of gravel. The view was concealed until one reached the south side of the house with its large plate glass windows; each bedroom had its own sleeping terrace, and the flat roof was to be used for sitting out. The interiors everywhere were white, with combed plaster walls, pale burr ash doors and woodwork, curtains woven by Marion Dorn, paintings by Ivon Hitchins, furniture (mostly very uncomfortable) by Hill, and a formal garden of white paving. From the west loggia one gazed on the paving and white concrete seats beside a long plain pool, with columnar dark evergreens in pots – all framed in a white rectangle supported by plain white pillars. Hill had captured, at first try, the essence of the Modern Movement garden – strict geometrical shapes, and the white frame for pristine pictures. In *Country Life* Christopher Hussey enthused: 'Such a view,

such a site, such a garden, were crying out like Youth to be enjoyed'. He announced that Joldwynds was the new approach to country houses: 'What ancient Rome was to the Renaissance, the Riviera is to the modern. Instead of making a Grand Tour, we take the Blue Train . . . the new house is giving a kick to life and relieving it of some of its petticoats'.

Apart from the structural difficulties with the house, Hill's furniture inflamed the wrath of Mrs Greene – it was too hard, too high and too upright: 'I notice that you sat on my best and softest cushion in order to be comfortable', she wrote to Hill. The result of a number of small difficulties was that, eventually, Joldwynds was pulled down and replaced.

Joldwynds. Designed by Oliver Hill, the perspective of the approach drive and entrance front was by J.D.M. Harvey, 1932.

The pool terrace at Joldwynds seen from the 'picture frame' loggia.

Garden at Hyères, France, by Gabriel Guevrekian. A much-imitated small garden of the early Modern Movement.

The best Modern Movement house and garden which survives to give a clue to its original delights is Amyas Connell's High and Over on Amersham Hill, built in 1934 for Professor Bernard Ashmole. High and Over perches like some revolutionary flying wing on its hill, surrounded by the woodland that had to be planted to shield the eyes of its more traditional neighbours. Looking back now, it is possible to see how brave the architect was with the garden, especially in suburban Buckinghamshire. The terraced rose beds on the uphill front of the house were planted in strictly layered but truncated triangles. At the entrance end there was another simple curving entrance drive with a turning circle around a plain white concrete plant container. On the garden side, facing down the hill, there are still the small triangular plant holes left by terrace paving at the diagonal, and the terrace gives way to a central flight of plain concrete steps down to a circular blue pool. The final touch is provided at the service end of the house (for the old divisions still ruled), where a white framework extends from the wall of the garage and outbuildings and provides the frame for numberless views of the garden. It is a tragedy that a modern development has been allowed to chew at the edges of this garden, for in the continuing saga of the 20th century garden High and Over (house and garden) is as important as any Lutyens house with a Jekyll garden.

But the only really substantial figure in 1930s garden and landscape design was Christopher Tunnard. Tunnard had the vital continental connections that allowed him to see what was coming before anyone else in England. He saw the effect of 'rational architecture' on Swedish gardens ridding them of conscious symmetrical planning, and introducing a freer and more mobile arrangement. Swedish architects were striving for a contrast 'between the disciplined outlines of the terrace walls, paved spaces, pools, etc, and a free and luxuriant vegetation designed to produce a happy decorative effect . . . that is the work of nature or of chance'. He had seen a much-imitated little garden at Hyères designed by a young Persian architect, Gabriel Guévrekian.

High and Over, Amersham, Buckinghamshire showing the rose garden on the south east and uphill side of the house, newly-constructed with a shuttered concrete framework. The geometry of the rose beds perfectly complements the house, but the shock High and Over gave to surburban Buckinghamshire can easily be understood from this raw, young photograph, when the kind of house in the distance on the right was more usual. Note the 'picture frame' on the left of the photograph and compare it with the colour illustration on page 122.

The Japanese influence. The interior garden of a Japanese house by Sutemi Horiguti, which was illustrated with the now familiar raked sand and symbolic stone gardens of the Zen tradition. English designers were seeing this restraint for the first time.

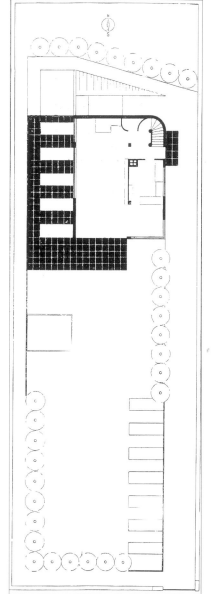

On a triangular site between white walls, the garden had square beds of flowers on a chequer-board pattern with mosaic between, and two Chinese orange trees. Tunnard knew the Belgian architect, Jean Caneel-Claes, who designed a series of stripped down gardens, and together they issued a manifesto: 'We believe . . . in the reliance of the designer on his own knowledge and experience and not on the academic symbolism of the styles or outworn systems of aesthetics, to create by experiment and invention new forms which are significant of the age from which they spring'.

The manifesto was enlarged into a series of articles which were printed in *The Architectural Review* in 1937 and 1938, and then collected into *Gardens in the Modern Landscape,* first published in 1938. Tunnard analysed the design of small gardens down to the bare minimum with a marked lack of sentimentality. Ruthlessness was necessary. 'Gracefulness, in things as in persons', wrote Raymond Mortimer in *The New Interior Design* in 1929, 'results from an elimination of the unnecessary'. 'Grace, it seems to me', wrote Oliver Hill in *Architectural Design*, September 1931, 'is the supreme desirability in fine architecture'. 'Grace', continued David Dean in *Aspects of the Thirties*, 'is a word not widely used in the credos of 20th century architects, but it has a rightness for Hill's work'. We have seen Hill's work and how he attempted to fit his gardens to this creed. Tunnard gave it much more thought and time and ruthlessly stripped away the emblems and symbols. He effectively stripped the whole of the picturesque ideal down to the influence of painting (which it was) and as such the need to produce a picture in a frame. Then he did an equivalent striptease on the English landscape style and produced, what it essentially was, the long view of a settled landscape, a prospect. Having evolved the picture and the prospect, said Tunnard, the art of garden design had then died – trampled to death by the bounty of the plant hunters tumbling into gardens and by a superfluity of other people's traditions brought back from all over the world along with the plants. The availability of so many interesting plants and the eagerness to cram every new idea and comforting tradition from the past and far away into an increasingly smaller space resulted in the overcrowded gardens that

Plan, opposite, and pictures of the architect Jean Caneel-Claes' garden near Brussels. The beds in paving beside the house are balanced by beds in grass at the end of the garden. The line of trees is of Lombardy poplars which afford a screen.

England had come to know (and love?).

Tunnard was not the total revolutionary; he was prepared to accept the opinion of the majority. 'The English garden, like the English Sunday dinner, is pretty much the same throughout the country . . . rose beds, herbaceous border, lawn and rockery . . . in all but the very smallest, there is a pergola garlanded with rambler roses'. Tunnard was quoting Jason Hill's *Gardener's Companion* of 1936, and he was prepared to accept that roses like the English soil and climate, that a herbaceous border, or preferably a mixed border, was an economical and decorative substitute for 'bedding out', that the lawn was the most valuable legacy from Brown and company, and that pergolas were useful to support good climbers. It was the way these things were thrown together that was wrong – that, and the intrinsic design of their parts. Grace was to be the aim.

After the stripping exercise Tunnard felt he was left with three sources of inspiration for modern gardens: fitness for purpose (the much vaunted functionalism of architecture), the influence of modern art, and the influence which he felt the strongest, that of Japanese gardens.

The modern philosophy dictated that, as the purpose of a garden remained rest, recreation and the provision of beauty, then these things must be provided in terms of the slimmed down economics and speeded up lifestyles of the modern house and its occupants. Garden design, Tunnard implied, was a matter of seeing the house and its setting (or better still, the projected house and its setting), then asking the client how much he wanted to spend on the garden and what he wanted the garden for: if, horror of horrors, this insensitive being insisted on a miniature alp or gothick summerhouse then you murmured about Le Corbusier and 'the styles are a lie', or loftily quoted Adolf Loos: 'The lower the standard of a people, the more lavish are its ornaments. To find beauty in form instead of making it depend on ornament, is the goal to which humanity is aspiring'. As a last resort, you suggested he try another designer.

A garden by Christopher Tunnard in Walton-on-Thames, Surrey. 'To the left a combined rose and tulip garden leads to a walk between flowering shrubs which borders the entire plot (about an acre) . . . A hedge divides the garden proper from the kitchen garden... Asymmetric as opposed to central axial planning saves the main lawn area from unnecessary sub-division'. The hedged circle on the right is a setting for sculpture.

The influence of modern art and artists, as explained by Tunnard, implied taking part. Tunnard and his friends, including the architects Raymond McGrath and Serge Chermayeff, took part in the Constructivist Movement of the 'thirties and the artists they most admired were the young Ben Nicholson and Henry Moore. Tunnard was thinking of Nicholson's early still lifes when he wrote of introducing spare, conceptual effects into planting design, of how the painter could introduce the planter to 'the interrelation of forms, plane and colour values'. He was thinking of the early work of Moore and Hepworth conveying 'new feelings for texture and masses, the need for [the artist] working outside his medium as well as in it, and the necessity for an unrestricted experimental technique'. In other words, the garden and planting designer must become just an artist as these others, drawing inspiration from the form and quality of the material of seats, walls and paving, but most of all from his plant materials, from the site and surroundings of his garden, and remain content to let Nature 'express his meaning in the simplest yet most convincing manner'.

Apart from the pure forms of Constructivist art, Tunnard felt that the garden designer should seek true beauty of form in the east, and make a pilgrimage to the temple gardens of Kyoto to understand the Japanese 'occult' symmetry. He banished that 'most snobbish form of Renaissance planning', the axial vista, where each side of the pattern mimicked the other, in favour of occult balance. What was more symmetrical than the human face? Yet the placing of a single red flower

Another Tunnard garden, this one for a country house near Leicester. 'The view from the principal rooms extends over a circular plunge pool and ha-ha and across thirty miles of typical shire landscape. The enclosed garden on the right is planted with alpines and dwarf shrubs set in flat beds between alternate squares of grass and paving'.

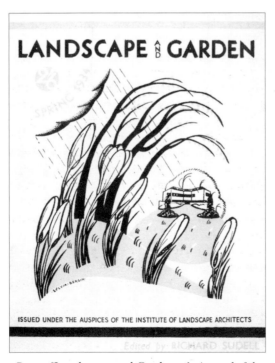

Cover of Landscape and Garden, *the journal of the Institute of Landscape Architects, 1934 – a fresh breeze blowing in the garden.*

A detail from 'Conifers', another of Cullen's drawings for Gardens in the Modern Landscape, *illustrating 'architectural' plants. 'The Monkey Puzzle or Chilian Pine'* (Araucaria imbricata), *wrote Tunnard, 'is best given a position by itself or grouped with its own kind – young plants on a lawn make a dark star-like pattern which is sometimes a pleasant change from the less precise growth of many other trees'.*

behind the right ear of a native girl heightened the appeal and allure, so expressing the idea of occult balance perfectly. This elusive merit was essentially a relative quality, depending on the interplay of background and foreground, height and depth, motion and rest – like Nicholson's paintings, of which abstract occult balance was the key, the effect in a garden and landscape could achieve the satisfaction of some innate desire of the human heart.

Implicit in the triumph of occult balance was the Japanese reverence for inanimate objects of which the Zen Buddhists were the most sensitive expressionists – reverence for simple things such as a branch of blossom waving against the sky, the shadow on a stone, or a single ivy trailing along a plain wall. Tunnard completely absorbed the oriental aesthetic in artistic terms (he presumably did realise that to take up Zen meditations and rake the sand garden every morning would mean shouldering another culture's old traditions and symbolism rather than those he so consciously rejected of his own!). It was, therefore, in purely aesthetic terms that he admired the Japanese gardens – the settings of the sliding-folding window walls of Japanese houses are 'echoed by screens placed near them, stone repeats stone on the simple terrace, plants encroach on the walls of the house and wreath themselves among its timbers . . . all calculated and under control. No great waves of vegetation beat upon the building; man shows his respect for Nature by allowing her admission into his scheme of planning but sees to it that the respect is mutual'.* And in return the designer does not exploit plants with 'barbaric massings of colour' but accepts form, line and economy of material as being of the first importance.

That word 'economy', used in its more material sense, was what was right about Tunnard's philosophy. Without even mentioning straitened circumstances, smaller gardens, even very small gardens, he had provided the aesthetic solutions to all these facts of 'thirties life.

He also, with the help of Gordon Cullen's drawings, established a new palette of plants in 'good' garden design terms. He introduced English gardeners to 'architectural' plants, plants with sufficient personality of their own to be effective in hard surroundings. Interesting leaf shapes, colours and textures, essential form and the ability to produce decorative fruits were suddenly rather more important than mere flowers. Architectural plants had to be hardy, and tolerant of dry sun and/or wet shade in their predominantly built environment of terrace, roof garden, courtyard pavings. They had to be of good value, i.e. provide some interest throughout the year, for they, unlike the wilder recesses of Munstead Wood, would be seen every day of the year. *Euonymus europaeus,* hebes, ivies, *Pachysandra terminalis,* frondy genistas, the famous *Fatsia japonica,* many a berberis and cotoneaster, bamboos, the New

* C. Tunnard, *Gardens in the Modern Landscape,* 1938, p.83.

'Plants with grey foliage', one of a set of Gordon Cullen drawings from Gardens in the Modern Landscape. *The drawing shows alliums,* Hosta fortunei, *and* Romneya trichocalyx *used in a modern architectural setting. Plants of good foliage, which produced white flowers, were especially valued, the whiteness complementing the whiteness of the concrete.*

Zealand flax, *Senecio greyii*, viburnums, especially *Virburnum davidii*, as well as hostas, euphorbias, *Tiarella cordifolia*, grasses and thymes – these and many, but not too many, others joined the ranks of approved plants and appeared on modern patios and in architects' illustrations. They eventually formed the basis for the Institute of Landscape Architects' basic plant list, a lifebelt for many young designers entering the stormy waters of horticulture. They were also to become rather too ubiquitous in after years, especially in new shopping malls and squares, but think how, in the 'thirties, they must have brought the revelation that garden design could be just such a 'spare and conceptual' art as painters and sculptors practised.

Tunnard's *Gardens in the Modern Landscape* still reigned in grand isolation as the only really original book of landscape design theory for the 20th century until Nan Fairbrother's *New Lives, New Landscapes* appeared in 1970. It still occupies a special place, largely for the nostalgia of what might have been, for much of it consisted of waspish accusations against more traditional designers that he did not stay to answer. With so many of those refugee artists and architects who thought they had found the freedom to work in the England of the 'thirties, he left for America when Hitler's war engulfed Britain in 1939. He spent the rest of his life making a large contribution to the reputation of Harvard's landscape school as the finest in the world.

Bentley Wood, looking at the south garden front from the edge of the coppice. The multi-stemmed birches were carefully selected and retained from the original coppice by Christopher Tunnard, who also ordained the mowing regime which linked the house to its landscape.

None the less, Tunnard also left behind two rare and tangible treasures of the Modern Movement garden, at the house that Serge Chermayeff designed for himself, Bentley Wood in Sussex, and at St Ann's Hill, Chertsey, Surrey, a house designed by Raymond McGrath in which Tunnard lived for a time.

In 1934 the burghers of rural Uckfield Rural District Council were raised to wrath by a planning application to erect something in their domain that was suspiciously flat roofed and made of wood, concrete and an awful lot of glass, and found themselves a place in architectural history by refusing the application. The architect, Serge Chermayeff – who was born in 1900, had come to England at the age of ten, been educated at Harrow and married the heiress of Waring and Gillow – appealed, won and his house was built. The main part is rectangular and weatherboarded, with a nod to the Sussex traditions, and is sited on sloping ground at the edge of a coppice, facing south over near fields and the more distant view of serene Sussex downs.

Bentley Wood is approached from the east along a plain concrete drive set into grass surrounded by the natural ground cover, bracken; the view to the south is realised but the whole of the house and its immediate garden are protected by a screen wall of yellow brick, above which rises the Canadian cedar

The dining room at Bentley Wood. Because of the large windows and glass sliding doors the relationship between indoor and outdoor spaces becomes very close. The window plants look like a Gordon Cullen illustration.

Bentley Wood. The sitting terrace and catwalk down to the landscape viewing frame at the end of the 'green gallery' – the epitome of Tunnard's picturesque concept in the modern manner. The plinth on the right was where the Henry Moore sculpture of a reclining woman was originally sited.

weatherboarding of the bedroom storey, faded to a soft mauve. Through the entrance arch the front door is at the far left corner, beside a group of berberis and other evergreens, in which the purply leaves of the berberis carefully reflect the colour of the weatherboarding. The front door is linked along the north side of the house to a separate garage block with a plain whitish 'pergola', without planting, but with a glass roof to give dry passage to the garage. The living and dining rooms, with their large glass walls, face south on to the terrace, and the main sitting and eating-out area is recessed beside the dining room next to a small rectangular pool, placed at the front of the sheltering east wall. This sheltering east wall extends the terrace southwards in grass – Tunnard nicely called it a 'green gallery' – to the very definite termination of the formal garden in a frame for viewing the landscape. The desire to view is satisfied by a catwalk which continues the terrace paving to the frame and ends in a plinth that was especially included to hold a Henry Moore reclining figure, now no longer there. The planting inside the wall is of shrubs rather than flowers, with contrasts in texture and, again, the touch of purple against the yellow brick wall reflecting the colour of the weatherboarding of the house.

To the west the mown lawn melts into mown paths through the coppice, with two special paths in curved paving stones; the edge of the coppice is linked towards the house by careful selection (by Tunnard) of groups of many-stemmed birches and single oaks, which complement the serenity of the whole setting and link the house to its landscape in miniature 18th century terms. Christopher Hussey visited Bentley Wood in 1939 and came away feeling a sense of 'sanity and freshness' in a house and garden that was so nearly not built, and where he had found a deep refuge from the world of an 'orgy of destruction' to which he had to return.

Tunnard's own home for a time, St Ann's Hill at Chertsey, Surrey, was designed by Raymond McGrath (1903-1977), an Australian who came to England and practised like a brilliant brief comet in the London 'thirties' sky, leaving St Ann's Hill as his only major house. This hill site was marvellous, the hill being a historic viewpoint over the Thames valley; the estate had belonged to Charles James Fox in the 18th century and some ornamental buildings were left from this time. It was the sense of history that encouraged Tunnard to leave most of the 'garden' as parkland in 18th century terms, but with a new twist of significance for the house. McGrath's house is dominated by the circle as the source of design (Bentley Wood was so definitely a 'rectangular' house); the entrance is into a circular court and one is met by the curve of the white house that is clearly part of a circle, but as yet cannot be seen as such. In fact the house occupies just over half a circle, the completion being made on the garden side by terrace paving. The circle is given a tail by the garden court, thus making a kind of question mark. The idea is very effective, especially in plan, so much so that the plan of house and garden was etched into glazing on a wall in the entrance hall.

St Ann's Hill is not a small house; it has a grand drawing room set within the curving wall of glass that overlooks the terrace and the 'park'. From the terrace outside the eye and the foot are directed towards a curving pool, set around the shape of existing rhododendrons, an almost overly explicit expression of the

St Ann's Hill. The courtyard garden, with its geometrical and astringent shapes, was designed to be enjoyed from the roof, as seen here, as well as at ground level.

dictum that nature inspires design, a rather shocking reversal of the usual soft plantings moulding themselves to hard walls in that a very substantial structure is moulded around a soft and ephemeral plant.

The major part of the sun-worshipping garden is set at the west end of the house, along the tail of the question mark, where the paved courtyard garden has been enclosed with a white framing wall, giving beautifully 'framed' pictures of the cedars down the park slope, so forming a very 20th century link. The modern walls actually connect cleverly with a fragment of 18th century walling from the original house which itself is part of a circle – mellowed old brickwork on the outside, rendered sparkling white on the inner side. The effect is totally Jekyll and Hyde. Originally the white walled

Modern art formed an essential part of the modern garden. Here Willi Soukop's fountain, in Hopton Wood stone, framed in the doorway of the garden at St Ann's Hill, pleases the eye at the end of the courtyard vista. Sadly, the fountain, like the Henry Moore sculpture at Bentley Wood, has long since been removed from its intended site.

interior formed a backdrop and frame for a fountain in Hopton Wood stone by Willi Soukop, but that, like the Moore at Bentley Wood, has disappeared from the scene. The courtyard garden, to be viewed from the roof as well as from within, was treated similarly to Bentley Wood's terrace, with plain rectangular pool, simple paving, a circular motif and circular pool for *this* place, and sparse, highly textural planting that was meant to soften but neither dominate nor disturb. Beyond the frames, beyond the pristine pavings, the parkland rolled away; the plan shows that originally its features were to be carefully controlled in circular motifs, short grass to long grass in circular movements through cedars and pines. St Ann's Hill is still intact, a rare and now almost unique inspiration from before the second deluge.

In overall terms it was but a trifling tragedy that the coming of Hitler's war frightened off so many potential leaders of design, though in the context of this chapter of my book, it was a tragedy. It was no wonder they left; the excitement in the air of a deep blue day of July 1939 was sniffed by Siegfried Giedion with Frank Lloyd Wright in far away Wisconsin: 'We stood on the top of the hill on which is built Wright's own home, Taliesin. The dome of the hill was so precise in shape, especially the hill crown which became a low-walled garden above the surrounding courts, reached by stone steps walled into the slopes, that I asked if

The picture frame wall of the garden court at St Ann's Hill, designed especially for viewing the old cedar of Lebanon which was a feature of the parkland.

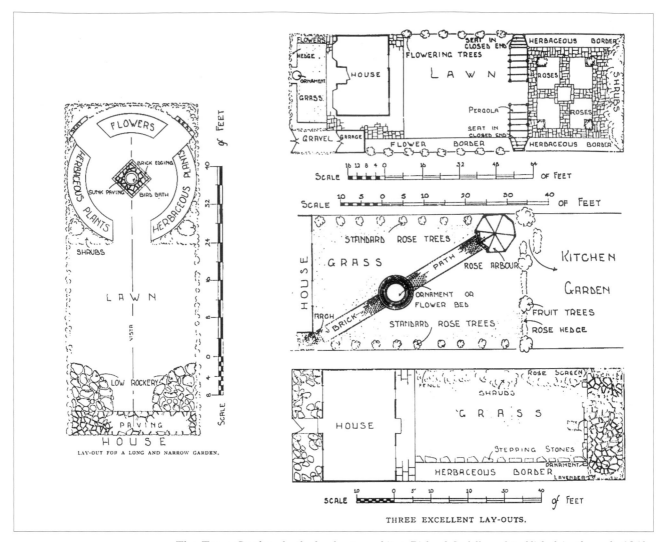

The Town Garden *by the landscape architect Richard Sudell, and published in the early 1940s, contained these layout designs for small gardens. Sudell was an early critic of the state of garden design in England in the inter-war period.*

it had been built up in artificial regularity from below. 'No, it is the natural soil', Wright said, 'I never build houses on the top of a hill. I build them around it, like an eyebrow...'.

Giedion continued, rather like St John: 'And I saw that it was indeed the house itself which brought into consciousness the pure curve of the ground, that in a certain sense its many-layered and unobtrusive forms gave meaning and definition to the contours from which it rose'.* With such a many-splendoured world awaiting how could so many talented artists and architects not leave for America? Here there was only war work to be done, and it must have been hard to believe that in a world after Hitler there would be any gardens at all.

* S. Giedion, *Space, Time and Architecture*, 1941, 8th. ed., 1949.

St Ann's Hill. The garden court as it is today. Where is the Willi Soukop fountain? See page 144.

Selected reading

The two editions of Christopher Tunnard's *Gardens in the Modern Landscape* (1938 and 1948) and Peter Shepheard's *Modern Gardens* (1953) are now only found in libraries or architectural booksellers. I have written more fully on Tunnard in *Eminent Gardeners* (1990) and Dorothee Imbert's *The Modernist Garden in France* is excellent on Le Corbusier, the Vera brothers and other designers who were so influential on English ideas. Ever since writing this chapter, originally in the mid-eighties, I have wanted to put the story of the modern garden in Europe, Britain and American into a book; this is now under way and will hopefully appear, simply titled *The Modern Garden*, in the year 2000.

Sissinghurst Castle. The entrance arch, looking into the Courtyard.

Opposite (above): The Rondel Rose Garden, in June, with South Cottage at the far end.

148

SIX
Sissinghurst Castle 1930-1962

The poet and novelist Vita Sackville-West and her husband Harold Nicolson bought Sissinghurst Castle virtually as an agricultural slum in 1930. By 1938 they had turned the dilapidated buildings into a home and the rubbish dumps into a beautiful garden and to them, as to thousands of others, the threat of war came as a threat to their very personal refuge and all they had worked so hard to achieve. But, unlike thousands of others, their personal fears were thrown into historical relief by their writings; in Harold Nicolson's 'war at the top' – at the Ministry of Information, at the BBC, in his daily encounters with ministers and politicians – his garden became an infinitely precious symbol of a peaceful happiness that had once been and when it was all over would be there once again. Vita Sackville-West wrote much of her epic poem *The Garden* during the war in an endeavour,

> To hold the graces and the courtesies
> Against a horrid wilderness.

Vita Sackville-West in her garden at Long Barn, about 1928. The photo was taken for an American magazine article celebrating her popularity as a novelist and poet. Writing was her chief activity in the 1920s, though she was already becoming enthusiastic about her gardening.

She also shepherded the Sissinghurst community of the old and very young, grew food for them, turned her lawns and orchard into hayfields, laboured to save her garden from damage beyond recall and wrote vivid prose and poetry on the mood of her Kent countryside laid open to the war in the air and possible invasion. Vita's war effort, which was her way of standing and fighting for what both she and Harold believed in, was typical of many private battles for many private worlds and such battles made up a national will.

Coming so soon after the effort of making the garden, the fight to keep it instilled another layer of history into its soul and added another reason for the

Knole, Kent. The sunken garden as it was in the early 1900s when Vita Sackville-West was in her teens. She wrote her many adolescent romances in the little summerhouse, and so wove herself into the history of the great house and her Sackville ancestors. The romance of this background was to remain the inspiration of her gardening for the rest of her life.

right and popular belief that the garden of Sissinghurst Castle represents the most significant of English 20th century gardening achievements. The making of the garden was very much a joint achievement and it has taken the present writer a whole book, *Vita's Other World*, to attempt an explanation of how it came about as an expression of both Harold and Vita's needs, hopes and beliefs, and of their love. To a very large extent Vita became a good gardener because Harold needed her to create a beautiful backdrop for his life, since the kind of 18th century mansion that, he felt, such a person of distinction should inhabit, was beyond their means. As it was Vita's lot to stay home and actually make the garden though, Sissinghurst's inspiration must begin with her.

She was born in 1892 and brought up at Knole in Kent, the great house that Elizabeth I had given to Thomas Sackville. Vita was an only child, strong willed and often lonely, and she grew up passionately loving the great house, believing that it had a 'soul, benign and mild', adoring to play in the splendid state rooms, accepting that the faces of her ancestors and the great men and women of England's past that stared down at her from the walls were her friends. She was utterly steeped in the history of Knole and the Sackvilles and quite naturally imagined that she would carry on in their tradition — caring for Knole and its garden, writing poetry and novels, with perhaps an occasional

Long Barn, Sevenoaks. The original cottage, left, and the added barn on the right.

foray into literary society or the outside world. If that life had been her lot we would be in some ways richer, in some poorer, but it was not. A notorious court case involving the Sackville inheritance ensured that Knole was entailed away from Vita; it was only to belong to the male members of the family.

So she had to step out and find a world of her own; she was by no means penniless and she was something of a celebrity for her eccentric aristocratic grace, her literary ability and her high degree of intelligence. She carried with her a love of Knole's garden, one that the Sackvilles' had consciously kept untouched by fashions since it had supported a household of two hundred souls in the early 17th century – a garden of walled rooms filled with salads, vegetables, flowers, orchards, inhabited by white doves, peacocks and tame bears (the walls kept them off the vegetables), with formal walks and bowling greens immediately near the house. Over the centuries the walls had crumbled and not been replaced, but in Vita's childhood she still felt it to be a large garden made up of smaller spaces – little square orchards with apple trees and iris, snapdragons, larkspur and pansies beneath them, arches through which she could catch differing glimpses of the great house, long green walks between herbaceous borders. In half the garden the trees that her forebears had planted had grown out of their straight lines into a wilderness of beech and chestnuts of great age, with mossy paths through bluebells and daffodils.

Vita had started her gardening 'late in life' – as she called it – when, in her twenty-second year, she came to the first home of her own in England, a cottage called Long Barn near Sevenoaks in Kent. She had left Knole when she married the young diplomat Harold Nicolson in October 1913 and the first months of their marriage were spent happily in Constantinople. The following year they had come home for Vita was expecting their first child in the summer of 1914. As a young mother at Long Barn Vita started her gardening in conventional ways: she gathered catalogues, visited nurseries and other people's gardens, made lists of her plants, but also in rather privileged ways. Her mother Lady Sackville took her to see Miss Jekyll and Munstead Wood and Sir Edwin Lutyens designed some formal beds, called a Dutch Garden, for Long Barn. Throughout the war and the 'twenties Long Barn and its garden formed the background to Harold and Vita's well-documented, tempestuous lives. The

Long Barn, Sevenoaks. The garden made by the Nicolsons between 1915 and about 1928.

Long Barn garden was a rustic English version of an Italian villa garden, with terraces of lawns, box-edged parterres of roses and lilies outside Harold and Vita's respective writing-room windows, small avenues of Lombardy poplars, a damp woodland of azaleas and wild flowers and Vita's triumphant mix of purple and blue, honesty and forget-me-not in a great sweep, and an Apple Garden, the enclosed orchard carpeted with spring flowers and roses in memory of Knole. In the raised brick-edged beds of Lutyens's Dutch Garden Vita practised her colour schemes of grey and blue, grey and orange, grey and pink.

Long Barn was a beloved flower-filled refuge for them both, but by 1929 it was under threat from development in the neighbouring fields. Harold's life was at a turning point, for he had given up diplomacy and was returning home to an uncertain career in journalism in London; Vita's father, Lord Sackville, had died in 1928 and Knole had become the home of her uncle Charles and his wife Anne, whom she did not like – a dislike exacerbated by a conflict of tastes and Vita's feeling that Knole was no longer her home. A new enterprise was needed.

It was at this point, through her friend Dorothy Wellesley and the Wellesley's land agent, Douglas Beale, that Vita discovered Sissinghurst Castle and fell 'flat in love' with it. Sissinghurst had been the great house of the Baker family, and Cicely Baker was the wife of Thomas Sackville. It had a tall slim tower of pink brick so like one at the Sackville home at Buckhurst in Sussex, it had touches of grandeur in fragments of cottages, it was in the middle of her favourite Wealden countryside, isolated in safe fields, and it was unutterably romantic. It was, in fact, also largely a ruin and in May 1930 the Nicolsons paid £12,375 for their ruin and Castle Farm with about three hundred and fifty acres of land. They hardly took a second look at the substantial Victorian farmhouse and its matured grounds with lawns and rhododendrons, but concentrated on the picturesque old cottages and stables, the bailiff's house (in want of immediate repair) and gateway and tower (in a passable state of repair) set among endless vegetable gardens and vast accumulations of rubbish – heaps of rusty iron, old bedsteads, old ploughshares, cabbage stalks, matted wire, mountains of sardine tins, bindweed, nettles and ground elder. Castle Farm and the farmhouse were let to Captain Oswald Beale, who became a stalwart friend of the Nicolsons and supporter of Sissinghurst's garden over the next quarter of a century.

The first priority was Vita's Tower – it was hers of right for the similar tower at Old Buckhurst had been the refuge of Anne Torrell, wife of Sir John Sackville, in Henry VIII's time. The Nicolsons spent their official first night in an upper room of the tower on camp beds on 18 September, 1930. The bailiff's house, now called South Cottage, was ready for occupation next and some furniture was moved over from Long Barn. They slept in South Cottage for the first time on 6 December. They never fully moved in until April 1932, but from that December on weekends and holidays were spent camping at the castle.

Vita's earliest joys were those of the treasure hunter – chunks of carved stone, old fireplaces and stone sinks were found in the rubbish and refurbished for use in the house and garden. The last thing the Nicolsons wanted to do was to destroy the magic of their Sleeping Beauty castle (very deeply asleep, some said) so they revealed it piece by piece. The ivy came off the walls, ugly lean-to buildings were stripped away, the courtyard was emptied of rubbish, levelled and seeded and the entrance arch was opened. Some of Vita's first plantings were around this arch; she planned a colour scheme of coral, white and green and planted *Chaenomeles japonica*, sweet bay, *Magnolia grandiflora* and her first two rarities, *Myrtus tarentina* ('Jenny Reitenbach') and *Plagianthus lyallii* (now *Hoheria lyallii*) with grey leaves and white flowers in July. A stone sink which she found in a pigsty was brought home in triumph as her first trough garden and filled with gentians, lithospermums and *Omphalodes luciliae.*

Despite Harold's almost immediate discovery that he disliked journalism, 1930 was a year of some success, even after the purchase of Sissinghurst. Vita's enormously successful *The Edwardians* and Harold's biography of his father, Lord Carnock, were published. After a late summer holiday Vita was working at Sissinghurst again in October and rejoicing in the discovery, underneath rubbish, of the south arm of the former moat and its wall: 'The moat wall is going to be very superb. They have uncovered its foot a bit . . . there are lovely

The view from Vita's Tower arch towards the entrance arch, the path bordered with rosemary and Irish yews.

Sissinghurst. The Orchard in full spring bloom.

big stones at the foot of the piers the piers are going to be lovely', she wrote. Clearing the nearby Nuttery revealed that the trees were in avenues and she made a first planting of narcissus and foxgloves which Harold collected from the woods in an old pram. In December 1930 Harold paid £125 for a dam to the Hammer stream in the lower field to make his lake.

The following year was the time of Harold's entanglement with Sir Oswald Mosley's New Party, and the consolation of Sissinghurst was much needed. South Cottage's garden was arranged on its simple crossing, with brick paths around the edges and a hedge of briar roses on the orchard side. On the cottage walls Vita planted the noisette rose 'Madame Alfred Carrière' which nearly took the cottage over, and the climbing hybrid tea 'Madame Edouard

Sissinghurst. Looking out from the Nuttery, across the Moat Walk and wall, into the orchard.

Herriot', the yellow lantern-flowered *Clematis tangutica*, and two honeysuckles.

She planted the climbing rose 'Richmond' on her tower, with clumps of rosemary at its feet and roses and figs on the courtyard walls. The Tower lawn had already been enclosed with a single yew hedge on the orchard side and the Bishopsgate wall (adorned with the plaque of three Greek bishops brought home from Constantinople) made the fourth side. It was planted with the rose 'Fortune's Yellow', *Abutilon vitifolium*, a ceanothus, rose 'Emily Gray' as a companion for sweet bay and a large flowered *Clematis* 'Gypsy Queen'. These were later joined by a precious *C. armandii* Harold brought home from La Mortola in Italy.

The Nicolsons moved into Sissinghurst on 9 April, 1932. Harold worried

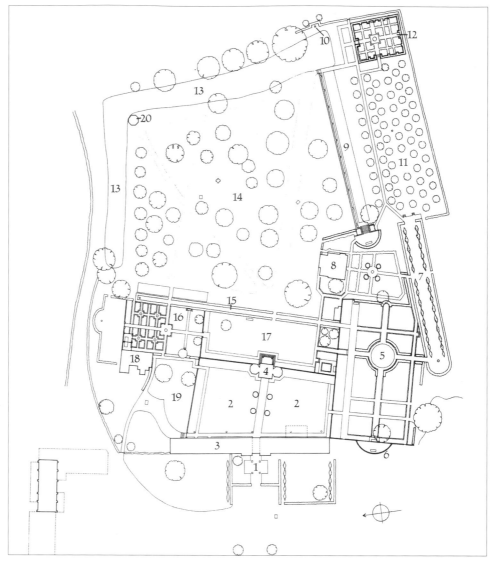

1	Entrance	11	Nuttery (Nut Plat)
2	Courtyard	12	Herb Garden
3	Big room	13	Moat
4	Vita's Tower	14	Orchard
5	Rondel Rose Garden with surrounding rose beds	15	Yew Walk
6	Powys's Wall	16	White Garden
7	Lime Walk	17	Tower lawn
8	South Cottage and its garden	18	Priest's House
9	Moat Walk	19	Delos
10	Statue of Dionysius	20	Gazebo erected in 1969 to the memory of Harold Nicolson

The plan surveyed and drawn by Stuart and Christine Page for the National Trust, makes an interesting comparison with the aerial photograph of Sissinghurst Castle taken in July 1932, after it had belonged to the Nicolsons for two years and they had lived in it for three months.

Opposite: the arch in the centre of the long 'barracks' range of buildings has been opened up, but there are still cottages to the right and stables to the left. The courtyard has been grassed over, and beyond the Tower the lawn has been enclosed by a single row of yews. In the top right corner the future Rondel Rose Garden is filled with rows of vegetables, but beyond it the pattern of the South Cottage front garden has been set out. To the left of the photograph the garden around the Priest's House (eventually to be the White Garden) is set out, but what will be Delos is still rows of cabbages.

about the castle as a drain on their income but at least he enjoyed it, spending most of the summer at home there writing *Public Faces* and *Peacemaking 1919*. That July the first aerial photographs were taken. Looking at them today they show the approach still through a ramshackle farmyard, and though the arch has been opened up, there are still only muddy tracks through grass towards it. The entrance range of buildings still consists of cottages to the right of the arch and stables and the old brewhouse to the left, and the awkward angle of this range of buildings which Harold will curse when he is trying to square up the courtyard paving is clearly seen. Inside the courtyard the marks of the once clinging cottages can still be seen on the walls, but the ground is level and looks green with a gardener reassuringly walking back to his wheelbarrow beside a flower border on the Tower wall. The courtyard has not yet been closed at the northern end – there were to be long arguments with their architect A.R. Powys as to how this gap should be filled. The photographs also show the bare outline of a rose garden (now the White Garden) outside the Priest's House and what is to be Delos is still filled with rows of cabbages. More cabbages fill the unhappy rectangle that is still called the kitchen garden, which is just beginning its transformation into the Rondel Rose Garden in this summer of 1932.

It was Harold Nicolson's endlessly patient measuring and sighting that coaxed

Above, left: the Yew Walk, planted to give a sheltered passage between South Cottage (the Nicolsons' sleeping quarters) and the Priest's House with the dining room.

Above, right: the Rondel Rose Garden looking north through to the courtyard. The roses are chiefly the Revd Pemberton's hybrid musks.

South Cottage, as it is today, still covered in roses, and with a crazy-paving path to the front door.

Opposite: close-up of the washing copper Vita found on the site and used as a centre-piece. She planted it with orange flowers so that with its verdigris coating she produced her favourite colour combination.

161

South Cottage at Sissinghurst, 1962, where Vita and Harold Nicolson had their bedrooms and Harold a writing room on the ground floor. The garden was always a bower, planted in a luxuriance of sunset colours. The climbing rose is 'Madame Alfred Carrière'.

Sissinghurst's obtuseness into shape. His hopes for a west-east vista through the whole garden were dashed by the unalterable angle of the moat wall, so he capitulated and planted his avenue of lime trees on the southern boundary of the garden in complementary parallels. The Moat Walk was divided from the slightly different angles of the lines of nut trees by a bank of azaleas, and a special purchase, the Statue of Dionysius, was placed to close the vista: what was so brilliant was that Dionysius also ruled the vista across the Orchard to the Tower.

For a vital four years, from 1932 till his death in 1936, the Nicolsons' architect for Sissinghurst's renovations was Albert Powys, the Secretary of the Society for the Protection of Ancient Buildings. Powys developed a fatherly affection for, and sometimes despair of, his clients' ideas; he was desperately sensitive to Sissinghurst's ancient fabric and atmosphere and determined that

The west end of the Rondel Rose Garden. This photograph, taken from the top of the Tower, shows the immaculate geometry which Harold Nicolson achieved out of Sissinghurst's 'obtuseness', and the importance of the semicircular wall designed by the architect Albert R. Powys.

all the materials and methods of renovation and addition should be in keeping. Vita, who felt she was equally sensitive to Sissinghurst's atmosphere, was always accusing him of over-elaboration and lavish expenditure. Out of all the fireworks (from which Harold was only too often absent) it must be appreciated Powys contributed a great deal to Sissinghurst's well-being; he made the Priest's House into a comfortable home for Ben and Nigel Nicolson, built the enclosing north wall in the Tower Courtyard, put forward the original suggestions for the double Yew Walk and the Erectheum, the summer loggia outside the Priest's House dining room, and, most important of all, he built (in the teeth of Vita's rage and disagreement) the west wall of the Rondel Rose Garden (Powys's Wall). This wall, with its lovely semicircular bay, raises the Rondel Rose Garden to the status of a garden room of the finest pedigree – the Nicolsons and Powys must have realised they were recreating the parterre of the Villa Gamberaia in the textures of a colder climate. It was shortly after the wall was finished, and Vita had buried a 1935 penny in it, and agreed it was *right*, that poor Powys died from overwork in May 1936.

In the autumn of 1935 Harold entered another place he felt to be a spiritual home, the House of Commons, where he was to be for the next ten years. He spent his weeks in London or in travelling and his weekends at Sissinghurst. Vita left her home less and less; her 'London season' slipped into three hectic days around Christmas, and she became content with her country life. When she wrote her poem, *Sissinghurst,* in 1931 she had given notice that she had found her refuge, where she could sink into her 'birthright far from present fashion' and live a quiet life in tune with country days and seasons.

Thus in the 'thirties Sissinghurst was shaped into the Nicolson family's home.

The Nuttery at Sissinghurst underplanted with polyanthus as it was in the Nicolsons' day.

Harold Nicolson's pots, originally oil jars he brought home from Italy, are spaced in the flower-filled pavings.

It had more than a little unconventionality about it – parts were really spartan – but it was well suited to the writers who lived there. Its special endearment is that it is a home *within* a garden rather than a home with garden merely attached. Vita used to say frequently that Sissinghurst was not a winter resort. The lifestyle was idyllic in summer but demanded goodly amounts of English fortitude in the cold and the wet. A car could get no nearer than the outer side of the entrance porch and Vita and Harold had to walk to South Cottage, where they slept, across wet grass and around dripping plants. Presumably there was a nightcap in Harold's sitting room downstairs in the cottage, and hopefully there was a fire in Vita's bedroom, where layers of Victorian wallpapers had been stripped to brick walls and the floors were bare boards with a Persian rug or two. For breakfast they had to come along the Yew Walk, almost across the whole width of the garden, to the Priest's House dining room – a route also to be taken in the dark after dinner every night; as Vita said, delightful on warm moonlit evenings, but less agreeable on snowy nights! Vita had to brave the gale gusting through the Tower arch to climb to her writing room with its one small radiator and wind howling round the turrets. But they all loved it more than anywhere else in the world.

The last summers before the war were when the visitors really began to come. Word had got around. There were requests from women's institutes, antiquarian societies, a party of Baker relatives, and the garden was opened for the first time on 1 May, 1938, for the National Gardens Scheme. There is no doubt that in the eyes of those who saw it Sissinghurst was at its most beautiful then, in the face of war. Imagine it, with its vistas direct but not quite fulfilled, its pavings crisp and new but the exception rather than the rule, its beds and borders overflowing in a perfect delicate partnership between flowers planted and those arrived by chance, and over all an easiness and ease that comes from nature and the gardener working in a harmony of mutual respect. By the entrance, the approach to the arch is now paved, and a pair of the exquisite vases that Lady Sackville brought from La Bagatelle outside Paris are full of purple violas; rosemary bushes in flower tumble across the pavings. Through the arch, past the carefree Irish yews, is the vista to another arch, another pair of vases and the blossom in the orchard beyond. The courtyard is serene and pretty with pots of lavender and more violas set against the mown green lawns; one has the feeling of a lot of 'activity' skywards, where gables, chimneys, turrets, weathervane and a vivid and new Sackville flag in black, red and yellow

Sissinghurst. Harold Nicolson's Lime Walk, the springtime event.

all rise into the blue. The grass is newly cut, but gently so, by the old machine pulled by Gracie Fields, the pony, in her leather boots.

In the Rondel Rose Garden the tiny rondel is a green toy of yew, but the earliest of the Revd Pemberton's hybrid musk roses, 'Danaë', was in bloom on 1 May, 1938, and the glossy fountains of her sisters were getting ready too; the iris spikes and flowers of purple and gold press over the grass paths, and inside the north wall of the garden the herbaceous border is a model of expectant neatness. In Harold's Lime Walk the edges of the new paving (much narrower than now) are awash with a hundred shades of blue and yellow – muscari, primroses, scillas and white-winged jonquils – and his newly acquired oil jars and terracotta pots are filled with red tulips. The Nuttery – the Nut Plat, as Vita

165

liked to call it – is that never-to-be-forgotten sight of the rainbow polyanthus carpet edge to edge. The moat is cool and still and slightly overgrown. The orchard has paths cut through nodding grasses and fritillaries and is full of birdsong and blossoms in all shades of pink. It is just becoming the wild garden of their dreams – wide green paths with bosky banks and tangles of wild roses, with drifts of iris, narcissi and white foxgloves. There was of course no White Garden to draw the gasps, only beds of roses and delphiniums.

The last picture is of Delos – in Vita's words 'small irises come through mats of aubretia and thyme, and the myrobalan plum trees overhead are white with blossom', which tumbles on to the ranks of old stones, treasures from Sissinghurst and treasures from Harold's ancestral home, Clandeboye.

This was the garden that Vita fought so hard to protect during the war. As he left, her energetic young head gardener, Jack Vass, implored her to look after the hedges and the paths even if the rest had to be let go. She did this. She scythed the orchard and lawns for hay, gathered the apples, said goodbye to Ben and Nigel who went into the army, prepared a gas-proof room for those that were left in the small community, and waited. The garden, in those first summers of the war, seemed more beautiful than ever as if defying the evil and the threats. At Sissinghurst they watched the bombers droning overhead, they saw the dogfights in the blue, they stood back as the army used the Tower as a lookout and crawled around the lake and woods, and they generally carried on as best they could. And then it was all over. The garden was opened as a celebration on 2 May, 1945 – the visitors must have seen spring flowers, blossoms and masses of ground elder, but what did it matter? Everyone was on their way home and Sissinghurst and its little community had survived intact.

For five years after the war, from 1946 to 1951, the garden was reworked by Jack Vass and his gardeners, and during those five years Vita and Harold's lives settled into a pattern which lasted until Vita's death. Harold worked his weeks in London on his writing, book reviews, lecturing, committees and travelling and spent his weekends at home. Vita was always at home, save for now rarer jaunts abroad and an annual trip around England looking at other people's gardens, usually in July and August when she did not think her own garden was worth looking at. But they were both getting older; Harold was sixty in November 1946, which depressed him profoundly, and on two weekends in the same month he found Vita propped against a tree in the garden, crying because her back hurt so much it stopped her working. They were both aware of their limitations, and of economies that had to be made, in efforts and finances. They both concluded that the post-war Sissinghurst would have to have a slightly different emphasis from that of their original dreams – simplicity, economy of labour and materials and lower upkeep costs would have to be the order of the new days.

But there were concepts that were symbols, of a value above all practical considerations, and these had to be protected and enhanced. The immediate task when work restarted was to cut the weeds in the Nut Plat and restore the carpet of polyanthus, the symbol of all that was bright and good. Then the courtyard and Tower lawns were ploughed and reseeded, and after such violent acts as these, Jack Vass set about removing the surviving plants, stripping the elder-ridden soil and replanting the Rondel flower beds. Then he moved into the Cottage Garden, but only after consultation with Harold for whom this garden had an 'elective affinity' though Vita did the planting.

Neither Vita nor Vass touched the Lime Walk, which was Harold's sole charge and looked after by its own gardener, Sydney Neve. Harold called his spring borders in the Lime Walk 'My Life's Work'. He had written from Leicester in the midst of the disastrous General Election campaign of 1945 when he was ousted: 'I am determined to make MLW the loveliest spring border in England', and added that if he could do that he would be happy. The Lime Walk is the most lavishly recorded of Sissinghurst's gardens, with Harold's efforts set out in meticulous detail in notebooks that he kept from 1947 until the late 1950s. The notebooks are a cavalcade of ideas: small crowds of the loveliest daffodils, 'Mrs R.O. Backhouse' (the first pink daffodil), *Narcissis bulbocodium conspicuus* (the hoop petticoat) and the jonquils he loved. There are delicate soft chrome yellow *Tulipa batalinii* mixed with *Sparaxis* 'Fire King', *Anemone* 'de Caen' and a patch of modest little myosotis; he loved cottage tulips, 'Couleur Cardinal' and 'Cottage Beauty', the frail 'Lady Tulip' *T. clusiana*, the old 'Clara Butt', and new ones from Peter Barr, 'Inglesworth', 'Rembrandt', 'Annie Laurie' and 'James Wild'. Each lime was numbered, and 'Lime Tree No. seven North' was a 'museum piece' of success surrounded by *Anemone fulgens*, jonquils and dog's tooth violets; an Etruscan vase was filled with *Iris pumila* and a jar from Ravello with *Clematis macropetala*, its delicate tendrils and violet blue flowers tumbling over the jar. Dwarf iris and muscari ran between the paving stones and *Gentiana acaulis* and even *Genista januensis*, the winged Genoa broom, were planted there; he cherished old varieties of polyanthus, especially yellow ones, and *Primula denticulata* which grew because Neve had the strictest instructions to swamp them with the snake irrigation.

Vita began writing her weekly column in *The Observer* in the autumn of 1946 and through these pieces her garden can be seen as it flowered in its prime, in the 'fifties.

She was extremely wary of Experts (with a capital E) but felt she was quite an expert herself on old roses. Her collection was at its peak during the 1950s and she must take much of the credit for showing off the old roses that first her friend Edward Bunyard and then Graham Stuart Thomas wrote about. She collected them passionately. Among the gallicas were 'Alain Blanchard', spotted crimson, maroon and purple, 'Anaïs Ségalas', mauvy crimson fading to lilac, the remarkable striped 'Camaieux', the practically thornless old rose pink 'Du Maitre d'Ecole' and the splendid 'Cardinal de Richelieu'. Besides her Pemberton hybrid musks 'Danaë', 'Pax', 'Cornelia', 'Felicia' and 'Pink Prosperity' (of which she had three each), and the hybrid perpetual 'Roger Lambelin' trained over the hazel hoops, she adored the romance of the Bourbons. Her Bourbons included the wonderfully scented 'Mme Isaac Pereire' with shaggy purple flowers, 'Mme Pierre Oger', a pale silvery pink lady, the blushing powder pink 'Souvenir de la Malmaison', the thornless cerise-pink 'Zéphirine Drouhin' and the splashed and striped rose-madder 'Commandant Beaurepaire'.

Though forever loyal to her old roses she did venture to consider others, as

The mixed border against the courtyard wall in the Rondel Rose Garden at Sissinghurst, June. This is the nearest the garden comes to having a herbaceous border.

long as they smelt like roses. She grudgingly admitted that floribundas had some merits – particularly the sumptuous red 'Frensham' and yellow 'Sandringham' and 'Sunny Maid'. Hybrid teas were a more secret vice – she had admired some she had seen in Regent's Park, in Queen Mary's Rose Garden, but at Sissinghurst they were confined to the vegetable and cutting garden behind Powys's wall. Her dozen bushes for cutting for the house were mostly old favourites: 'Emma Wright', a pure orange, the coppery orange 'Mrs Sam McGredy', crimson scarlet 'Ena Harkness', darkest crimson 'Charles Mallerin' and the silvery pink, verbena-scented 'The Doctor'.

The Rondel roses were the yardstick of the Sissinghurst year: 'The garden has been really lovely this summer', she wrote to an American admirer in July 1955, 'the roses have flowered as never before, and now they have been

The Herb Garden in Vita's time. It was laid out immediately before the Second World War, but planted afterwards. Vita collected as many as sixty varieties of herb for their texture, colour and fragrance. She was no cook, and her gardens at both Long Barn and Sissinghurst were a long way from the kitchens.

succeeded by masses of white lilies'. *Lilium regale* massed against the neat green of the Rondel hedges were Harold's dream – along with the waving spires of white eremurus and pink and white peonies.

The Herb Garden beyond the Nut Plat was actually planted, rather timidly, before the war. Afterwards potatoes were used to clean the ground and Vita and Vass discussed the divisions of the beds by grass paths into the pattern that exists today. That the Herb Garden is the furthest garden from the kitchen bears witness to the fact that Vita was no cook; her collection was far more for colour and foliage contrasts and for her bees and, according to the list for her Acme labels, she collected over sixty varieties of herb – all the expected ones and the more unusual: melilot, clary, elecampane, costmary, woad, herba barona, vervain, horehound, Old Lady, Old Man, comfrey and Good King Henry. Thymes were rather special: she tracked down twenty-four varieties and grew about six – 'To smell the thyme', she noted with satisfaction, was a Greek phrase to express a literary elegance of style.

The orchard and the Moat Walk were homes for some of the rarest plantings, highly individual ideas which were of their nature transitory, except for the billowing white crinolines of the rose 'Madame Plantier' trained up the old apple trees. For a while Vita grew beds of gentians over the old foundations of the former castle – like the Mediterranean at her feet – but watering them with mains water, when it arrived, killed them. In the orchard Vita spread generous

The orchard and moat in spring. A rare photograph taken in 1955 when Vita was still in charge of her garden.

sheets of spring colour with trumpet daffodils mixed in drifts with flat-faced narcissi, followed by fritillaries, cowslips, fine grasses and wild flowers. She let the flowers and grasses wave into high summer, for her bees and for themselves, and although paths were cut through them the orchard was never completely cut until after seed time in July, in the best wild-flower meadow manner.

We have seen that in the creation of Sissinghurst's garden Vita had indelibly stamped her romantic personality, leavened with her fine good taste, on the courtyard, dominated by her Tower, in the Rondel Rose Garden and in the orchard. Harold's classicism, tinged with the sentimentality of which he was only too aware and which overcame him at times, rules the Lombardy poplared entrance, his Lime Walk, the Nuttery and the Yew Walk. That these elements combine with such harmony is the measure of their complementary souls; it was indeed a joint effort – 'our lovely garden', as they never ceased to remind each other and everyone else. It is fitting therefore, that the last great Sissinghurst effort was a joint one – the White Garden belongs to both of them.

There are many reasons why the White Garden was made. Vita was a 'night owl' – she loved walking in the dusk and darkness, and it was then that she saw how the white lilies gleamed in the twilight or moonlight; she first thought of planting white flowers in the south-west corner of the Tower lawn, a dark corner where a pond was drained. Then Vita and Harold contemplated what to do with the area in front of the Priest's House, which they both felt was unsatisfactory. Vita, the romantic, watched the snowflakes falling and thought how wonderful their resident 'great ghostly barn owl' would look swooping over a pale garden in the gloom; Harold considered grey and white – cineraria

The White Garden: the crossing. A photograph recalling the character of the garden in Vita's day, with the narrowest of arches in the hedge and a crowd of pots of pelargoniums around the central oil jar. Now that Sissinghurst has become the most famous of the 20th century gardens it is these intimate details that are sacrificed to crowds of visitors.

in masses, rabbits' ears in masses, lad's love, santolina, a jungle from which *Lilium regale* would rise, would be good, and would prolong the garden's interest through July, which he felt was important. Eventually, to the box and lavender-edged beds of what Vita at first called her White Garth, she added to Harold's original planting ideas the new things that he found by scouring the Royal Horticultural Society's shows, a long-held habit. There were white gladiolus, an English iris 'White Pearl', pompon dahlias, a small eremurus and the very large *Verbascum broussa* (*bombyciferum*) - with white delphiniums, a foam of gypsophila, *Hydrangea grandiflora*, white cistus, white tree peonies, *Buddleia nivea* and white campanulas.

The White Garden completed Sissinghurst as Vita knew it. During the 'fifties she reached the crest of her life. She was so famous that dealing with her post took a major part of her mornings. Her Companion of Honour awarded in the New Years Honours of 1959 had given her dignity (if she needed it) and her *Observer* column was bringing her ever more popularity (if she desired it). A

The White Garden. This was the last of Sissinghurst's 'garden rooms' to be completed. It was planted in 1951 especially for the summer of the Festival of Britain.

The White Garden with masses of alliums, snapdragons and Stachys lanata. In the background is the Priest's House, where Vita died in 1962.

The Virgin Statue in the White Garden.

Vita Sackville-West's memorial plaque on the wall beneath the Tower arch.

letter addressed to 'The Hon Mrs Nicolson, A Castle Somewhere in Kent' would find her, and so would one marked simply 'V Sackville-West, The Novelist'; both delighted her. She spent her days writing letters, supervising her garden, being a Magistrate on the Cranbrook Bench or attending a Committee for the Preservation of Rural Kent meeting in Maidstone. Rarely, but regularly, she went to London for a meeting of the National Trust Gardens' Committee of which she was a founder member. Otherwise she was at home to streams of visitors – and finest of all, in June 1952, came the day when Queen Elizabeth the Queen Mother came to lunch and walk around the garden.

During the later 'fifties Vita and Harold relished their now famous garden, the thing of beauty they had made where none was before. They hoped it would pass to their grandchildren. In practical terms Vita was content about her gardening – her two young head gardeners, Pamela Schwerdt and Sybille Kreutzberger, joined her in the autumn of 1959 – and she soon knew that her garden was in expert hands. She died, of a cancer, at Sissinghurst on 2 June, 1962. Harold, lost without her, drifted on quietly for another six years. At a joint memorial service in St James's, Piccadilly, on 16 May, 1968, their friend John Sparrow, Warden of All Souls, Oxford, spoke of their literary achievements and of the love of their friends; but many thoughts must have left the sublime Wren interior and flown and settled amongst the spring flowers and blossoms of a garden somewhere in Kent, in the prime of its blooming.

The Tower where Vita had her writing room on the first floor, viewed from the White Garden.

Selected reading

Victoria Glendinning's *Vita* (1983) and James Lees-Milne's 2-volume *Harold Nicolson* (1980) provide the biographical backgrounds. It is essential to read V. Sackville-West's own words about her gardening; there is a 1986 edition of her *Observer* pieces, edited by Robin Lane Fox, and the long poems, *The Land* (1928) and *The Garden* (1946) appear in a joint new edition (1989) edited by Nigel Nicolson. He has also edited his father's diaries and letters in several volumes, and *Vita and Harold, The Letters of Vita Sackville-West and Harold Nicolson* (1992).

At Sissinghurst Castle, the two head gardeners, Pamela Schwerdt and Sybille Kreutzberger, have retired to their own garden in the Cotswolds after spending longer in the garden than Vita was allowed. Tony Lord's *Gardening at Sissinghurst* (1995) gives an admirable account of the development and maintenance of the garden. The opening times are published annually by the Trust and would-be visitors are advised to check carefully as numbers are sometimes limited.

SEVEN

Hidcote Manor and The 'New Georgian' Gardens

The idea that gardens for their own sakes could be legitimate cases for conservation was established by the formation of the National Trust Gardens' Committee in 1948. This was an act of tremendous foresight. The founding members of the committee were Lord Aberconway, second Baron of Bodnant who was then President of the Royal Horticultural Society, the Earl of Rosse, the Hon. David Bowes-Lyon, Sir Edward Salisbury, Dr H.V. Taylor and Vita Sackville-West. The aim of the committee was to raise money for the care and restoration of great gardens the Trust already owned (including Charlecote, Bramham Park and Montacute) as well as to consider which gardens were 'suitable' (great enough) to be acquired by the Trust in the future. Some urgency was given to the committee's deliberations by the knowledge that Major Lawrence Johnston wished to leave his wonderful garden at Hidcote Manor in Gloucestershire and retire to his French home, La Serre de la Madrone, near Nice. The committee immediately decided that Hidcote Manor should be saved 'for the nation', and it was through the members' efforts that this was successfully accomplished and that Hidcote became the first property acquired by the Trust for the sake of its garden.

Above: Hidcote Manor. Pink borders and the original Cedar of Lebanon near the house. Opposite: the garden is famous for the 'living walls', the luxury and variety of fine hedges.

Inevitably, the existence of the Gardens Committee, an alliance of the Trust and the Royal Horticultural Society, implied a hierarchy; there would be gardens that were acceptable and gardens that were not. Of the latter, little is known and little said. The reasons for, and against, acquisition by the National Trust of any property are complex; one only has to dip into James Lees-Milne's diary volumes to see just how complex, how much a matter of personalities, of being in the right or wrong place at the right or wrong time, of the confusions of politics and finances. The 'politics' of conservation are not part of this book, but there is no doubt that the acquisition of Hidcote was the equivalent to the founding of a dynasty of taste, a kind of Hidcote connection, that leads through other gardens and garden makers and may add up to a 20th century style.

The connection does not actually begin with Hidcote Manor, but in a village beside the Thames, a few miles south of Abingdon, called Sutton Courtenay. The Old Manor House in Sutton Courtenay, Oxfordshire, was given as a wedding present, in 1895, by Lady Wantage to her nephew Harry Lindsay and his wife Norah. It was not to be a happy marriage, and for the next fifty years, Norah Lindsay devoted her boundless energies and talents to the making of her own garden and the gardens of friends. She is undoubtedly the most brilliant and elusive gardener of this century, she had a strong influence on

The Long Garden at Sutton Courtenay Manor House as it was in Norah Lindsay's time. The photograph illustrates her allegiance to the garden gods of ancient Florence and Rome, and her genius for laissez-faire and planting that was more a matter of spires and turrets of flower form rather than of Miss Jekyll's broad sweeps and drifts.

Mrs Lindsay's garden at Sutton Courtenay was full of plants that she felt had planted themselves in just the right places.

many other gardeners, and her strongest influence of all was on her friend Lawrence Johnston.

The garden of Sutton Courtenay's manor house was captured for us in a *Country Life* article which Mrs Lindsay, as a signal honour, was allowed to write herself in 1931. I would like to reproduce the whole of it, but one paragraph will have to give a taste of her theatrical approach. She owed her allegiance, she wrote,

> 'to the crumbling shrines of the ancient garden gods of Florence and Rome'; she believed that her garden should offer a 'perpetual refreshment to the spirit . . . which becomes a wonder and a blessing'. 'You feel you never want to leave this source of enchantment where peace and beauty beckon and colour and shade and fountains and long green alleys invite and promise a shelter from the unbearable noise of the world without... The tremendous solemn trees, the smooth green lawns which one remembers holding long evening shadows on their laps, the beguiling wild flowers which give and give and give, rushing in and out of the real garden with a reckless joy and a dancing grace; the old sun-burnt walls, pink as a malmaison and wreathed in wistaria tassels; the moonlit evenings when the turf is dry and warm, covered in rose petals like strange exotic shells; and the scent of the syringa and

Hidcote Manor, the Old Garden, with Alfred Parsons' 'nook quality'. Parsons, both artist and garden designer, lived in Broadway and almost certainly helped with the first stages of Hidcote's design.

honeysuckle weaves invisible webs of sweetness across one's dreaming face – these are the enduring possessions that the garden bestows, a happiness not made with hands'.

Mrs Lindsay was so emphatically not a professional – but a charismatic amateur – she never drew anything or wrote anything down. She was a brilliantly intuitive artist of the moment. Only fragmentary memories remain; we know she worked for the Gilbert Russells at Mottisfont Abbey, and Vita Sackville-West (who was only too well aware of Norah's talents) wrote of a lovely border beginning with white and pale blue flowers, working up through pinks to flames and oranges, for the Trittons at Godmersham Park. Blickling Hall in Norfolk maintains the huge herbaceous beds that she designed for Lord Lothian in the 1930s. Norah certainly worked at Cliveden because Nancy Astor was one of her closest friends; Russell Page remembered the audacity of the beds on Cliveden's terrace being crammed with Nepeta (catmint), but then it seems likely that he varnished over her work for Philip Sassoon (who was another of her great friends) at Port Lympne. Lanning Roper admired the remnants of her blue borders reflected in the long pool at Trent Park, Middlesex, Sassoon's other garden, in the 1950s. Norah's daughter, Nancy Lindsay, who collected rarities into her own garden at the Manor Cottage, Sutton Courtenay, wrote to Vita Sackville-West about two large rose gardens that her mother was making, using a collection of old roses that she had

Hidcote Manor, Mrs Winthrop's garden, named for Lawrence Johnston's mother.

sheltered during the war years. In 1945, Norah had to sell Sutton Courtenay; she had long struggled financially, helped out by her friends, and especially Lawrence Johnston, who wanted to give her Hidcote Manor. It was Norah's sudden death, in the spring of 1948, that left Hidcote to the National Trust.

It seems likely therefore that much of the credit for the wonder of Hidcote's planting in the 1930s must go jointly to Norah and Lawrence Johnston. Johnston was born in 1871, of American parents, and brought up in France. He entered Trinity College, Cambridge in 1894 and then became a British citizen in order to fight in the Boer War. After a spell farming in Northumberland in

1907 his mother, Mrs Winthrop, bought him a modest farmstead of 280 acres with a small stone house and some cottages at Hidcote Bartrim, high in the Cotswolds – the high and windy place he had chosen for the good of his weak lungs. Johnston was first a farmer, and soon a gardener – he took ten acres in from his fields to make the garden and his only notable asset was a large cedar of Lebanon.

One of today's paradoxes is that so many people speak of the gardens of Sissinghurst and Hidcote in the same breath, for they could not be, or should not be, more different in their atmosphere. It is impossible to experience Sissinghurst without the all-pervasiveness of Vita and constant reminders of the well-known details of the Nicolsons' marriage and lives. But Hidcote can be fully appreciated – indeed, to a large extent has to be – without more than a nodding aquaintance with its maker. The makers could not have been more different: Vita Sackville-West – tall and dark, literary, godless, melancholy, almost imprisoned in her traditions and castle walls, with a passion for alsatians, loving her flowers for their innocence, beauty and historical pedigrees; and Lawrence Johnston – the fair, blue-eyed, dapper Major, devoutly Roman Catholic, scrupulous in his tastes, inseparable from his pack of dachsunds, who loved painting and reading horticultural books but never left a written word about his garden let alone himself. People love Sissinghurst, but they admire Hidcote. It is arguable that in terms of a great garden Sissinghurst is too emotional a place, too dominated by its makers' tastes of a wide world. Perhaps a great garden should be sterner in its dominance of the arts of design, less susceptible to history, even less susceptible to nature and more demonstrative of horticultural niceties and achievements. Hidcote is a perfect expression of Major Johnston's talents, but then his talents were almost perfectly bestowed for the making of an ideal gardener.

Besides his one cedar and some pleasant beech trees, Johnston had other useful assets: plenty of money and a bravura which allowed him to impose a strict formality upon his empty fields. He was extremely, compulsively, scrupulous and thorough in everything he did; he had apprenticed himself to an English farmer before he took up farming, and he studied architectural design before he laid out his garden.

Hidcote has a T-shaped layout; the crossing of the T runs from east to west, from the old garden around the farmhouse and through double borders of pink then red flowers, to the pair of Pavilions on their stepped platform; beyond them the Stilt Garden rises gently to the garden's highest point and a pair of ornamental gates. From the Pavilions' platform the 'leg' of the T is thrust grandly southwards as the Long Walk, which ends in a larger pair of ornamental gates against the sky and the distant southwards view. With this geometrically pleasing plan Hidcote displays not only Johnston's skill in the manipulation of his levels, but also his equal skill in turning ten open, windy acres into walks and enclosures of comforting human scale. The levelling, or rather careful grading, of the slopes, not possible without farm machinery (Johnston undoubtedly drove the tractor himself) plays tricks with the mind's eye. The sloping walk westwards through the pink and red borders to the Pavilions and the Stilt Garden appears foreshortened, so that the pleasure of

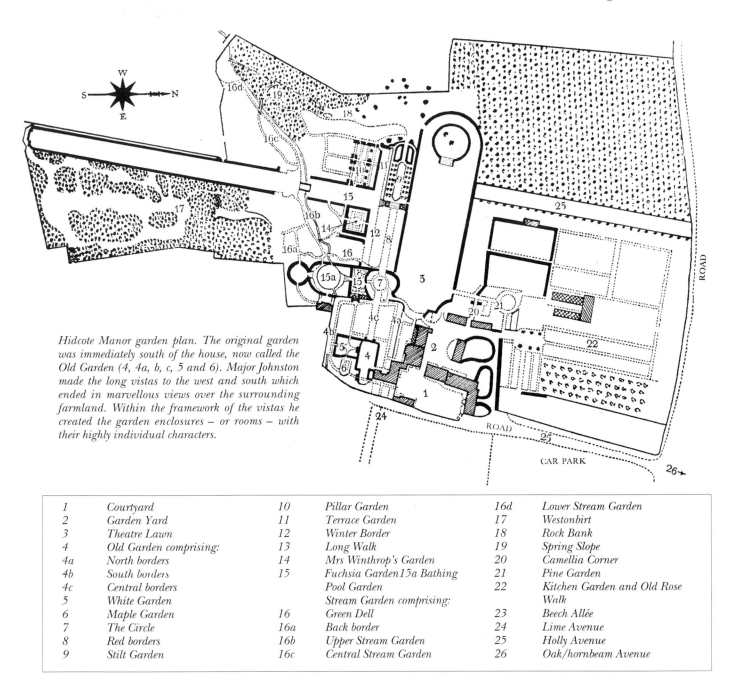

Hidcote Manor garden plan. The original garden was immediately south of the house, now called the Old Garden (4, 4a, b, c, 5 and 6). Major Johnston made the long vistas to the west and south which ended in marvellous views over the surrounding farmland. Within the framework of the vistas he created the garden enclosures – or rooms – with their highly individual characters.

1	Courtyard	10	Pillar Garden	16d	Lower Stream Garden
2	Garden Yard	11	Terrace Garden	17	Westonbirt
3	Theatre Lawn	12	Winter Border	18	Rock Bank
4	Old Garden comprising:	13	Long Walk	19	Spring Slope
4a	North borders	14	Mrs Winthrop's Garden	20	Camellia Corner
4b	South borders	15	Fuchsia Garden 15a Bathing	21	Pine Garden
4c	Central borders		Pool Garden	22	Kitchen Garden and Old Rose
5	White Garden		Stream Garden comprising:		Walk
6	Maple Garden	16	Green Dell	23	Beech Allée
7	The Circle	16a	Back border	24	Lime Avenue
8	Red borders	16b	Upper Stream Garden	25	Holly Avenue
9	Stilt Garden	16c	Central Stream Garden	26	Oak/hornbeam Avenue

pacing through the flowers is longer than expected, then the view back from the Pavilion steps is a surprise. This trick is also played with the Long Walk, which dips, apparently in the middle, but really at a point one-third of its length. The sense of enclosures of human scale is given by the Hidcote hedges which were, of course, primarily necessary for shelter so that almost any desirable garden flowers could grow. The triumph of Hidcote is that so many tender rarities did survive there, the treasures that Major Johnston brought home from his own plant-hunting expeditions to Kenya and the Victoria Falls and from his last expedition to China with George Forrest – again, part of his thoroughness, he wanted rare plants so he went out to collect them.

It is the hedges of Hidcote – the living walls – that give it a different quality to so many other English gardens that merely have brick or stone walls. The

Hidcote Manor, the Stilt garden of pleached hornbeams, architectural severity in living walls, much imitated in later 20th century gardens.

hedges add so much to the quality of luxuriance of textures in the garden; Vita Sackville-West rhapsodised over them in her original article* on Hidcote:

'There is a great deal of Yew, but Major Johnston was not content with plain Yew, beautifully as he employed it. In one place there is a mixed hedge of Yew and Box, an attractive combination with its two shades of green: he has realised how many different shades of green there are in Nature, not forgetting the value of dark pools of water and their *chatoyant* reflections, and he has made use of all these greens in a way that would have delighted Andrew Marvell. Different textures of leaf have also been made to play their part in the "flatness" of Yew contrasted with the inter-planted shine of Holly – there is one harlequin of a hedge, with five different things . . . Yew, Box, Holly, Beech and Hornbeam. Like a green-and-black tartan'.

Into his spaces, sky-lighted rooms, Major Johnston poured his plants – he planted, planted and planted – so that Hidcote became a jungle of beauty, beautifully controlled. The garden rooms displayed their individual characters by their furnishing and ornament, be it rich and pretty or classically severe. The latter came as especially surprising, as it was classical severity achieved, not in stone and brick, but in living plants: the Stilt Garden, with pleached hornbeams, box like, not a leaf out of place, on flawlessly straight trunks, and the Pillar Garden, dominated by Irish yew pillars of immaculate proportions, again not a leaf out of place, rising from beds of Hidcote lavender, *Philadelphus*

* Originally printed in the *RHS Journal,* November 1949, and subsequently reprinted as part of the National Trust guide.

The main garden vista at Hidcote. Seen from the Old Garden it passes clipped hedges (living walls) and the pink and red borders, before leading up to the Pavilions, the Stilt Garden and the sky beyond.

'Belle Etoile' and peonies. The contrast between the strict architecturally clipped shapes and the abundant prettiness of the planting was the mark of Hidcote as Major Johnston made it: everywhere the rich and pretty was seen against an immaculate background – masses of phlox playing around chunky topiary birds in the Old Garden, the wonderful trails of scarlet *Tropaeolum speciosum* through yew hedges, ribbons of a bright mauve campanula along the foot of a wall, linaria creeping along the steps, masses of old roses everywhere (he and Mrs Lindsay made Hidcote's collection one of the finest in England). And the rare and the beautiful flowered at Hidcote too – treasures of iris and clematis given to him by Miss Ellen Willmott and rare varieties of shrubs he had brought home himself to his semi-tropical border and heated plant houses. The particularity of Hidcote's planting was that it was what Miss Jekyll would have dismissed as 'spotty'; there was no need to stick to Miss Jekyll's safe drifts of single textures and graded colours and Mrs Lindsay and Major Johnston actually broke most of her rules.

Vita Sackville-West felt that Major Johnston would want to have been thought of as a botanist and plant hunter; he was in that great tradition, but it was his outstanding skill as a designer, or rather his thoroughness in mastering the skills of design, as he mastered other matters, that makes Hidcote an outstanding garden. The contrast of treatment between one 'room' and another, one walk and another, the clear pattern of progression that leads one around the garden with never a doubt as to what follows, the cohesion and

The Bathing Pool Garden at Hidcote expresses Major Johnston's taste for perfect geometry in the Italian manner transported to a very English setting.

harmony of the garden's whole design, allows Sylvia Crowe in her *Garden Design* to say that 'It is this application of the universal laws of composition which lifts Hidcote so far above a mere plant collection and makes it something more than a re-hash of other garden styles'.

I think that Sissinghurst and Hidcote do have one essential in common – they reveal how the making of a great garden, especially in unsympathetic times, demands total devotion on the part of its maker, and will swallow up every considerable resource and more. Perhaps the gardens of the 20th century have to be set upon a scale of obsessiveness, determination, talents and means?

An interesting garden, contemporary with Hidcote, was made by a friend of Lawrence Johnston's, the Hon. Robert James, at St Nicholas, Richmond, Yorkshire. Robert James, the younger son of Lord Northbourne, was Managing Director of a steel company in Barrow, and gardening was his greatest hobby; he was ultra-fastidious in his tastes, not allowing bright yellows into his garden (he did not think they suited the northern light) and he thought the colours of autumn vulgar. But he was immensely skilful with his – again – highly intuitive and individual plantings and in persuading tender plants to grow in his northern clime.

In design James's garden was an expression of his own taste and derived from the romantic setting of his Tudor manor house that had once been a rest house for Easby Abbey. The garden consisted of a series of rooms with immaculate yew walls, old brick walls covered with lovely plants and straight grass walks between richly planted borders. He had wonderful double borders: '130 yards long and 18 feet wide backed by hornbeam hedges . . . unlike any others I know', wrote Lanning Roper.* 'Planted to require the minimum of staking, there are large numbers of fine shrub roses, ceanothus, tree peonies, eleagnus, phlomis and potentillas, some of which are very large...a Wolly Dod [rose] is over 12 feet tall and as much across . . . Plants are chosen for colour, for foliage and for fragrance.

* 'A Garden for Reflection', *Gardening Illustrated*, November 1953.

The formal garden at St Nicholas, Richmond, Yorkshire, with ornamented yew walls and beds of China roses, fuchsias, pinks and geranium.

Viola cornuta creeps through the border like a breaking wave of mauve . . . grey and silver foliage plants . . . are a foil for the deep crimson and cherry of sweet williams'. James also had red borders of *Phlox drummondii, Lobelia cardinalis,* verbena, alonsoa, dahlias, penstemons and centaureas, peat walls made to house a collection of Asiatic primulas, lewisias, ramondas, haberleas, soldanellas and meconopsis, as well as carefully cosseted climbing gazanias, *Mutisia ilicifolia* and *M. oligodon* and *Berberidopsis corallina* with heart-shaped leaves and long sprays of crimson flowers set with *Nerine bowdenii* and *Alstroemeria ligtu* hybrids.

St Nicholas in its heyday with double borders beside an immaculate green walk and backed by hornbeam hedges. These were the borders that Lanning Roper saw and commented on in 1953 – 'unlike any others I know'. The walk ends in a semicircle of grass with a William Kent seat.

Tintinhull House, Somerset. Opposite below: the view from the house door through the Eagle Court as it was in the days of the maker of the garden, Mrs Phyllis Reiss. Opposite, above: the pool, lawn and borders made by Mrs Reiss out of an old tennis court, with the dominant cedar, a tree which she treasured. This page, above: the vista from the house continuing beyond the pool garden. These two more recent photographs show the fine quality of the garden enhanced by the care of Penelope Hobhouse and her husband, Professor John Malins.

Tintinhull House. A further view of the pool and garden, with the dominant cedar.

Major Johnston, Robert James, Johnston's neighbour Heather Muir at Kiftsgate Court, Phyllis Reiss at Tintinhull and the Hornbys at Pusey House were perpetuating and continuing certain traditions of English taste in gardening into the unsympathetic air of the mid-20th century. Between the wars this taste could be identified, as it has been by John Cornforth, as 'the manor house cult'. Extravagant tastes needed foreign fortunes, and the extravaganzas at Hever and at Leeds Castle, and of the Trittons at Godmersham Park, of William Randolph Hearst at St Donat's and of Philip Sassoon at Port Lympne were all a little un-English. Though Lawrence Johnston too had had American money, his own fastidious taste captured a style of gardening that was acceptable to the kind of people who bought and lovingly restored the old manor houses and their gardens. Among them were the Jenner family who restored Lytes Cary in Somerset and then bought Avebury Manor in Wiltshire, Sir Ernest Wills at Littlecote Manor, and Colonel Reginald Cooper with his string of lovely houses, Cold Ashton near Bath, Julians in Hertfordshire and Knightstone in Devon. These houses and their gardens were very much the world of *Country Life* in the 'thirties.

The work continued quietly during the Second War, but afterwards, as after the First War, nothing could be the same. The First War had destroyed in an ideological, perhaps even an emotional, sense; the Second War destroyed in a more practical way. Gardens were destroyed by neglect and there were neither the manpower nor the resources to revive them in the former spacious terms. There were no longer to be any gentlemanly professions or businesses upon which the making of a garden could be supported; diplomacy, directorships and even farming were now full-time occupations from which neither time nor energy was left over for a demanding hobby. In the world of gardening the terms

Tintinhull House, Somerset. The garden as in Colonel and Mrs Reiss's time, showing what was then a new use of ground cover planting. Shortages of manpower and resources after the Second World War meant certain adjustments in garden design, but at Tintinhull the tradition of English taste in gardening continued, in spite of the unsympathetic air of the mid-20th century.

'labour saving', 'economy of planting' and 'low maintenance' became the order of the days. Everyone wanted ground-covering plants to defeat the weeds, all-seasons' colour to avoid the constant change over of plants that had occupied the old-fashioned gardener's summer, and bigger, brighter, more foolproof plants in any case. In other words, the garden had to become as trouble-free and wipe-clean as the plastic-surfaced kitchen, and this implied a permanence that is anathema to nature. Gardening on these terms was set to become a national hobby and a profitable business – because so many of the plants died they frequently needed replacement. A very few people continued to insist that good design had a part to play in popular gardening, but this was mostly seen as an attempt to squeeze the elements of the English landscape style into the long thin plot of the average suburban garden, the subject of my next chapter.

The few that did care about good design and a certain elegant restraint in taste, cared about it in their houses and in their gardens. Before the war the

Avebury Manor, Wiltshire. Bays of evergreen holding yellow roses and silver foliage form the unusual rose garden around the lawn. Mainly Elizabethan, but set amidst the much older stones of the Avebury circle, Avebury Manor is one of the most important houses of the 'manor house cult'. The garden also has an unusual curved herb walk; sculptured yews of enormous size around beds of flowers, an Italian court, formal vistas and secret arbours; over it all is the kind of ancient English peace and easiness that are perhaps the most elusive of the qualities that the formal revivals of recent years have tried to recapture.

East Lambrook Manor, Somerset. The garden was made by Walter and Margery Fish and begun in 1938. During the 1950s Margery Fish began writing about the garden and especially her love of cottage garden flowers which she collected and used to great effect. She was largely responsible for the return to fashion of astrantias, alchemillas, bleeding hearts, many decorative herbs and silvery-leaved plants, as well as many other old-fashioned flowers which Gertrude Jekyll had used but which had gone out of vogue since the First World War.

The Hunting Lodge, Odiham. The formal garden made by the interior decorator John Fowler for his own country retreat after the war.

'manor house cult' had subtly moved into the Georgian era, with the work of decorators such as Syrie Maugham and Sybil Colefax, and John Fowler who worked with Mrs Nancy Lancaster (formerly Tree) at Ditchley and then at Haseley Court in Oxfordshire. John Fowler's creation of his own highly stylised yet romantic garden around his little Hunting Lodge at Odiham in Hampshire reminded everyone that interiors and exteriors were all one really, and the tastes and rules of one could equally be applied to the other. Indeed, a knowledge and understanding of the total art of living was essential to a successful assault on the problems of those who were rich in imagination and tastes, but now comparatively poor in means. It was an assault that demanded tremendous agility, for the standards must never be seen to drop and yet the price must be a fraction of what it seemed. According to these demanding rules, and in the Norah Lindsay, Maugham, Colefax and Fowler tradition, there arose a discreet coterie of professionals in gardening terms who have brought the Hidcote connection through unscathed through fifty years. By being able to write entertainingly to various degrees, but even more by combining sound gardening practice with the ability to discuss the matter and others over the client's dinner table or at a picnic at Glyndebourne, these gentle professionals, have triumphed. Among their number I would include Beverley Nichols, Peter Coats, John Codrington, Russell Page, Lanning Roper, Graham Stuart Thomas, Christopher Lloyd, Rosemary Verey, Beth Chatto and Penelope Hobhouse.

Interestingly, Russell Page is the only professional landscape architect in this

One of John Fowler's twin 'Gothick' pavilions at Odiham. They repeat the fantasy of his cottage ornée in garden terms.

list; though he was English, educated at Charterhouse and the Slade School, Page did most of his life's work abroad. His considerable influence in this country is through his one book, *The Education of a Gardener*, first published in 1962. It is an infuriating, entertaining, infinitely wise and inspiring book; infuriating because he is repeatedly vague and confusing about the actual garden he is writing about, and hardly ever identifies a place or a garden clearly. But what denies posterity (and a great store of his garden drawings

The Dower House, Badminton. The rose-covered fretwork folly or arbour in the garden Russell Page made with Lady Caroline Somerset.

survived his death in 1985) makes for enchanting reading. Page offers a disarmingly frank insight into the gentleman designer's world, 'being passed from house to house' among friends who became clients and vice versa.

Before the war Page had worked in informal partnership with Geoffrey Jellicoe, and their differing personalities had been usefully tailored to different clients. Jellicoe had fared best with the Trees at Ditchley, but after only a brief encounter with Lord Bath doing the Caveman Restaurant at Cheddar, it was Page who continued to advise on extensive planting in Longleat's park. Jellicoe was called in to design the terrace and its setting for the unspoiled Georgian

Pusey House, Berkshire. The 'Chinese Chippendale' pattern bridge, which may have originated with Jellicoe and Page's ' thirties collaboration.

house, Pusey House at Faringdon in Berkshire which Michael and Nicole Hornby found themselves in 1935, a terrace that gave them the key to continue the garden on their own. Page had the upper hand in what he called 'a rather sumptuous terrace' for a Decimus Burton house, Holme House in Regent's Park. He then worked abroad from the outbreak of war until 1962, largely in America and France. The English garden that best expresses his fine taste in design is the *jardin potager* which he helped Lady Caroline Somerset to make at the Dower House, Badminton in Gloucestershire. The centrepiece is a white fretwork folly, Page's favourite kind of garden building, which has become covered with pink and white roses and clematis. Brick paths edged with box hedges outline borders of flowers backed with espaliered apples and neat military rows of vegetables. The revival of the once French but Jekyll-approved *jardin potager* in this manner, so fitting for the modern lifestyle that does not have the space to be decorative and functional in separate rooms, is one of the strongest aspects of what may be called the 'New Georgian' garden.

Almost an *alter ego* for Russell Page was the American, Lanning Roper, who was only vaguely aware of the charms of English gardens until he came over here as a serving naval officer in the D-Day campaign and remained on naval duties until after the end of the war. He found particular inspiration at Bampton Manor in the Cotswolds and at Margery Fish's East Lambrook Manor. Released from the Navy, he eventually decided to return to England and work in gardens; he studied at Kew and Edinburgh Royal Botanic Gardens, started in garden journalism and gradually built up his garden design work until it was the mainstay of his income. Lanning Roper's greatest assets were his fine arts background (he had graduated from Harvard in that subject in 1933), his innate good taste and a modesty which allowed him to listen to his client's point of view first before finding good reasons for changing it. He also had a lifelong and disarming belief in what he was doing.

In 1948 Lanning Roper married the artist Primrose Harley, formerly Mrs John Codrington, who painted flowers and was a friend of the painter/gardeners Cedric Morris and John Nash. John Codrington and Primrose had made an unusual wild garden around Park House in Onslow Square, Kensington; as the home of Lanning and Primrose the garden at Park House became celebrated and its fame did a great deal to launch Lanning's career. Park House was essentially a country cottage in the heart of London. The soil was of the poorest and plants that were easy to grow – ferns, bamboos, hostas, ivies, shrub roses, elders, limes, laurels, laburnums and willows – were used in profusion. There were certain special plants – a paulownia, a catalpa, masses of Cedric Morris's irises and pots of unusual pelargoniums in varieties that Primrose bought home from Spain and Madeira, clouds of cherry blossoms, dramatic *Fatsia japonica*, wisterias, vines, *Yucca gloriosa* sprouting next to a classical balustrade and the giant heracleums attended by lesser Queen Anne's Lace. It was a bower garden, a glorious mixing of the wild and cultivated to defeat the polluted air and greyness of city living. It had an entrance drive like a country lane with bluebells and blackberries, its carefree pavings were crammed with sedums, saxifrages, *Alchemilla mollis* and ivies, and through it all an elegance that brought it to the pages of *Vogue* through the camera of Cecil Beaton. Park House did wonders for town gardening, and Lanning Roper's *Successful Town Gardening*, first published in 1957, enshrined its ideas.

The longing for familiar plants, from the wild or from the memories of childhood, became a consistent theme in the return of gardening popularity after the war. Judging the virtues of rampant growers like the heracleum or Russian Vine demanded a fine and precise knowledge, which only came from a great deal of practice and usually some travelling and plant hunting. John Codrington, the initial inspiration for Park House, designed just such a combination of the rare, precious and wild into the garden of Stone Cottage at Hambleton in Rutland for his sister in the early 'fifties. He inherited the house and garden ten years later, and it became a mecca for garden visitors for the next twenty years. He was well in the van of the environmental revolution, with his love of wild flowers, his much too large gravel drive which flowered with corn cockle rare clovers, grasses and campanulas and his jungle of bird-filled woodland. He used to say that he had always longed for water in his hill-top garden, and found his wish granted by the flooding of Rutland Water, to Sylvia Crowe's careful design, which gave him a splendid lake view. He also told me that he would never write his autobiography – which I was also assured on another occasion by Codrington's contemporary James Russell, whose ownership of Sunningdale Nurseries did so much for the revival of old roses and hardy perennials after the war. Russell sold Sunningdale into the garden centre age, and went to live and work at Castle Howard, where his gardens are a fine legacy but, as with John Codrington, it is so difficult to know exactly what else he did; he was also a

Park House, Kensington. The garden was created by Primrose Harley and her husband, John Codrington. It was later made famous by her second husband, Lanning Roper.

rhododendron expert and planted new gardens in the tradition of this 19th century passion. James Russell was part of a discerning élite of New Georgian gardeners presided over by Queen Elizabeth the Queen Mother, who began her serious interest in the subject at Royal Lodge and with the development of the Savill and Valley Gardens at Windsor with King George VI, in the immediate post-war years.

Both John Codrington and James Russell tended to remain in the shadows beyond the media spotlight that was increasingly searching out the gardeners of taste and fashion. It was no longer enough to be a good gardener, with a garden open to visitors, but it became necessary to write, broadcast, and eventually be seen on television, as well.

The media demands, which reflected the growing popularity of gardening tastefully, were excessive from the start. Lanning Roper, who wrote for *Country Life*, had a column in *The Sunday Times* (a successor in mood and time to V. Sackville-West's pioneering *Observer* column) but he was so devoted to working in his clients' gardens that he had no time for a garden of his own. His too early

death in 1983 was probably partly due to overwork. Lanning Roper was a unique survivor from a vanished breed of consultants who wanted to do the bulk of the work themselves; his successors as columnists were to be wiser. Christopher Lloyd has a seemingly perennial column somewhere, but has concentrated upon his books and his garden at Great Dixter, rather than upon consultancy. Robin Lane Fox is an academic who writes brilliantly about his garden in the *Financial Times*. Beth Chatto has managed her nursery, with its wonderfully influential catalogues, and her books and articles, but Penelope Hobhouse admitted that she could never have managed the garden at Tintinhull House and her books and garden designs without the help and support of her

Opposite and above: Great Dixter, Sussex. The ancient house, enlarged and given a garden by Nathaniel Lloyd, with the help of Edwin Lutyens, before the First World War, was chaperoned into present fame by the gardening genius of Christopher Lloyd.

Unusual plants – part of Beth Chatto's stand at the Chelsea Flower Show. Among the vast mounds of coloured monocultures, Mrs Chatto's exhibit always made the point to hundreds of thousands of pairs of eyes that careful choice of colour and interesting contrasts in textures make for more interesting garden planting.

Left: title page decoration by Rex Whistler for Beverley Nichols's Down the Garden Path, *first published in 1932, and popular ever since.*
Centre: 'Autumn', also drawn by Rex Whistler, evokes the elegance and well being – and almost the smell of the firesmoke – of the New Georgian garden.

Right: the Royal Academy's 217th Summer Exhibition poster, 1985, showing Levens Hall Garden, a lithograph by Norman Stevens, RA, with additional design by Gordon House. The choice of this illustration heralded the acceptance of a return to formalism, albeit with a little English eccentricity added, in the worlds of art and design in the 1980s.

West Green Manor, Hampshire. A gravel walk between box edging passes a garden pavilion and ends at the 18th century brick house – the image of New Georgian gardening par excellence.

late husband, John Malins. And to be a modern consultant, to serve the new élite who want gardens as a sign of their success but who have neither the time nor the knowledge themselves, is often a thankless task. Having imparted enthusiasm, usually with large doses of tact and discretion, the consultant has to assume invisibility, whilst the owner happily and proudly takes the credit.

The watchword for the New Georgian garden is prestige. The handbook to all gardens desirable is the ever-plumper *Yellow Book*, appearing annually with the daffodils, to list the gardens open for charities supported by the National Gardens Scheme. The idea began in 1927, but has flourished particularly as a later 20th century phenomenon because of the commitment of its county by county organisation, the high standard of gardens that qualify and the consequent status acquired by being 'in'. Enjoyment in a good cause has caught the public imagination and hundreds of thousands spend Sunday afternoons in summer visiting large and small gardens, where the elements of the 'private' and the 'ordinary' are an irresistible draw. No self-respecting garden can afford to be left out of the *Yellow Book* – nor can any gardener of ambition – for it is in the best English tradition that casual conversations during Sunday visits are a fertile growth medium for all matters of taste and fashion in gardening society.

Along with the *Yellow Book* and openings for other charities (the Red Cross has a strong county scheme) has come a heightened interest in conservation. The Garden History Society and the National Council for the Conservation of Plants and Gardens (NCCPG) were both founded in the 'sixties, and have encouraged parallel agendas to research and conserve both historical gardens and save the older varieties of plants. The National Trust's Gardens Committee thus soon found itself working in a sympathetic field; the Trust's first Gardens Adviser was

Hillbarn House, Great Bedwyn, Wiltshire.
Fruit trees on metal arches, flowers and vegetables together in a family garden made by Lanning Roper in the early 1970s.

Lanning Roper's planting at The Mill House, Woodspeen, Berkshire, illustrates his skill in bringing together varied textures and colours in the most intimate of settings.

Mottisfont Abbey, Hampshire. A Stilt Avenue in the Hidcote tradition, possibly introduced here by Norah Lindsay while she was designing plantings for the Gilbert Russells in the 1930s. This actual planting and the silver and white border are by Geoffrey Jellicoe.

Graham Stuart Thomas and he did a great deal to establish the high standards of garden management and the improved status of gardening staff, as well as plant the Trust's collection of old shrub roses at Mottisfont Abbey. His successor, John Sales, has worked in even more enlightened times, and historical research into design and planting informs the maintenance of almost all of the Trust's gardens. In fact, the taste has come full circle, for gardens are now realised as the most attractive properties that the Trust owns, 'the world's greatest collection' in terms of historic places and precious plant collections, and thus the 'past times' of gardens seem to have caught the public imagination as well. The National Trust's 20th century gardens that fall into a Neo-Georgian, new-formalist, style include Hidcote Manor (of course) but also Polesden Lacey, Nymans, Mottisfont Abbey, Lytes Cary, Tintinhull House, Hinton Ampner and Sissinghurst Castle. This new historical concept of a garden having a place in time, of 'old-fashioned' plants, has interested a large section of the English gardening world, and encouraged this 'period' turn of mind into many gardens.

The serious implications of a view of gardens as the reservoirs of good taste, peace and purity within a world of ugliness, exploitation and pollution cannot be the subject of this book. Equally that idea must be held at the back of the mind for it is the basis of the success of revivalist garden tastes and conservation, and has been used as such by marketing and advertising. The purity of 'The English Garden' pervades chemist shops, fabric and dress design and much of the food we eat. Herbs and their uses have become subjects of great interest and encouraged the growing and designing of herb gardens in necessarily the medieval and Elizabethan style. The mixtures of herbs, vegetables and flowers – advocated by Gertrude Jekyll, who in revival can be seen to loom over this century's gardening in so many ways – encourage a return to vegetable growing in attractive *jardin potagers*, inspired both by Villandry (near Tours) as well as by Jekyll's restored plot at Lindisfarne Castle and in her other plans. Likewise potpourris, lavenders, thymes (planting on seats and for lawns) and a whole world of fragrance has returned, not forgetting the old roses restored to modern gardeners by James Russell, Graham Stuart Thomas, David Austin, Peter Beales and many more in their train.

Not by accident most of the devotees of 'The English Garden' style live in 18th century houses – why, is another subject in itself. It seems that the late 20th century has had to make up for an oversight on the part of the 18th and provide the gardens to fit 18th century tastes as conceived by 20th century people. The blackguard in the case is definitely seen as Lancelot 'Capability' Brown, who was scorned in the 1979 Exhibition at the Victoria & Albert Museum to celebrate one thousand years of British Gardening for sweeping away the old gardens in his campaign to cover England, making her more beautiful than at any other time in her history, according to G.M. Trevelyan, with the English Landscape Style. Why the one great achievement of the English at originating a great movement in the world of art, not just landscape gardening, has to be lightly dismissed is also beyond the scope of this book – largely as it eludes me. But dismissed it has been by the New Georgians.

So, to summarise, the New Georgian garden can be found around a mansion or behind a terraced cottage. It can be a small herb plot or flower parterre surrounded by box hedges, or one garden room with a paved floor, *trompe-l'œil* gateway, classical vase, lush shrubs and old roses; or it can be any multiplication or ramification of these spaces by walks, alleys, vistas, pergolas and arbours. No larger version is complete without a *jardin potager* within walls or hedges, with borders of roses and pinks and cordon apples and pears fronting neat rows of unusual vegetables, the decorative Ruby Chard, the splotched and frilled ornamental cabbages, a mixture of Brussels sprouts and bright green lettuce. Another necessity is an orchard, not just apples and plums, but a true Jekyll orchard with the picturesque sounding old varieties, Blenheim Orange, Devonshire Quarrenden, crabs, medlars, walnuts and with old trees retained as frames for climbing shrub roses. As a bow to the ecological movement, part of the conservation conscience, the orchard grass is burnished with sequences of wild flowers – crocus, daffodils, narcissi, fritillaries, orchids, ox-eye daisies – and

The moon gate and eye catcher at West Green House, Hampshire, viewed from the jardin potager. Alistair McAlpine, who acquired the lease of the house from the National Trust in 1973, remade the garden in and around the bones of the remains. The area around the house is strictly formal, with box parterres in gravel and a terraced lawn overlooked by busts of Roman emperors.

never cut until after flowering and seed set. The New Georgian garden is contemplated from a terrace or planted pavement furnished with white Chinese Chippendale latticed chairs and a wave-backed seat copied from Lutyens's original design for his own gardens, with white lattice trellis strung with Kiftsgate roses and clematis 'Perle d'Azur'. The New Georgian garden embodies the most desirable virtues of sanity, sobriety and good taste as well as much beauty, but is it the best we can do?

Selected Reading

Lanning Roper's *Sunday Times Gardening Book* (1961) is still my favourite guide to the post-war English gardening planting style; it is a comforting gardening companion. The people and gardens of the Hidcote connection appear in *The Englishwoman's Garden* (1980) and *The Englishman's Garden* (1982) both edited by Alvilde Lees-Milne and Rosemary Verey. John Cornforth's *The Inspiration of the Past* (1985) richly describes John Fowler's work for the National Trust which led to the resurgence of historic taste in interiors, and Rosemary Verey's *Classic Garden Design* (1984) identifies all the related methods, features and ornaments. Many of Margery Fish's books are reprinted and her garden and nursery at East Lambrook Manor in Somerset have been revived; John Codrington's garden at Stone Cottage, Hambleton, Rutland, has new owners and is still open for the National Gardens Scheme. Rosemary Verey's many books on her planting, along with those of Penelope Hobhouse, are the most inspirational in the Neo-Georgian tradition.

Turn End, Haddenham, Buckinghamshire. Peter Aldington's sempervivum collection in a corner of the sunny garden, with rose 'Felicite et Perpetue' spilling over the wall from the shady lobby.

EIGHT
The Post-Modern Garden

The idea of conserving old gardens did not enter the heads of young designers, landscape architects and architects, returning to their professions after the Second World War. Most of them had been educated in the stimulating air of the 'thirties, they had learned of fitness for function and spoke in terms of a contemporary relevance for design. They wanted to put these ideas into practice for post-war living.

In terms of garden design the prospect seemed bleak. The client for a large private garden was a vanished species; designers who needed to make a living would have to turn elsewhere. The major pre-war voice in modern design, Christopher Tunnard, had, like others, gone to America, where he was appreciated and where he stayed. In England the Institute of Landscape Architects, only ten years old at the outbreak of war, had survived because Geoffrey and Susan Jellicoe had kept in touch with members during the war. Now the profession had to concentrate on reconstruction, on the revival of its education syllabus and the setting up of university courses (the first began at Reading in 1946 under Frank Clark, the second at Durham in 1948 under Brian Hackett), and the infiltration of landscape architects into local authority

Harvey's Store, High Street, Guildford with roof garden by Geoffrey Jellicoe to capture the mood of the 1950s.

209

Garden at Newport, Rhode Island, by Christopher Tunnard, 1949. The pattern is, of course, designed to be seen from the ground, where its curves interlock and turn back on themselves, and not from the higher viewpoint of the photograph. The trees are limes (eventually to be pleached), with a row of thuja to screen the garage court on the extreme right; ivy, box and yew are the sculptural plants, and the ivy is on mounds edged with purple and white petunias and other summer flowers as desired. Below: plan of the same garden.

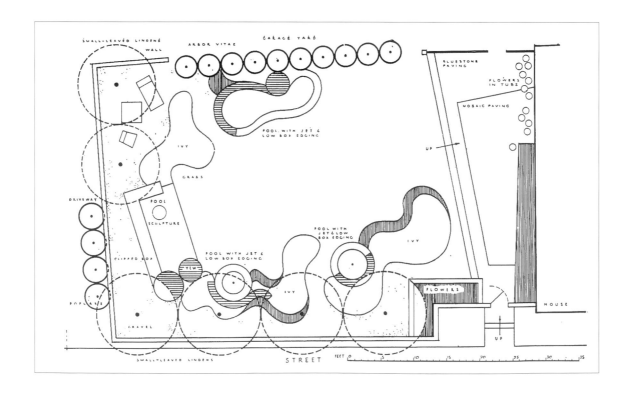

Roof garden of an insurance building in Rio de Janeiro by Burle Marx, 1938. The pattern is created from the textures and colours (red, green and silver) of the native plants.

teams. In this mood it was understandable that garden design seemed largely irrelevant, unless it could be transmuted into good design for semi-public and public landscapes. The idea of living, going to school and working in garden-like surroundings had run as an arcadian thread through the thoughts of architects and town planners since Ebenezer Howard had first reminded them of Eden when he wrote of 'Garden Cities' in 1898. He had called his dreams *Tomorrow: A Peaceful Path to Real Reform.* With the designation of the new towns, and large areas of old ones to be rebuilt, it seemed not unlikely that tomorrow had come. It was, after all, only a matter of scale. Designing a garden had become a preliminary task in the training of a landscape architect, because the relationship between our human scale and a given space is the basis of all good design. The challenge would be to translate the elements of garden design, the harmony and unity, the clear direction and good organisation of space, the interesting use of plants and the control of colour and form, to semi-public and public spaces. Then, clearly, other elements had to be added – all-the-year-round durability and attraction with as little expense for maintenance as possible. This was the challenge the young designers wished to accept; beside this garden design was seen as trivial and an uncertain living. For most landscape architects gardens have become an indulgence, a sideline, though still regarded with proprietary feelings as the place of their profession's origin.

Designers returning from the war soon became aware of two strong influences from abroad that had filled the vacuum at home. They first heard of the painter and plantsman Roberto Burle Marx from an article by Claude Vincent in the *Architectural Review* in 1946. Burle Marx was born in Sao Paulo in 1909 and was encouraged in gardening as a child. At first he had studied music but was subsequently so inspired by seeing the work of Van Gogh that he

211

Roberto Burle Marx's typically curvaceous planting of exotic Brazilian natives in the Odette Monteiro Garden in Rio, 1948.

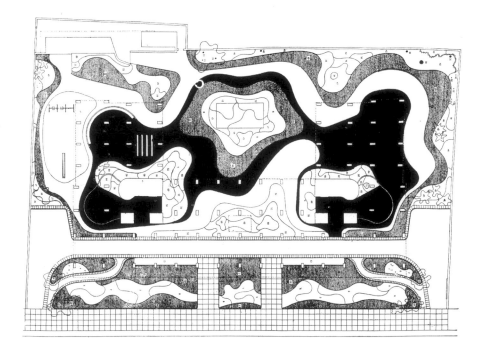

Plan of a garden for an apartment house in Sao Paolo by Burle Marx. The dark area is mosaic paving, while the white rectangular marks represent the pilotis supporting the building.

Copacabana Beach, Rio de Janeiro. Burle Marx's lively modernism in mosaic paving.

decided to become a painter. As well as painting prolifically he studied architecture and botany in Rio, and he and a number of friends formed a caucus in support of native traditions in Brazil in the 'thirties, when the western influence was so strong. His first design commission was for his friend, the architect Lucio Costa, who asked him to design a garden for a house in Rio using only native plants. From there Burle Marx went on to become Director of Parks in Recife and the designer of a large number of gardens, parks and public open spaces in Brazil and Venezuela. His strength was in his talent as a painter, and in his loyalty and a certain chauvinism in his philosophy which meant that he kept to his native plants: 'I have five thousand trees and fifty thousand plants to choose from' being his sound reasoning. He also felt that a strict loyalty to surrounding nature meant that his gardens could not be 'artificial'. He designed his gardens adhering to these two loyalties, and as a painter speaking 'in an art language', so that the strength of form of the painting was made reality in the garden. In later years he had made a

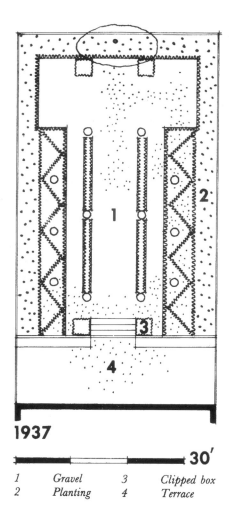

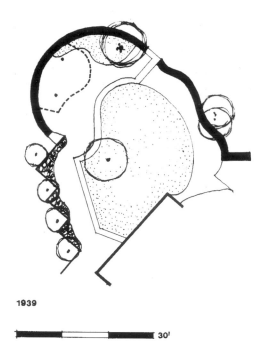

Formal town garden design by Thomas Church, 1937. The design is a product of Church's first idea of a garden as an outdoor room.
1 *Gravel*
2 *Planting*
3 *Clipped box*
4 *Terrace*

1937

1	*Gravel*	3	*Clipped box*
2	*Planting*	4	*Terrace*

1939

Exhibition design, 1939, by Church. It is an early attempt at the flexible, free design which resulted in the Sonoma pool garden nine years later. The thick black lines are fences, while the other shapes denote ground form in woodblock paving, brick edgings, grass and plantings.

tremendous collection of his favourite plants, with his own nursery to supply his schemes; he became increasingly outspoken in the cause of nature conservation in Brazil where so many western-style developments threatened the habitats of his plants and the conditions in which they might prosper.

It seems hardly surprising that Burle Marx has continued to inspire British designers; could they be more than envious of his palette of wonderful plants or his opportunities in the sun-lightened spaces of Brazil, or was there a more universal element of inspiration? After some of his work was shown in a London exhibition at the ICA in 1956, Geoffrey Jellicoe wrote a review in which he identified the element of delight which only a designer with such a belief in himself and in his theatre of design could muster. Jellicoe concluded: 'Landscape design is concerned with the co-ordination of space into a composition which not only fulfils its function but which also gives pleasure and is poetic as well as being tectonic in quality'.

Thomas Church, the second source of inspiration, was motivated by a different set of talents and circumstances. We may think of Californian culture as 'only Hollywood', but in the 1930s it was looking for a return to its Mexican-Spanish roots after the imposition of smart Eastern seaboard taste that had come with integration into the United States almost a century earlier. The Californian climate encouraged outdoor living and there were so many things that the average family wanted to do out of doors. But the average family in the burgeoning development also had at least one large automobile

The swimming pool garden for Mr and Mrs Dewey Donnell at Sonoma, California, by Thomas Church with Lawrence Halprin and George Rockrise, 1948. The photograph was taken before completion, but the garden relies on the existing trees and natural landscape, rather than new planting.

to be parked on the 'front lot', where fences and gates were a nuisance and an open green landscape was encouraged. Thus the 'back lot' was increasingly smaller and had to fulfil many uses.

Church started work in 1930. He had been traditionally trained and his first gardens were rooms – he contended that if the garden was an extension to the house it must be equally formally organised. Then, throughout the 'thirties, he became aware of the Modern Movement, and a trip to Europe in 1937 convinced him that his gardens should move in harmony with modern architecture, especially with the curving, flowing buildings of Alvar Aalto, whom he met in Finland. Church's philosophy is beautifully expressed by his advocate, Michael Laurie of the School of Landscape Design at Berkeley:

'He came to believe that a garden should have no beginning and no end and that it should be pleasing when seen from any angle, not only from the house. Asymmetric lines were used to create greater apparent dimensions. Simplicity of form, line and shape were regarded as more restful to look at and easier to maintain. Form, shape and pattern in the gardens were provided by pavings, walls and espaliered or trained plants...The central axis was abandoned in favour of multiplicity of viewpoints, simple planes and flowing lines. Texture and colour, space and form were manipulated in a manner reminiscent of the Cubist painters. At the same time all practical criteria were satisfied'.*

Church's most famous garden, the Donnell garden at Sonoma, 'one of the most beautiful gardens in the world, ranking with Villa Lante, continues Laurie, is undeniably an exquisite work of art, or rather a series of works of art as every view as well as the plan conveys delight and pleasure. As if the inspiration of his art were not enough, Church was also blessed with a practical zeal and an ability to transmit the quality of his creativity to thousands of garden owners. For forty years his influence worked through *Sunset Magazine* and its subsidiary publications (brought home by literature-starved generations of English landscape architects) which were eagerly read by many house owners and gardeners. The *Sunset* look, based on Church's original designs, was achievable by overall planning, especially of paths and sight lines and a close relationship between these elements indoors and outdoors; by constant attention to details, especially in pavings, edgings, plant containers, deckings and walls; by the use of low-maintenance planting which made the most use of contrast in texture, colour and form; and by the belief that there should be a sense of freedom, of doing whatever seemed right to make the garden liveable in rather than conforming to stiff old rules. Church's inspiration, no less than Burle Marx's, was the encouraging climate of his native landscape which gave so many advantages to the art of landscape design. Could it ever happen in grey, chilly, misty old England?

In 1950 there was only a handful of landscape architects working in Britain to try, but the young profession had friends in the right places, including Gordon Russell and Hugh Casson. The first demonstration of what they could do was at the Festival of Britain on the South Bank in London in the summer of 1951. With its Dome of Discovery and Skylon, pavilions devoted to the sea and ships, power and production, the new schools, health, sport, the seaside and 'The Lion and the Unicorn', and with the Pleasure Gardens at Battersea Park based on the follies of a mad Venetian with a Roland Emmett railway and a dragon-infested Tree Walk, the Festival was, as Roy Strong has written, a '*ville imaginaire*'. It was 'presented in a flight of surrealist fantasy as the life style of the new technological age . . . of a land teeming with natural resources to be tapped by valiant workers in field and factory, where traditional skills and crafts were cherished, where industry and commerce were about to boom and bring a hitherto unknown universal prosperity'.* It was an image of a land of a people whose character combined realism and strength on one hand, and fantasy, independence and imagination on the other. All this may have been a political dream, but it was the perfect environment for a landscape designer.

The landscape of the South Bank site, around the present Festival Hall, was a different matter from the Pleasure Gardens in Battersea Park. The latter were conceived and created in terms of traditional fantasy by the Chief Designer James Gardner, with an array of additional talents including those of John Piper and Osbert Lancaster. James Gardner 'designed' the hard surface areas of the gardens by calculating two square yards per person on a peak Bank Holiday – 'that would keep people off the flowerbeds'. There was little

*M. Laurie, *An Introduction to Landscape Architecture*, 1976, p.46.
* In prologue to *A Tonic to the Nation*, eds. M. Banham and B. Hillier, 1976, p.8.

Peter Shepheard's planting for the Moat Garden around the tented tea restaurant at the Festival of Britain, 1951. An element of wilderness, using 'architectural' plants, made a visual and practical barrier.

subtlety there! He continued by making a continuous route round the edge of the site, with a number of 'way-throughs' to keep circulation fairly even over the whole area. Luckily, plenty of fantasy was added by John Piper and Osbert Lancaster. Last but not quite least, Russell Page was called in to do the actual planting. There was a large area of spring bulbs, which he planted in the autumn of 1950 into mushroom compost covering cinders. Shrubs, particularly rhododendrons in flower, were transported from Exbury, while the formal flower beds in the central area held traditional 'bedding plants'. There was nothing revolutionary about the Pleasure Gardens, just good fun.

On the South Bank site itself rather more was achieved. Landscape architects Frank Clark, Maria Shephard, Peter Shepheard and Peter Youngman shared the responsibility for creating an all-pervasive garden atmosphere between the buildings. In many instances they did this by design but also, when inevitably the money or time ran out, they filled in with plants those sites intended for buildings or other features. Illusion was all. Along the walks and avenues and around groups of seats the planting was in concrete edged squares and rectangles or in the cone-shaped concrete and plaster flower pots especially designed for the Festival, a design which has become a classic in the intervening years. Bedding plants, tulips and petunias, as well as masses of a wonderful marguerite, magical under the floodlights, filled these planters, but there were also plants new to the public, those 'architectural' plants that the designers had identified in the 'thirties. These, polygonums,

The Regetta Restaurant garden by H.F. Clark and Maria Shephard at the Festival of Britain. The planting was partly of shrubs and herbaceous plants, such as Senecio greyi *and* Ligularia clivorum, *azaleas, iris, and partly of bedding plants. The bronze sculpture is by Lynn Chadwick.*

heracleum, *Rheum palmatum, Crambe orientalis*, ligularias and fine-leaved bamboos were used to dramatic effect, in particular where they were for looking at only among the stones and boulders of Peter Shepheard's Moat Garden and in contrast to the sinuous island that Frank Clark and Maria Shephard made for the Regatta Restaurant garden.

The Festival gave the British people a taste for planting that was more attainable than those complex bedding schemes they were used to at Eastbourne, Blackpool and in city parks. It also gave them other ideas – if all these lovely gardens could be produced 'instantly', and people never ceased to remark on that, why couldn't everyone have an instant plant or an instant garden? It was all so delightful and such fun, if one didn't know the traumas and battles that the designers and makers had gone through, that it was all accepted 'as though there was no surprise in five hundred trees springing to

The Homes and Gardens Pavilion and the Shot Tower at the Festival of Britain, 1951. Bays for sitting out were formed by the planting and, for the first time, the British public came close to plants in an urban setting markedly different from the familiar seaside bedding out.

immediate leaf-laden life in what, only a few months previously, had been a building contractors' desert'. Misha Black, one of the Festival's chief designers wrote this twenty-five years afterwards in *A Tonic to the Nation*. He continued: 'The ten thousands of tulips (changed overnight into summer flowers), the turf, rocks, streams and waterfalls were all accepted as normality while I remained amazed that nature could be harnessed by our command into instantaneous activity'.*

It is the big parties of life that we remember best, especially when they come after difficult times. The British public came away from the Festival of Britain convinced that a new breed of miracle gardeners had been born; the architects, planners and engineers, equally amazed as Misha Black, laughed at the idea that landscape architects could have a hotline to Mother Nature (or even higher), but from now on they too would demand cosmetic miracles.

* In 'Architecture, Art and Design in Unison', *A Tonic to the Nation*, eds. M. Banham and B. Hillier, 1976, p.84.

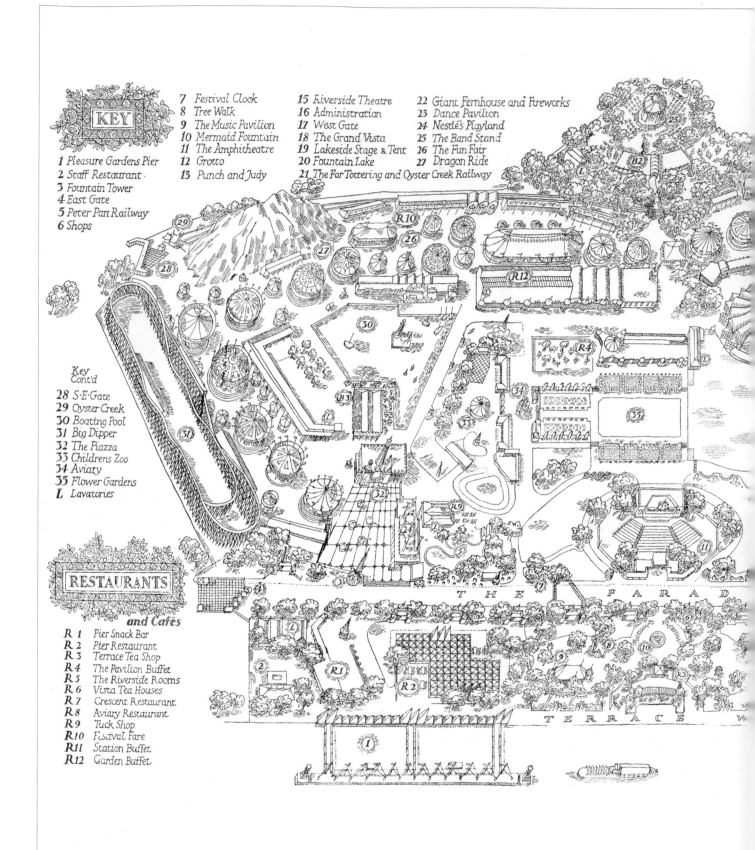

KEY

1 Pleasure Gardens Pier
2 Staff Restaurant
3 Fountain Tower
4 East Gate
5 Peter Pan Railway
6 Shops
7 Festival Clock
8 Tree Walk
9 The Music Pavilion
10 Mermaid Fountain
11 The Amphitheatre
12 Grotto
13 Punch and Judy
15 Riverside Theatre
16 Administration
17 West Gate
18 The Grand Vista
19 Lakeside Stage & Tent
20 Fountain Lake
21 The Far Tottering and Oyster Creek Railway
22 Giant Fernhouse and Fireworks
23 Dance Pavilion
24 Nestlé's Playland
25 The Band Stand
26 The Fun Fair
27 Dragon Ride

Key Cont'd

28 S·E·Gate
29 Oyster Creek
30 Boating Pool
31 Big Dipper
32 The Piazza
33 Childrens Zoo
34 Aviary
35 Flower Gardens
L Lavatories

RESTAURANTS

and Cafes

R 1 Pier Snack Bar
R 2 Pier Restaurant
R 3 Terrace Tea Shop
R 4 The Pavilion Buffet
R 5 The Riverside Rooms
R 6 Vista Tea Houses
R 7 Crescent Restaurant
R 8 Aviary Restaurant
R 9 Tuck Shop
R 10 Festival Fare
R 11 Station Buffet
R 12 Garden Buffet

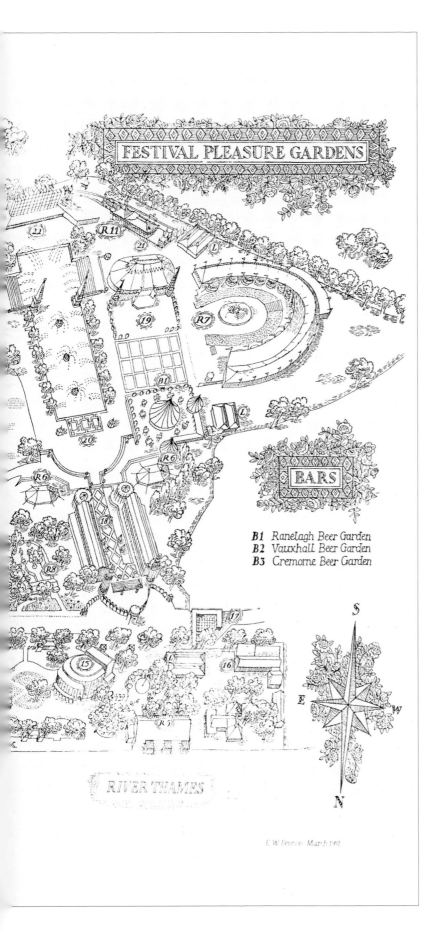

BARS

B1 Ranelagh Beer Garden
B2 Vauxhall Beer Garden
B3 Cremorne Beer Garden

E W Fenton March 1961

RIVER THAMES

Plan of the Festival of Britain Pleasure Gardens in Battersea Park, 1951, drawn for the Festival guidebook by E.W. Fenton. The emphasis was on pleasure in a garden setting, but with far less gardening than was found in the old London pleasure gardens at Ranelagh, Cremorne and Vauxhall (after which the bars were named!). The flower gardens, by Russell Page, are in the centre, number 35 on the plan. The rest of the plan was masterminded by the chief exhibition, and graphic, designer, James Gardner, who created enough hard surfacing to carry peak afternoon crowds around the site and then devoted the left hand half of the site to the fairground and the right hand half to music, dancing and performing. The differing moods of the two halves are symbolised by the water features – the practical boating pool (30) near the fairground, and the more formal Fountain Lake (20) between the Dance Pavilion (23) and the large Crescent Restaurant (R7). The influence of contemporary modern design, which would have made the water features and the gardens simpler and perhaps sinuous, is notably absent. This is because of the predominant fantasy element of the gardens, inspired by the artists Osbert Lancaster and John Piper and realised in The Far Tottering and Oyster Creek Railway (21), the Tree Walk (8) and Grotto (12), and the capricious folly detailing which was everywhere evident. The gardens must have seemed a kaleidoscope of medieval joust, Merry England fairing, the Sleeping Beauty's village and Never-Never Land, and much of its magic lay in the confusion of images, when nothing is quite what it seems. It was just this sort of confusion that the Modern Movement before the war had sought to sweep away.

Model design for a small garden twenty feet square by Geoffrey Jellicoe, 1951. This garden – to show that even the smallest pocket handkerchief could be well designed – was part of the 'extra-mural' Festival of Britain. It was designed for a small housing development (at Lansbury, north London) that was in the 'real' world.

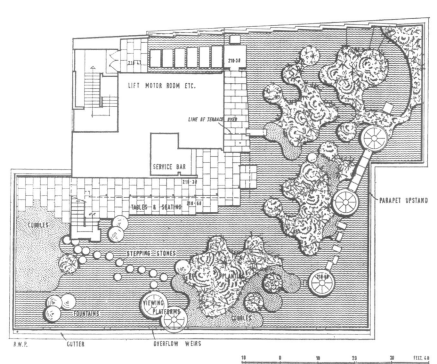

Harvey's Roof Garden, Guildford, site plan by Geoffrey Jellicoe, 1956, and opposite, in its heyday. The design was inspired by the 'Sputnik' satellite, and the first view of earth from space.

An interesting postscript to the Festival came in a more permanent form in 1958 with Geoffrey Jellicoe's Roof Garden for Harvey's Store in Guildford High Street. Jellicoe called it a 'Sky Garden' because the ever-changing sky was reflected in the sheets of water as well as, as he explained, because he designed the garden while the first Sputnik 'spun miraculously round and far above the earth'. This garden contains all those 'fifties elements of fantasy, the influence of abstract art, of Burle Marx and Thomas Church, of hope in miracles of science that would change the world beyond our imaginings. It was also a small miracle in itself – water on a roof? – how preposterous and impractical. But apparently not so: the water, concrete islands, soil and plants had been accommodated upon an ordinary 'live' load roof with an asphalt surface that would have been used anyway. The store's owners, with fond memories of the fame of Derry & Tom's Roof Garden in Kensington High Street and how that had drawn the shoppers, were confident in their

Gateway House, Basingstoke, headquarters building for Wiggins Teape and the only flat-roofed office building in a whole town of such developments to provide a roof garden.

investment. With large, flat-roofed buildings springing up everywhere, the techniques safe and sound, the land values on the ground soaring too high to be left unused by building, it seemed that the age of the roof garden had come and British cities would be robed in green and scented bowers.

That they are not is an effective symbolic expression of what has happened to that ideal of garden-like design softening the built environment that boomed during the 'sixties and early 'seventies. There was no room for it, either in the developer's mind or on his site or in his balance sheet. In 1969, with tremendous verve and foresight, the young architects Darborne and Darke built a large development in Lillington Street for Westminster City Council, with a successful rich planting of trees and shrubs on the access balconies at various levels. In 1979 Wiggins Teape's new headquarters, Gateway House at Basingstoke, Hampshire, revealed roof terraces bursting with greenery for the pleasure of passing motorists as well as for the office staff indoors. Both these buildings have been given every architectural award in the book, they have become much-visited legends in their own lifetimes, they remain admired and almost unique.

After the Festival of Britain the gardening world revived to attend to what would clearly be a popular interest in gardening. *The Studio's* annual volume on gardening returned in utility format, edited by Frank Mercer and Roy Hay and full of a high standard of horticultural advice. Among the plethora of crazy paving, the rock walls and pergolas of tradition, there was, in the 1952 volume, a short article by Brenda Colvin, entitled *Gardens to Enjoy*. In her third paragraph she summed up the situation: 'Where formal gardens are concerned we have borrowed from every available source, and we have never really jettisoned our appreciation of formal design. But the "landscape" style of the 18th century was our first great contribution to the art of garden design, and in this present century the world has been watching our

Hailey House, Oxfordshire. Designed by Sylvia Crowe in the 1960s, it made a feature of the round paving stones of German manufacture and displayed at the continental gartenschau *at that time.*

experiments in the free groupings of an enormously increased range of plants within the framework of widely differing garden styles. Those experiments have often been more successful from a horticultural point of view than for their aesthetic value. But we are learning . . .'

Brenda Colvin's hint was elaborated by her friend and colleague Sylvia Crowe, then the President of the Institute of Landscape Architects, in her book *Garden Design* published by *Country Life* in 1958. This was rather like the voice from Olympus, for it was well known that she spent most of her time dealing with new towns, nuclear power stations and the routing of supergrid lines. 'Gardens are the link between men and the world in which they live', she explained in her opening sentence; 'men in every age have felt the need to reconcile themselves with their surroundings, and have created gardens to satisfy their ideals and aspirations'.

Garden Design allows only two and a half pages, out of over two hundred, to the 'Contemporary Garden'. This section is illustrated with the work of Roberto Burle Marx and Thomas Church's Californian contemporary, Lawrence Halprin, and concludes: 'The danger of their influence lies in imitations, which render the shapes anaemic or arbitrary, whereas their success is in the dynamic and individual form, which can only issue from the spirit of an artist'. Sylvia Crowe felt Burle Marx and Halprin's contribution to be the bringing of the vocabulary of design of gardens 'into concord with the contemporary spirit of the other arts'. But in much of the rest of the book her admiration for Hidcote Manor is very evident.

So, had the professional designers failed to escape the revivalist net after all? Well, no, rather they slipped out underneath. *Garden Design* is a complex book; it weaves in and out of historical 'styles', choosing the best elements for use in modern gardens, parks, allotments, factory, school and housing landscapes. It has never been bettered for an explanation of the elements of good design. Besides drawing upon the expected sources of Persia, Spain, Italy, France, Sissinghurst and Hidcote, Sylvia Crowe manages to weave in the English landscape style, keeping her professional loyalty to Brown and Repton. Even small gardens may make use of land moulding, sculptural planting and the misty, meandering water for which the English soul most yearns.

Garden Design revealed all those free curves, sinuous waterlines and ribbons of planting of apparently 'modern' design to have perfectly sound English 18th century roots. 'A whole garden may be hidden from view, to be suddenly revealed from a chosen spot…gentle contouring can be used to conceal some part of the garden …a small garden of the in-looking type can be made more interesting, secluded, self-contained by raising the sides and back in a horse-shoe formation, which gives background to a saucer of garden in the centre. Or a gentle mound may be brought a little forward from the far boundary, allowing the garden to continue around the back of the hill …'* One of the reasons for failure of the imitations of the English landscape style, she added, was that this vital contouring was omitted.

Sculptural planting, the Brownian adventure of sinuous walks curving through masses of bold greenery, could also be achieved in miniature provided that the bywords were 'discrimination' and 'restraint'. Even more welcome was the recommendation that a soft-edged lake of misty inlets, so beloved of the English memory, could be brought into the garden in miniature as a plant-edged pool, as long as it nestled naturally in ground- shaping.

The later 20th century task of the best landscape designers has been an endeavour to encapsulate the qualities of the English landscape style into gardens that have grown ever smaller and are most usually of harsh rectangular shapes. This is an extraordinarily difficult task and graceful outcomes are difficult to find; both Brenda Colvin and Sylvia Crowe had too few chances to demonstrate how it should be done, but the two gardens illustrated, Sylvia Crowe's garden at Whalebones, Barnet, and Brenda Colvin's work at Sutton Courtenay Manor House to simplify Norah Lindsay's garden (p.231) are both expressive examples and further examples follow.

Michael Branch, also a landscape architect, has maintained a practice in

* S Crowe, *Garden Design*, 1968, p10

The garden at Whalebones by Sylvia Crowe with a view from the house terrace. Sylvia Crowe has written: 'A whole garden may be hidden from view, to be suddenly revealed from a chosen spot.'

exquisite gardens; his work emphasises the opportunities of seemingly ordinary sites. The garden in Oxford is for a bungalow with a small, narrow garden, but the owner had added the ends of four other gardens to give him the long Y-shaped site. In his second garden, in Hampstead, Michael Branch combines a romantic rock pool and a 'landscape' lawn. John Brookes is in my long-held opinion, the most talented Modernist who has worked in Britain since the war; his garden for Penguin Books was a landmark, but also the kind of stroke of youthful genius that it is difficult to emulate. He has worked in many elaborations of modernism, but his introduction of timber for paviours, steps and structures in English gardens was of pioneering importance. Some of his best work can be seen in his own garden at Denmans near Fontwell in Sussex, where he teaches and runs courses, and all his books should be in every serious gardening library.

Anthony du Gard Pasley is a landscape architect who has been more successful than most in maintaining a private garden design practice; with Rosemary Alexander he set up The English Gardening School, based at Chelsea Physic Garden, which was innovatory in the teaching of garden – as opposed to landscape – design. Preben Jakobsen is a Dane, with all his

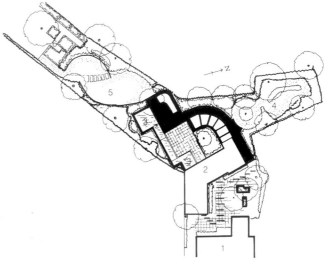

Plan for a garden in Oxford by Michael Branch, showing the bungalow in the original narrow garden, together with the extra land bought to make the present Y-shaped garden. A sheltered court of patterned paving connects the bungalow (1) with the summer house (2); the pivot of the Y is emphasised with a substantial curving pergola around a court with water rills between the two pools (3). A secluded, lushly planted wing of the garden (4) contrasts with the more open lawn (5) which leads to a small vegetable garden (6).

The design for an ordinary-sized 'country garden' in Hampstead by Michael Branch fulfils both a desire for 'romantic' water and for a modern treatment, as stipulated by the client. The water springs from a naturally-planted rock pool and flows over a rocky waterfall into a carefully shaped, sinuous stream lined with slate. The slates were cut at the quarry into three sizes which allowed the curves to be subtly shaped.

Anthony du Gard Pasley. The serenely curving green rear garden in the 'landscape' style, for which plan and planting are on page 231.

Garden at Denmans, Sussex by John Brookes. The creation of a picture viewed from inside the house invites the viewer to explore the garden.

country's native instinct for Modernism. Most of his work, besides the famous garden at Stanmore, much illustrated (p.239), has been on the landscape scale, but he has a Europe-wide reputation and regularly contributes to the annual garden festival at Chaumont-sur-Loire in France.

The last two 'post-Moderns' illustrated epitomise everything about these gardens: they are secluded, private, made in these two cases by architects in time left over from their professions, they are essentially Modernist but with accretions and additional influences, and they only came into the limelight in their maturity. Sir Frederick Gibberd's garden at Marsh Lane, Old Harlow, was featured in *The Englishman's Garden*, and well known to his friends and local people in his lifetime; now it has become most famous and most visited in a battle to save it which was launched by a band of supporters, The Gibberd Garden Trust, in 1995. The garden was made 'as a private pleasure' reflecting Sir Frederick's outstanding career as an architect, landscape architect and landscape planner, notably as the designer of Harlow New Town, Heathrow Airport, Liverpool Roman Catholic Cathedral and Coutts Bank in the Strand, London. It also reflected his collection of modern paintings and his interest in sculpture, and with a supreme understanding of his site, around a bungalow on sloping fields on the outskirts of the new town, and a collector's passion for plants. This is a combination that has produced one of the most

John Brookes's courtyard garden for Penguin Books Ltd., Harmondsworth, Middlesex. This garden caused a stir in post-war Britain, both in design circles and in public opinion. It was the first notable expression of modern art in a landscape form, its inspiration being drawn from a geometric abstract by Piet Mondrian.

Above: Sutton Courtenay Manor House garden by Brenda Colvin, 1959, is an informal garden of vistas and mown grass walks between groups of trees.
Left: the garden plan of Sutton Courtenay Manor House. It shows how sculpture in the garden is so sited as to make focal points from the house.

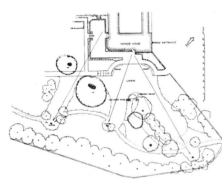

The rear garden of the house in Hurst Avenue by Anthony du Gard Pasley. See also page 229.

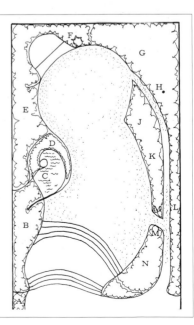

A Philadelphus 'Belle Etoile'.
B Fuchsias, lilies, daphne 'Somerset', and azaleas 'Rosebud' *in front of an existing fig tree,* Leycesteria formosa, *rose 'Wedding Day'.*
C The pool.
D Bog bed of primulas, Royal fern, Iris laevigata, Rodgersia pinnata, *mimulus, anthericum and* Mentha aquatica.
E Yuccas, rue, hellebores and Juniperus sabina tamariscifolia *in front of arundinaria, viburnums,* Cotoneaster cornubia *and existing camellias.*
F Erica carnea *'Springwood Pink' around* Prunus yedoensis pendula.
G Weigela rosea *and* Potentilla arbuscula *in front of large viburnums,* Sorbaria aitchisonii *and* Cotoneaster frigida.
H Rose 'The Garland' with existing cherry tree and Forsythia aucaulis nymans.
J Masses of senecio, lavenders with Yucca gloriosa, *rose 'Golden Wings',* Caryopteris clandonensis *and* Rhus continus *'Notcutt's Purple'.*
K Peonies, mallows, iris, rose 'Marguerite Hilling' and Ceratostigma willmottianum.
L Row of Escallonia macrantha.
M Phlomis fruticosa.
N Sedums, Stachys lanata *and* Salvia officinalis purpurea *in front of rose 'Nypels Perfection',* Rosa rubrifolia, *tree peonies,* Philadelphus virginale *and* Daphne mez ereum.

Marsh Lane, Harlow. Frederick Gibberd's garden, showing the bronze dogs by Robert Clatworthy gambolling across the glade, in front of the tapestry hedge.

beautiful gardens anywhere. Gibberd wrote of his garden, 'Garden design is an art of space, like architecture and town design. The space, to be a recognisable design, must be contained and the plants and walls enclosing it then become part of the adjacent spaces. The garden has thus become a series of rooms each with its own character, from small intimate spaces to large enclosed prospects'. Clearly this is familiar, it could have been written about Sissinghurst, etc., so what is new? The Gibberd Garden has to be experienced to find out, for his wizardry is such that as one moves, the spaces change, the walls dispose themselves differently, the shrubs melt into the mist and emerge in differing guises, the shapes and sculptural objects evaporate and return to enchant and surprise. There is a real mystery of form and movement in this garden; it is, of course, the only garden he made.

Peter Aldington's garden at Turn End, Haddenham in Buckinghamshire, is the outcome of his desire to build modern houses – three – that grew out of cottage traditions, yet made the most of state-of-the-art 1960s technology to create refuges from the stressful everyday world. The three low-slung houses with white roughcast walls and burnt-orange pantiled roofs, are grouped around an entrance close and shaded by mature trees. In 1964 the Aldingtons had to fight to save these trees on their old garden site as the normal practice was then to clear every living thing: the houses were completed in about five

Turn End, Haddenham, Buckinghamshire. Two plantings of infinite variety that exist within a few feet of each other. Above: bold foliage beside the sleeper steps. Below: a gathering of pelargoniums in the Daisy Garden.

years, and through the 1970s Peter Aldington gradually made his garden, also in the spare time left over from a busy architectural practice. The original site was half an acre, but he has added surrounding properties to make a series of gardens, which still add up to less than an acre, but seem much more. The interpretation of flowing glades that forms the main garden is now flanked by more formal spaces: the last garden to be made, in 1981-2, was the Sunny Garden or No-Mans, a rectangle of formal L-shaped beds, raised in double-sleeper edgings. A particular asset of these raised 'island' beds is that the delicate array of irises, alliums, artemisias, penstemons, grasses and verbascums that flower here are transformed hourly as the light moves behind them.

Marsh Lane and Turn End, both acknowledged as 'the twentieth century's finest', loyal to their Modernist philosophies yet embroidered with luxuriant plantings, a tapestried hedge at Marsh Lane, indulgent collections of potted sedums and pelargoniums at Turn End, and both of the 1980s, might then have been called old-fashioned. They are both direct descendants, on a lesser scale, from the 18th century landscape style, and they both have a traditional purity of design. They are totally concerned with design motives, and the same preoccupations to which Thomas Love Peacock so famously devoted a chapter of *Headlong Hall* (published in 1816) – that is the variation in the weather, the light, the temperature, the health of the plants, the view or lack of it: the design is the entertainment, to stroll and comment or hide in the summer house, fulfils its purposes.

But our century is the century of activity, of doing rather than merely being, and commenting upon the scenery. It was, by the 1980s, no longer enough for a garden just to be a garden, it had to be an extension to the house, or of the personality, tough enough to stand the pace of modern life, insubstantial enough to be adaptable to whim and fashion and, above all, useful. A garden now is not just an outside living room, it has to be an outside kitchen, utility room, dining room, playroom, gym, bathing and sleeping area and pet pad. Solace and refreshment are no longer enough, there must be the wherewithal for flower arranging, culinary masterpieces, the feeding and breeding of the local wildlife, showing off the bronze shepherdess or a mock 'Coca Cola' tin disguised as a fountain. In August 1980, *Landscape Design*, the professional journal which only rarely and choosily illustrated gardens, revelled in a design brief for a garden 'to provide for seven young children and their friends, their bicycles, two dogs, a clothes drying area and sand pit, a swing and a climbing tower . . . a small vegetable patch, a secluded area for sun bathing and granny's garden seat'. Surely time for granny to leave the country? And where, oh where, is the place for day-dreams, make-believe and cultivating the imagination? Or where indeed, was any scope or interest for the designer?

The designers saw a new and bigger (than 14 metres by 36 metres long of the nightmare garden) stage on which to demonstrate ingenious solutions with the announcement that the shade of the 1951 Festival of Britain had been revived into the 1984 International Garden Festival at Liverpool. It was to be the professional designer's coming of age: by decreeing that Merseyside should have the festival, with something under two and a half years' preparation time, on a vast and bleak site full of methane-bubbling refuse tips,

Above: the early award-winning Span housing developments of the 1960s by Eric Lyons and Ivor Cunningham included these small adjoining estates, Grasmere and Weymede, at Byfleet, Surrey. Houses and surrounding landscape are so obviously designed together with great care that the effect of the whole is to capture the wellbeing of living in a garden village.

Right: Span's Mallard Place, Teddington, of the 1980s. Twenty years after the first 'estate' was made both architecture and planting are more exuberant, but the effect of garden spaces within buildings is just as reassuring.

Mrs Thatcher's Government issued a challenge that was taken up, and met. In that incredibly short time a sea of dereliction was turned into a lovely rolling landscape, with an exciting, rock-strewn water park and a long Marine Esplanade beside the Mersey. It is good to know that modern professionals can create in the Brown tradition and work miracles at the same time, and if the idea of garden festivals brings to present-day Britain a string of large-scale landscapes for leisure, it must be applauded. But large-scale landscapes are another story and not the subject of this book.

It is the 'garden' aspect of the festival that is not so appealing in terms of the traditions of good design. For, in fulfilling their actual purpose – to provide a summer-long jamboree that brings in the crowds and, hopefully, makes the money (and, some say, diverts the eyes from the real living conditions of Britain's inner cities) garden festivals have brought us the *theme* garden.

Theme gardens have to be crammed with, to the point of obsession, the symbols and fantasies of their subjects. They are not gardens at all in the traditional sense of a peaceful refuge. Liverpool's festival intrigued and amused the British public with a Beatles' Garden complete with yellow submarine and apple-shaped maze, a jam garden (with strawberry jam moat and marmalade cascade), a quiz garden and a Liverpool street garden; it also offered stage-set versions of foreign traditions – from Holland, Japan, Turkey, Ancient Egypt and the not so foreign diminutive lochs and miniature moors of heather.

The idea of flower festivals – summer outdoors – which has arrived from the Continent is absolutely wonderful and encourages laughter. It is just rather a pity that the name 'garden' has become attached. Or is it? Are theme gardens – the playing out of hobbies, fantasies and passions that so often crowd our homes – such an odd idea after all? They are certainly not new – the Victorians made gardens as dreams of the mystic east, and gardens for dinosaurs and

International Garden Festival
Masterplan LIVERPOOL '84

OCTOBER 1983

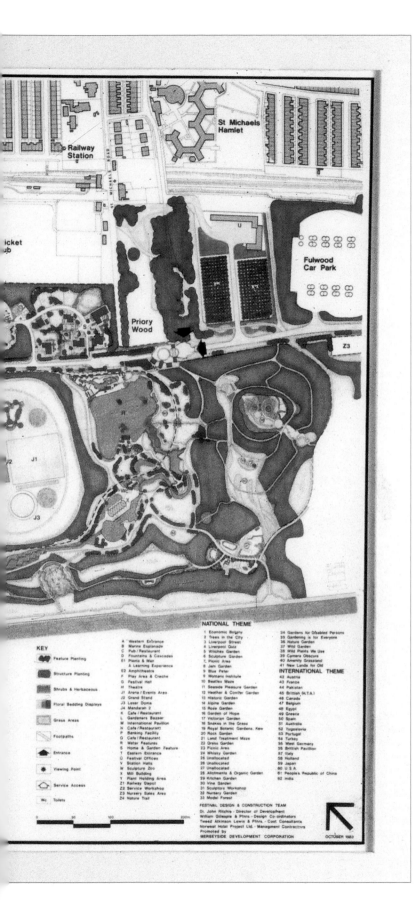

From a visual standpoint this master plan for Liverpool's International Garden Festival by the Design Co-ordinators, William Gillespie & Partners, is in the tradition of Victorian public parks and the Festival of Britain Pleasure Gardens (see pages 220-221). The progress at Liverpool was in technological terms, creating this park-like setting from methane-bubbling rubbish tips on wind-swept and derelict Merseyside acres.

International Garden Festival, Liverpool. The real triumph was in the technical achievement epitomised by this elegant gravel sculpture by Brian Clouston & Partners (landscape architects) created on a mound of compacted rubbish.

miniature alpine chalets. 'Gardens are the link between men and the world in which they live', wrote Sylvia Crowe; in a world of disappearing wild places, vanishing natural wonders, where the creations of obsessively scientific minds rampage beyond our control, perhaps fantasy in the garden is just the buffer we need?

Selected reading

John Brookes' garden at Denmans in Sussex, the Gibberd Garden at Marsh Lane, Old Harlow, and Peter and Margaret Aldington's Turn End at Haddenham are all open to visitors and details will be found in the annual *Yellow Book*. The Gibberd Garden is open also more frequently, and an appeal has been launched to save and support the garden; further details from The Gibberd Garden Trust, The House, Marsh Lane, Gilden Way, Harlow, Essex, CM17 0NA. Tel 01279 442112.

The Post-Modern garden has been little documented. *Town Gardens to Live In*, by Susan Jellicoe and Marjory Allen (1977) has a wealth of good advice, and Sylvia Crowe's *Garden Design* (1958) has been revised and re-issued (1981 and 1994). The avalanche of books that have set the gardening shelves groaning since the early 1980s (with only brief let-up during the economic gloom of the early 'nineties) have rather more to do with publishing than gardening. Gardening has been a buzz-word for publishing prosperity and, however much I adore (and am personally grateful to) the wonderful RHS bookshop at Wisley, it does make me smile to see that when I decide it

Planting and poolside detail from Preben Jakobsen's garden in Stanmore. Serenity is implied by the use of good modern materials, exact geometry and a Japanese-inspired respect for objects and plants.

would be nice to have a clematis, for my one or three plants there are about twenty-five books to choose from! Orchids rate about six shelves of books, and as they are the plant I most dislike, I can only conclude that this vigorous variety of gardening tastes is indicative of a healthy gardening state. The wealth of choice is overwhelming: with roses, clematis, dahlias, carnations, chrysanthemums, lilies, heathers, auriculas, rhododendrons or any other chosen blossom, it can only be personal taste, or simply exhaustion at ploughing through them, that prompts a decision. However, there are aspects of gardening that are important and have been well-aired in recent years: we now easily assume a sophisticated taste in colour schemes, largely interpreted by Penelope Hobhouse in *Colour in Your Garden*; we are coming to terms with long, hot summers, hence Beth Chatto's *The Dry Garden* leads a trail of good books to help. The even wider implications of wildlife friendly and organic gardening have been a repeated theme of the last ten years, and activities in the garden are tackled by Bunny Guinness in *The Family Garden*, also one of several on this subject. Finally, and even more essentially, Sue Minter, Curator of the Chelsea Physic Garden, has written *The Healing Garden* and Bob Flowerdew's *Complete Book of Companion Gardening* (both 1993) are just two which deal with the relationships between plants and humans, and plants and plants.

NINE

Geoffrey Jellicoe and *The Garden of the Mind*

I t is an irresistible fancy that the patron saint of gardeners sought to lead us out of the 20th century maze simply by giving our luminaries the same initials – Gertrude Jekyll and Geoffrey Jellicoe.

As I wrote earlier, Geoffrey Jellicoe was the original inspiration to this book. His work seemed to hold the key to the kind of gardens that we need in the later 20th century. He has already filtered into several of my chosen themes, especially through his influence on our perception of the Italian Renaissance gardens. In the 1920s when the century was young, he saw and studied those gardens when he was young, and they exerted such a strong influence on his thinking because he saw them as an exact expression of the consciousness of an era. Since then, he absorbed some of the artistic consciousness of his own time, and he retained the true artist's uncompromising innocence and

Above: Shute House, Wiltshire. The Canal Garden, as an essay in perspective.

Opposite: The Rill, with water planting by Lady Anne Tree.

241

modesty whilst working through over one hundred landscape commissions, most of them on a very large scale.

As he observed in 1961, architecture is a cumbersome art, slow to materialise, but landscape design is even more laggard: 'Of all the arts none takes so long to come to maturity, and none is so liable to deterioration and destruction. Nevertheless, landscape design has proved itself to be one of the great arts'.* The fruition of his life's influences seemed to come with his eighth decade and large-scale park landscapes, for the cities of Brescia and Modena in Italy and Galveston in Texas, which will not be realised until the 21st century. The commission for Modena came at the same time as the commission for the garden at Sutton Place in Surrey – in the late summer of 1980, just prior to Jellicoe's eightieth birthday. 'Both were far larger than any I had had previously, and the basic design of both was completed and accepted after one visit'.** Such is the surety when one has been considering one's theories and working on them for thirty years! By some wonderful justice Geoffrey Jellicoe was able to express his life's ideas in the garden at Sutton Place. This garden is the subject of my final chapter because I believe it expresses many facets of 20th century life and art, and offers solutions to so many of the quandaries. But what of those preceding thirty years? Or forty, or longer?

Geoffrey Jellicoe was born in London, 8 October, 1900. His general education ended with three years at Cheltenham College and he became an architect after studying at the Architectural Association School in 1923. It was then that he went to Italy, on a Rome Scholarship, to study the gardens. He began private practice as an architect in 1925, but was already convinced that 'architecture was part of the environment and therefore incomplete when considered in isolation'. For him this meant that the actual building was only important in direct relationship to its unity with its setting, and thus it has been buildings with landscapes or landscape commissions around existing buildings that have made up the bulk of his life's work. He had also been continually involved with teaching in one form or another: he was Studio Master at the Architectural Association 1929-34 (and later Principal of the School), President of the Institute of Landscape Architects 1939-49 (as well as a Founder Member), a Founder Member and President of the International Federation of Landscape Architects, and served on the Royal Fine Arts Commission and as a Trustee of the Tate Gallery. He was knighted in 1979.

After *Italian Gardens of the Renaissance* appeared in 1925, fourteen more books followed including the monumental *Landscape of Man*, written with his wife Susan, and the three-volume *Studies in Landscape Design* which explain, through lectures he gave, his view of the artistic and other influences upon his work. Before the war Jellicoe worked on several gardens – Ditchley and Pusey have already been mentioned – including gardens at Royal Lodge, Windsor, and Mottisfont Abbey, in Hampshire. Even during the war he started on a long string of commissions for industry when thoughts were being turned to restructuring and revival, and afterwards he worked in old city centres and new towns, housing landscapes, town hall settings and civic centres, schools, hospitals, motorways, power stations, steadily building towards those prestigious commissions for which he is best known – the pool at the Royal Horticultural

* G. Jellicoe, *Studies in Landscape Design*, vol II, 1966, p.1.
** *Architectural Review*, March 1985, p.49.

Fitzroy Square, London. Free of traffic and with its human scale restored, the square once again becomes an expression of an age-old geometrical theme, the circle within a square. The paving pattern, with setts lining drainage gullies, is directly inspired by Giovanni Bellini's painting 'The Allegory of Souls' (see page 267).

Society's garden at Wisley, Surrey and the Kennedy Memorial at Runnymede.

Sir Geoffrey 'retired' from his private practice in 1973 to continue working hard as ever as a consultant. In this latter capacity he had several private garden jobs, including a scheme for the Duke of Wellington at Stratfield Saye in Hampshire, as well as a landscape development plan for the oil-rig construction works at Kishorn, Wester Ross. It was into this scenario that the commissions for Modena and Sutton Place came – in both cases he found clients who responded to his thinking, that had, by this time, confirmed itself: 'This theory is that all man-made environment is a projection of our psyche, whether individual or collective, and when this is not so [i.e. a projection of our brain only] then there is disruption and unhappiness that is mainly due to the dislocation or repression of subconscious instincts'.*

It was my very conscious instinct, as I started this book, that the whole of the

* *Architectural Review*, March 1985, p.49.

Above: Shute House, the flower garden.

Below: The Rill looking north. The bubbling fountain is worked by gravity, an idea learned in Kashmiri gardens.

Opposite: the apple porch.

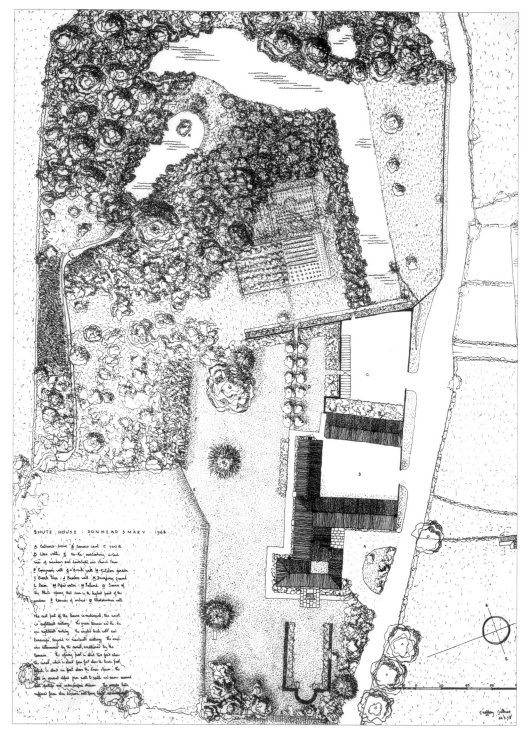

Above: the 'before' drawing of Shute House garden, in 1968.

Opposite: the 'after' drawing of Shute House garden, 1978. The land immediately around the house has been cleared and formal touches added, including a 'green bedroom' on the west end. Jellicoe's new designs, largely inspired by his clients, Mr Michael and Lady Anne Tree, are in the 19th century area, where Dutch elm disease had made much clearing and replanting necessary. Winding paths encounter statues in wooded clearings; the kitchen garden has been moved to the road boundary to make room for large square beds of flower and shrub planting. Jellicoe's most notable feature is the musical Water Garden – rills designed for harmonious sounds – which crosses the centre of the plan.

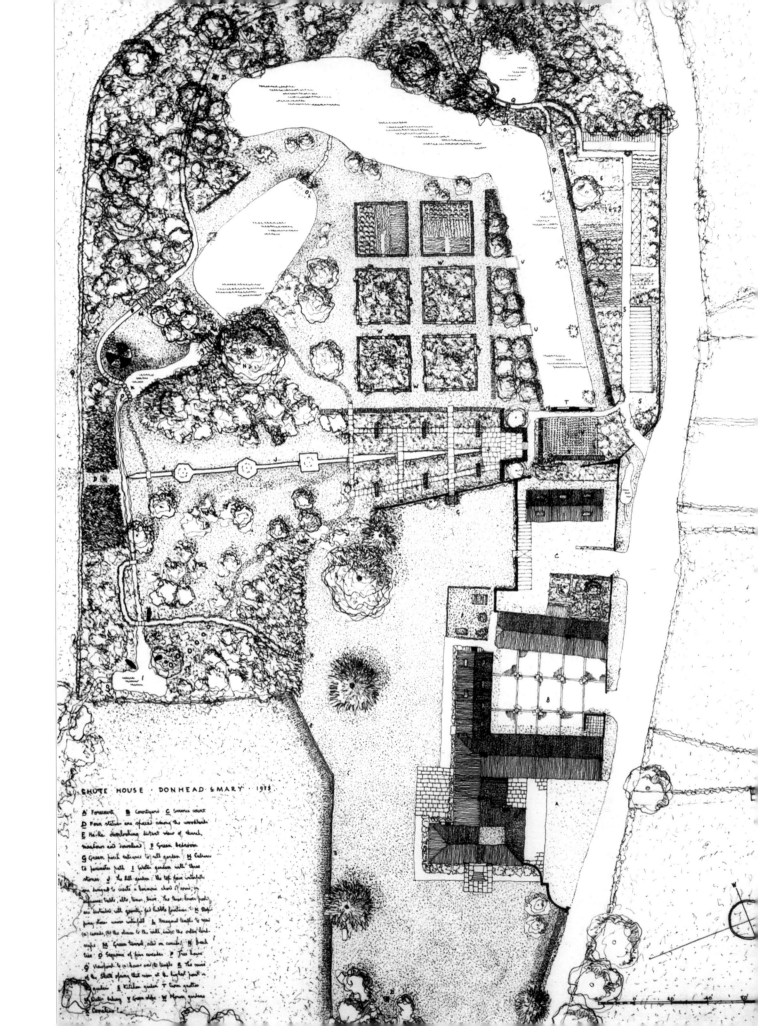

SHUTE HOUSE · DONHEAD ST MARY · 1973

20th century was tumbling towards Jellicoe's solution. In conversations with him, in the spring of 1983, I sought his guidance as to the steps towards the realisation of his theory, and it is these steps that this chapter seeks to identify. Our conversations took place in the small Georgian house with its long London garden, that had been Geoffrey and Susan Jellicoe's home for over forty years. As other artists use a mouse or a butterfly, Sir Geoffrey has repeatedly drawn his little garden plot, to scale, in the corner of layouts for massive schemes; he has never forgotten our precious human scale.

As a preliminary to conversation we looked at the collection of drawings and paintings throughout the house. Most of them were given to him by, or bought by him from, the artists when they were young and poor together. He has some drawings by Henry Moore, several of Ben Nicholson's architectural sketches – crisply drawn arches framing soft fields and hedges, human order balanced to natural order – some irises by Matthew Smith, a sea of bracken by Ivon Hitchens, four Sutherland sketches, a John Tunnard, an early abstract by John Piper, an Alan Sorrell. He wished he had a work by Paul Klee, who had always inspired him but was equally always beyond his means, and I am not sure whether there was anything by Victor Pasmore, for whom Jellicoe has always had the greatest respect, though he admits he has never quite 'reached him'. Jellicoe modestly insisted he had always only been reaching where these other artists led him, groping his way to transmute their art into landscape terms – though he remembered with delight joking with Nicholson and Moore on this subject, and how at least they dubbed him a 'top groper'.

If the Italian villa gardens had made Jellicoe realise how much architecture was part of landscape, then the Constructivist Movement of 1930s' art endorsed and enlarged his view. 'A new cultural unity is slowly emerging out of the fundamental changes which are taking place in our present-day civilisation', was the opening statement of *Circle*, published in 1937. *Circle*

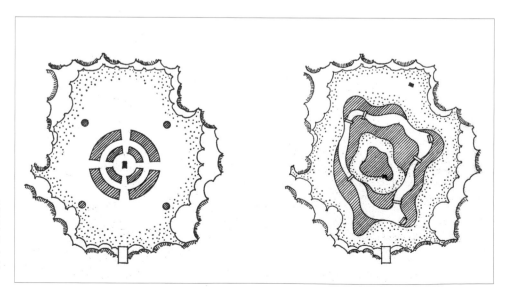

Drawings of the Rose Garden at Cliveden. The original design (left) is static and restrictive, while Jellicoe's new design (right) expresses the freedom, fascination and rhythms of modern art.

*Geoffrey and Susan Jellicoe's final
London house, a flat in Lubetkin's,
Highpoint (see p.123). On the wall, the
precious collection of early works by
Sutherland, Moore, Nicholson, Piper
and others, who were both friends and a
lifelong inspiration.*

*The 'tower block' view that Jellicoe the
modernist found comforting in his last
years.*

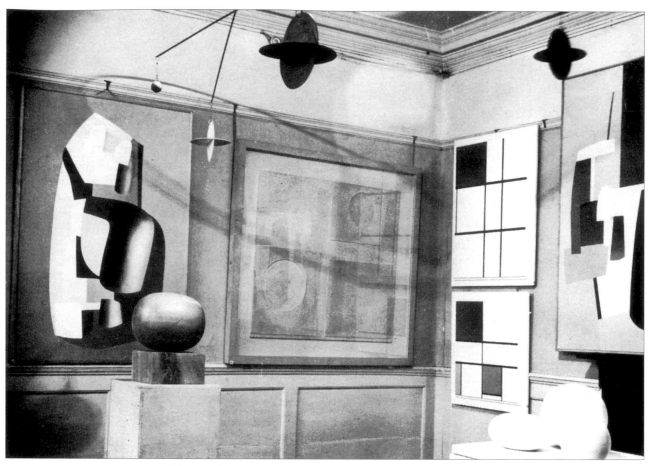

Photograph of part of the 'Abstract and Concrete' exhibition held in Oxford in 1936, at which paintings and sculpture by artists of the Constructivist Movement were on display, including works by Ben Nicholson, Barbara Hepworth and Piet Mondrian. The exhibition reflected the artistic mood of the period. The Constructivist Movement endorsed and enlarged Jellicoe's view that architecture was in fact part of landscape and that ideas could be transmuted into landscape design.

expressed the unity of a group of abstract artists, Naum Gabo, Nicholson, Barbara Hepworth and Henry Moore especially; in architecture the ideas are seen in Amyas Connell's High and Over, Tait's Le Chateau at Silver End in Essex, Lubetkin's Highpoint flats in Highgate and the Penguin Pool, then newly opened in Regent's Park Zoo, and in Mendelsohn and Chermayeff's De La Warr Pavilion at Bexhill-on-Sea. Among the ideas of the architects, with which he was already familiar, Jellicoe found the words of the artists, and especially in Barbara Hepworth's skill at explaining her art:

'Full sculptural expression is spatial – it is a three-dimensional realisation of an idea, either by mass or space construction . . . For the imaginative idea to be fully and freely projected into stone, wood or any plastic substance, a complete sensibility to material . . . is required. There must be perfect unity between the idea, the substance and the dimension . . . The idea . . . actually *is* the giving of life and vitality to material'.*

She continues, analysing the qualities of a great sculpture:

'Vitality is not a physical, organic attribute … it is a spiritual inner life. Power is not man power or physical capacity – it is an inner force and energy. Form … is the chosen perfected form … perfect … for the embodiment of the idea. Vision is not sight – it is the perception of the mind. It is the discernment of the

*'Sculpture', *Circle* 1937 (reprinted 1971) p.113.

reality of life, a piercing of the superficial surfaces of material existence, that gives a work of art its own life and purpose and significant power'.

Henry Moore argued that contemporary art was not an escape from life because it avoided reproducing natural appearances: 'It may be penetrating into reality . . . an expression of the significance of life, a stimulaton to greater effort in living'.**

Ben Nicholson emphasised the search for reality as the 'principal objective' of abstract art: 'A different painting, a differing sculpture are different experiences, just as walking in a field or over a mountain are different experiences . . . it is only at the point at which a painting becomes an actual experience in the artist's life, more or less profound and more or less capable of universal application according to the artist's capacity to live, that it is capable of becoming a part, also, of the lives of other people . . . It must be understood that a good idea can have a universal application which is not solved in its own terms and if any extraneous elements are introduced the application ceases to be universal'.***

Moore expressed his envy of architects who could create to great size and scale, but realised that function shackled them. But what about landscape architects? Did not so much of the Hepworth theory that applied to 'stone, wood or any plastic substance' have implications in landscape terms? And what about Nicholson's belief in the power of the idea, equally shared by the others? It was with these beliefs, and the work of these artists especially, that the vaguest hunch was born in Jellicoe's mind that the power of 'the idea' could be transmuted into landscape design. Moore, Nicholson and Hepworth in particular had sparked something off not just in his mind, in his psyche, his soul. From now on their philosophies must be traced through his work as, slowly and spasmodically at first, he found commissions that sent him searching for answers beyond the obvious. Unlike a sculptor, though, who can roam in search of his wood and stone, the right material that will allow his idea 'to be fully and freely projected' into it, a landscape architect has to wait for commissions and sites to turn up. And the client was also of supreme importance.

'Client' is an interesting term. In designing a garden, where there is a one-to one relationship with a personality, harmony is essential, and there may or may not be a strong aura of history or 'style' present in the house and its setting. In the 1930s Jellicoe had rejoiced in the 'true Palladian' taste of Ronald Tree at Ditchley, and he said that Stanley Seeger at Sutton Place in 1980 gave him a full and free response to his own ideas. In the intervening forty-five years he found a few equally satisfactory relationships with clients like the Trees at Shute in Wiltshire. He also learned that the 'collective' client – a board of directors or a city council – has the ability to convey a sense of sympathy, or otherwise. Dealing with 'collective' psyche has become just as important as with the individual. A final possibility that I put forward myself, because Jellicoe had been extremely sensitive to it, is that of an invisible but powerful ethos pervading from a person no longer living, as with the memorial to President Kennedy at Runnymede, or from an idea – the idea of nuclear power.

** 'Quotations' *Circle*, p.118.
*** Ibid, p.75.

Horsted Place, Sussex, as designed for Lord and Lady Rupert Nevill in 1965.

The straight path from the house to the woods is rhythmically punctuated with arches to form green laburnum tunnels.

The Repton-style baskets on the lawn represent a more random progress, also between the house and woodland.

Barbara Hepworth's studio and garden, St Ives, Cornwall. A tiny space which contains great sculptures in an almost magical companionship.

Below: Horsted Place, Sussex. The circular baskets are related in thought to this large circle of immaculate grass in the heart of the woodland.

The Guinness Brewery, Park Royal, London. Geoffrey Jellicoe's earliest landscape sculpture using the excavated soil from the A40 Hanger Lane underpass.

In 1959 the sculptural material and a willing client turned up at the Guinness Brewery at Park Royal outside London. To use a large amount of subsoil, excavated when building the A40 Hanger Lane underpass, rather than go to the expense of carting it away, was an attractive proposition, and the result was the abstract sculpture of two hills beside the 1930s' 'Palace of Industry', as the Guinness Building was known.

The following year Jellicoe received the commission for a landscape around the nuclear power station at Oldbury-upon-Severn in Worcestershire. The terms of reference were straightforward and intimidating enough: to dispose of two million cubic yards of subsoil from the river bed (excavated to form a reserve lake), and to form a plateau on the adjoining land, level with an existing towpath. The landscape was of flat, irregular fields, protected from river flooding by the towpath on a twelve-foot high embankment. The new level of the land would improve drainage and prevent flooding; the philosophical problem was to provide a link between the small fields of the surrounding countryside and the vast bulk of the power station. This idea directly linked back to the 'thirties, when Jellicoe had first encountered the Ben Nicholson series of 'White Reliefs'. Nicholson's work bore the comforting

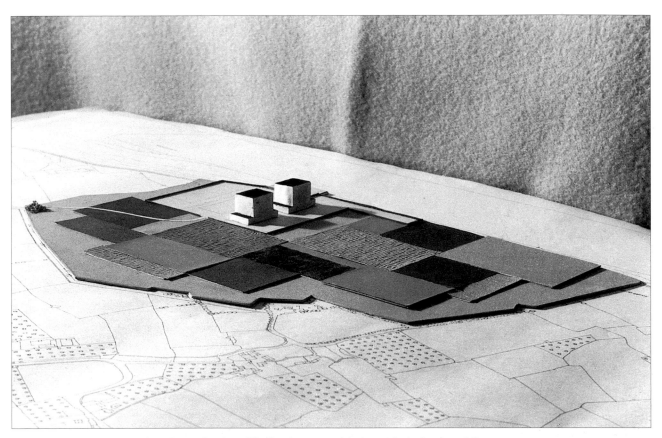

Oldbury-upon-Severn Nuclear Power Station. The landscape model shows the influence of Ben Nicholson's 'White Relief' paintings on Jellicoe's new field pattern, which unites the bulk of the power station buildings with the old landscape.

implication that, with 'the outside world too disorderly to contemplate', he had to create an inner world of order. Nicholson also found much of his inspiration in nature. The techniques of the Oldbury contract (levelling vast areas of soil to predetermined contours, replacing fences and hedges, grading banks and planting new trees) had to be taken for granted; they were a known quantity that can be taught and learned. But making the philosophical link between a familiar landscape and the elemental, perhaps frightening, symbol of the power station was the task of the designer's own experience. In Jellicoe's terms this was solved by an appeal to the subconscious by creating a landscape pattern that reflected the order of a Nicholson abstract.

In *Studies in Landscape Design* Jellicoe speculated on the enormous advantages that could have been gained by using the soil from the Hyde Park car park excavations (160,000 tons of London clay dragged through the streets to Heston): 'This gorgeous substance could have been released to become a mountainous serpent whose ripples would have extended down Park Lane to the very heel of Achilles himself', its head to rear up in front of Stanhope Place and its body protecting the park from the 'eruption' of Marble Arch; partly soft and turfy, partly bristling with trees, there could have been a grandstand, an amphitheatre, a fairy tale: 'a summary of how much the imagination inherent in the landscape profession could give to society, if only, like the clay, it were called upon to do so'.*

So the inspiration of abstract art brings even monumental structures into a believable relationship with human scale; Jellicoe is creating a world of imagery within one of fact, primarily through the relationship of objects with their

* G. Jellicoe, *Studies in Landscape Design*, vol. III, 1970, p.83.

The Kennedy Memorial, Runnymede. Pilgrims enter by the wicket gate (above) and follow the winding path to the stone (opposite) which records the purpose of the memorial.

settings. Like other powerful artists, he is creating from the materials of nature.

The acre of English ground, the hallowed ground of Runnymede, that was given to the American nation as an British memorial to President John F. Kennedy after his assassination, was clearly almost sacred in the giving, replete as it was with memories and emotions within itself. The memorial stone would have to be of a suitable stature to commemorate the holder of the most powerful office in the world; the difficulty would be to provide the 'furnishings' of such a memorial without conflicting with its aura. Jellicoe thought of President Kennedy as a champion of individual liberty, and a gentle man, with a zest for life and great reserves of strength within himself.

The sloping acre on the side of Runnymede was approached across the meadow and traversed by a path upwards through the trees to where the hillside opened to a view across Runnymede and the Thames.

It was logical to place a memorial stone at the head of this path. There were five elements, therefore, that needed to be harmonised by design: the site, the path, the memorial stone, the view from the top of the slope and seats to enjoy this view. Geoffrey Jellicoe was visiting Japan during part of the 'gestation' period for the design, and was there reminded vividly of the 'thirties appreciation of how the Japanese revered inanimate objects in their garden traditions; Nicholson's 'White Reliefs' and Moore's feeling, akin to the Japanese, for the inherent beauty of form of any craftsman-moulded piece of stone were also at the back of his mind. The resulting design is at Runnymede for all to see; it is more of an interpretation of all these elements, explained by

Jellicoe as the visual impressions that all visitors find plus the 'grey world' of allegory that lies behind the obvious.

The following is a paraphase of Jellicoe's own description of the Kennedy Memorial at Runnymede from *Studies in Landscape Design*:*

> Entrance to the acre is via a wicket gate (from *Pilgrim's Progress*); the visitor is assumed to be a pilgrim, at times the entry is difficult because of the wet ground (purposely *not* surfaced in any way) and a few granite setts have been inserted into the grass to help. Through the gate, the path winds upwards through the wood. It is made of hand-hewn granite setts, hand hewn so that no two are the same, and random laid; they represent some of the souls for whom President Kennedy symbolised freedom. The wood, which is emphatically not good forestry, symbolises 'the virility and mystery of nature as a life force' with trees and bushes of all ages, some past their best. It offers a completely enclosed journey to the crest of the slope and the memorial stone. The stone is rectangular and white, completely covered with its inscription so that it is a message in itself. The facts are followed by the President's words: 'Let every nation know whether it wishes us well or ill, that we shall pay any price, bear any burden, meet any hardship, support any friend or oppose any foe in order to ensure the survival and success of liberty'. A scarlet American oak, rich red in autumn, stands guardian behind the stone.

> After the stone, 'the twilight of the woods gives way to full light. The path to the seats is direct, like Jacob's Ladder. The upper seat is the public image of the President, the secondary seat that of his consort. The idea for this came from Henry Moore's 'King and Queen' in the solitary landscape at Shawhead'. The two seats are placed side by side, but separate, the second being subtly deferential to the first in the King-Queen, man-woman relationship. They both look out on to the same lovely view, across the meadow of Runnymede and the river Thames among the trees.

> This sophisticated design is fitted into an intentionally natural landscape: 'There is no compromise of neatly cut grass and trim flower-beds . . . The intention is to convey the same impression as that of a Greek temple, whose presence lends meaning to a primitive scene'.

The Kennedy Memorial represents a climax in Jellicoe's achievements in imbuing a piece of landscape with an idea or series of ideas. The concept of a memorial, particularly this memorial, lends itself to the emphasis on the spiritual values of a place. In a garden that element of spirituality can be lightened to fantasy, and it is the element of fantasy, another country for the mind to explore, that Jellicoe believes the 20th century mind most longs for. A very small and simply grasped example is found in the Rose Garden at Cliveden in Buckinghamshire. It was 'formal' in the Victorian sense – neat, precise, stunted and static in plan. In 1962 it was redesigned, based on the mind's-eye view of Paul Klee's 'The Fruit', painted in 1932, an embryonic or foetal-like representation of life inside an apple. The new Rose Garden has that quality of freedom, fascination, intrigue and rhythm that Jellicoe feels the modern soul seeks.

Thus, with all these associations – the inspiration of a person, a sympathy with the genius of the place, with elements of impeccably classical design, and the pursuance of an idea behind the obvious, Geoffrey Jellicoe has accomplished feasts for the imagination within factual settings. He has brought fantasy,

* Vol. III, 1970, pp.28-32.

Kennedy Memorial, Runnymede. Winding upwards through the woods of the English acre of land, the path to the memorial stone is an allegorical expression of crowds of pilgrim souls who saw President Kennedy as a champion of their freedom. Jellicoe wanted the individually cut granite setts laid at random, like a crowd of pilgrims. In Volume III of Studies in Landscape Design *he wrote: 'They emerged from the craftsman's hand with too much regularity. Then the idea was revealed to him, and he was asked to imagine that they were a crowd attending a football match. With this in mind the craftsman went ahead and virtually positioned every sett himself. They are, I think, a considerable work of art'.*

intrigue and delight into an increasingly prosaic, trivial and chaotic world. Which seems to be the very best purpose for which late 20th gardens can be made. As well as the tiny Rose Garden at Cliveden, he has achieved these kind of delights at Horsted Place in Sussex and for Shute House in Wiltshire. But the most conscious achievement, a wholeness of design philosophy, was for Sutton Place in Surrey, which is fittingly the subject of my last chapter.

Selected Reading
To a greater extent than any other professional landscape architect, Geoffrey Jellicoe kept the thread of gardens running throughout his career. This is beautifully celebrated in Michael Spens *The Complete Landscape Designs* and *Gardens of Geoffrey Jellicoe* (1994). Michael Spens has also devoted a whole book to the garden at Shute – *Jellicoe at Shute* (1993). The Garden Art Press has issued three of the four volumes comprising *The Complete Works of Geoffrey Jellicoe*, beginning 1993.

Note: Sutton Place can be visited by prior arrangement: please address enquiries to The Sutton Place Foundation, Sutton Place, Guildford, Surrey GU4 7QN (Tel: 01483 504455).

The Nicholson Wall at Sutton Place. The work of transforming his 'White Reliefs' into the giant realisation in Carrara marble was supervised by Ben Nicholson especially for this setting. The original design was for a rectangular pool.

TEN
Sutton Place

Sutton Place is a 16th century manor house set within a loop of the river Wey in rural Surrey, to the north-west of Guildford. It is, according to Pevsner's *Buildings of England* 'side by side with Layer Marney, the most important English house of the years following Hampton Court'.* Built in warm brick with terracotta panels of ornament, it has many an incised RW for its builder, Richard Weston, and large windows of shimmering glass. It is all the more intriguing because so little is known about its building. Sir Richard Weston was granted the estate in 1521, but no one knows when he started his house, and the puzzlingly early appearance of the terracotta by Italian craftsmen and centuries of subsequent rural obscurity add to its fascination. In the 1930s it was much talked of for the parties given by the Duchess of Sutherland, at which the Prince of Wales courted Mrs Simpson, and after the war it became the well-

Above: The Paradise Garden at Sutton Place. The view from the house roof shows how paths weave through flowers and arbours.

* Nikolaus Pevsner, *The Buildings of England: Surrey,* 1971.

The yews on the south lawn, Sutton Place. This part of the garden is the intended site for the avenue of fountains designed by Jellicoe to lead to a grotto and the river.

known but rarely seen home of the reclusive millionaire Paul Getty. The outside world passed by the gilded gates that face on to the A3 London to Portsmouth road, and though anyone with a boat and a licence could drift through the park on the Wey Navigation, the house was little seen or heard.

When Getty died Sutton Place was eventually leased by another American, Stanley Seeger, who wanted his treasure house – and its fast accumulating content of treasures – to be appreciated by a discerning public, who would come in carefully organised parties of manageable numbers ('because houses are very special and need knowledgeable guidance') to listen to concerts and view exhibitions. Stanley Seeger also wanted to add distinguished gardens to his house, and he had been told that Sir Geoffrey Jellicoe would be his man.

Sir Geoffrey paid his first visit to Sutton Place in July, 1980. He had not met Stanley Seeger before, but on the way to this encounter he recalls how he almost fell over a Henry Moore sculpture in the hall and became aware that the works of Ben Nicholson, Claude Monet and Graham Sutherland were all present around him. He realised, even before he was told, that he was not being asked to restore an historical garden (which would not have interested him) but to create a garden 'which expresses the modern mind, was sympathetic to the ethos of the place, which comprehends the past, the present and the future'.*

* G. Jellicoe, *Sutton Place*, 1983.

The entrance front at Sutton Place as it is today. The house was built in the 16th century by Sir Richard Weston, and this façade is decorated with carved terracotta panels, some of the earliest known workmanship of Italian craftsmen in England. There has always been a direct approach, via an avenue, across the park to this front, which formerly had a gatehouse. This was pulled down in the 18th century, but its outline in box-edged borders of ground-cover planting can be seen.

In terms of Jellicoe's career and interests, even in terms of the progression of 20th century garden design, this was a remarkable commission. Stanley Seeger apparently insisted on grand scale but stipulated nothing more. Sir Geoffrey, fired with enthusiasm, agile and energetic for all his years, produced his first diagrammatic plan in four days at his drawing board, and was later told that Stanley Seeger apparently approved this first concept in ten minutes. Much of Geoffrey Jellicoe's inspiration had come from the surprise of the commission, a feeling that his client knew what he wanted and that it was his task to express it, and a kind of *déjà vu*, that here he was, in his eighties, once again in the presence of those shadowy Italian craftsmen who had created his beloved Italian villa gardens, the inspiration of his twenties.

The point about the history of the garden is interesting. Like most artists, Jellicoe was too creative to be interested in purist restoration; but he was far more sensitive than many restorers, in that he carefully

Plan of the garden at Sutton Place by Geoffrey Jellicoe. The vertical of the cross stretches from the lake through the series of cascades which will be below the grotto and meets the horizontal of the South Walk on the south front of the house. The Paradise Garden and the Secret or Moss Garden are on the east of the house, the Swimming Pool Garden and the Kitchen Garden on the west. The Nicholson Wall faces the rectangular enclosure on the extreme left.

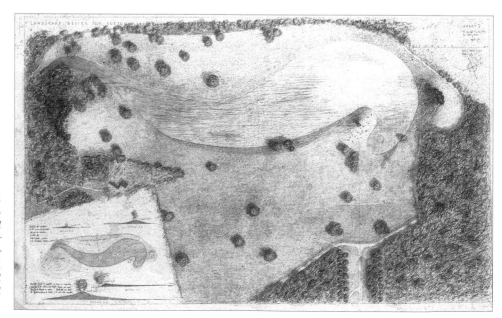

The plan for the lake at Sutton Place, 1981. The lake is entirely man made at a level higher than the adjacent river Wey. The spur of land jutting out into the water at the eastern end is the site Jellicoe prepared for Henry Moore's 'Divided Oval'.

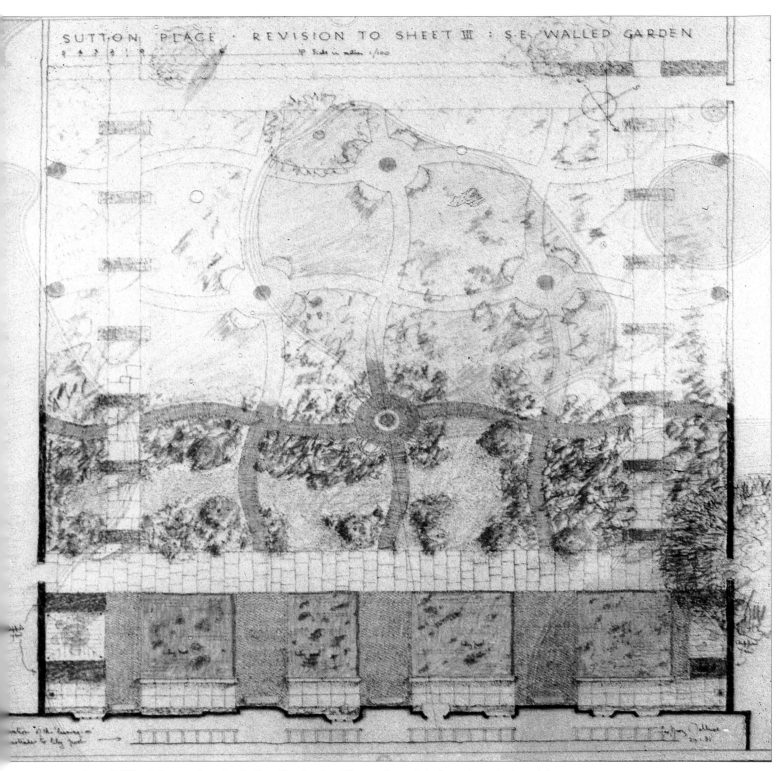

One of Jellicoe's layout plans for the Paradise Garden. The east front of the house is at the foot of the plan, with the moat to be crossed to gain the paths, arbours and flowers of the walled, sunny and scented garden.

The Paradise Garden with detail of the brick paths winding through flowers and showing the ironwork arbours, reminiscent of birdcages, which are for climbing roses and jasmines. The garden does, in fact, attract hundreds of small birds who find it a suitable preening and gathering ground so there is always the sound of birdsong.

Detail of Susan Jellicoe's planting in the Paradise Garden. It is seen here in its second season.

Giovanni Bellini's 'The Allegory of Souls'. Geoffrey Jellicoe has always been inspired by this Renaissance painting and used the balustrade in the same way in which Bellini had used it – as a division between the familiar and the unknown.

Sutton Place. The east façade and the moat – a device for spanning the time between the old house and new garden. The stepping stones introduce an element of risk that needs to be taken to reach the Paradise Garden.

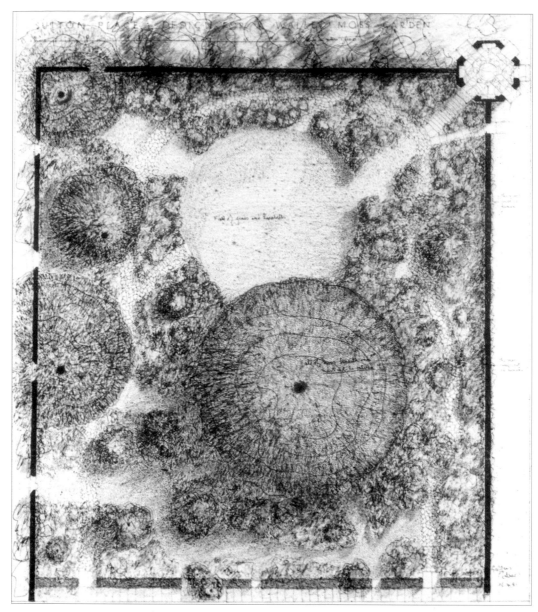

The Secret or Moss Garden plan, 1981, showing the circles inspired by the canopy of the plane tree, which is undercarpeted with moss, and a second circle of grass. This is a garden for individual interpretation, writes Geoffrey Jellicoe, 'with this proviso only: that you can enter the grass circle, but not the moss under the plane tree'. The flowers here are those of a child's nature book – bluebells, foxgloves, anemones.

Opposite above: the gazebo at Sutton Place seen from amongst the wild flowers of the Secret or Moss Garden.

Opposite below right: the gazebo at Sutton Place designed by Geoffrey Jellicoe along the lines of traditional garden buildings, especially those in 17th century gardens like Montacute in Somerset and Pitmedden in Grampian where they sit demurely at wall angles. From this gazebo one can look back at childhood in the Moss Garden, out to the distant fields or nearer woods and along the highly sophisticated South Walk.

Opposite below left: the steps to the South Walk.

'Divided Oval' by Henry Moore. This original in the Stanley Seeger collection was to be enlarged eight times and cast in bronze for the lake setting.

examined the past, so that his work created another harmonious layer in time, a kind of continuum of thought and expression. Sutton Place had originally had a gatehouse on its north entrance front, which was pulled down in the 18th century, but the form of this influenced his treatment of the front. An early print shows the house with walled gardens on both sides, but those on the east were never built; the kitchen garden range occupied the west side. For most of its life Sutton Place existed in a simple parkland setting; the English landscape style of Capability Brown, or even his successor William Eames, did not touch it. For this Jellicoe was thankful for he would have found it difficult to tangle with that. Most of the garden, including a long terrace on the south front and the avenue of formal yews there, was made for Lord and Lady Northcliffe in the early 1900s. There are Jekyll plans for a rose garden and some borders but it seemed these were not carried out. For such an old house, the garden was a lightly marked canvas on which to begin work.

The only way to describe Geoffrey Jellicoe's Sutton Place is by exploration. Either from the A3 entrance through the gilded gates and over the Wey, or from the longer drive from Jacob's Well and Send, past the cottages, farm buildings and church, one arrives at the north entrance front of the house. Where the parkland rolls down to the river channel to the north there is now the new lake, 4.6 hectares of it dug out of a sloping pasture field, with the excavated material so skilfully contoured around the banks as to make a seemingly natural setting while still preserving as many of the original trees as possible. The lake is a serpentine shape (strongly reminiscent of the serpentine mound that Jellicoe dreamed of making in Hyde Park), primeval, like a sea monster, with a softly moulded spur of land jutting into it. This is Jellicoe's setting for Henry Moore's 'Divided Oval'; the original in Carrara marble is in Stanley Seeger's collection, and for this site it was intended to be cast in bronze, eight times larger than life. The lake is a 20th century tribute to the English landscape

The South Walk looking back towards the gazebo. The laburnums on iron frames will, in the fullness of time, form a tunnel.

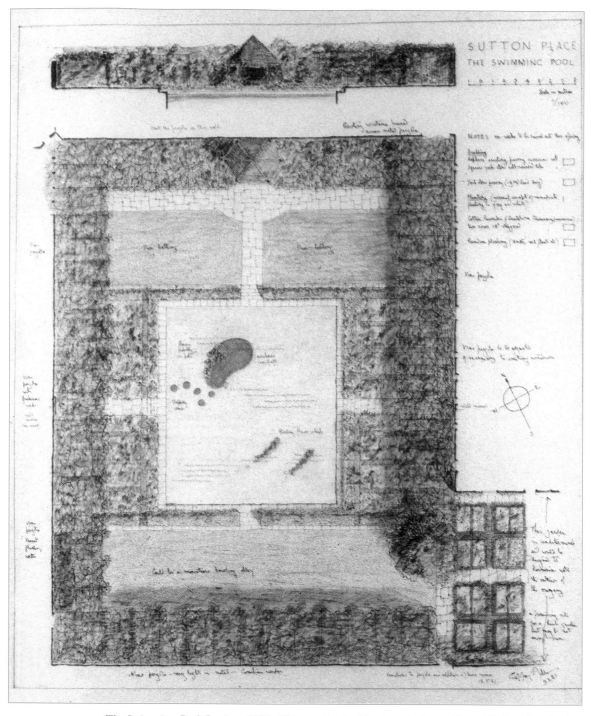

The Swimming Pool Garden, 1981. This was inspired by the paintings of Joan Miró, with a floating sun raft of abstract shape.

Opposite, above: the plan for the Kitchen Garden 1981. The two main squares of the Kitchen Garden are defined by espaliers of apples and pears, with central towers topped with a golden apple and pear respectively. The northern part of the garden is the fruit cage, with wide borders of cutting flowers.

Opposite, below: plan of the avenue of fountains, cascade and grotto, 1981. The fountains between the yews lead to a climax fountain, named Persephone, which stands on a glass basin lighting a grotto below. The only way into the grotto is under the falling water of the fountain, then, after a second, darker grotto, which is presided over by Pluto, one escapes back into the sunlight and the falling waters that cascade down the slope to the riverside.

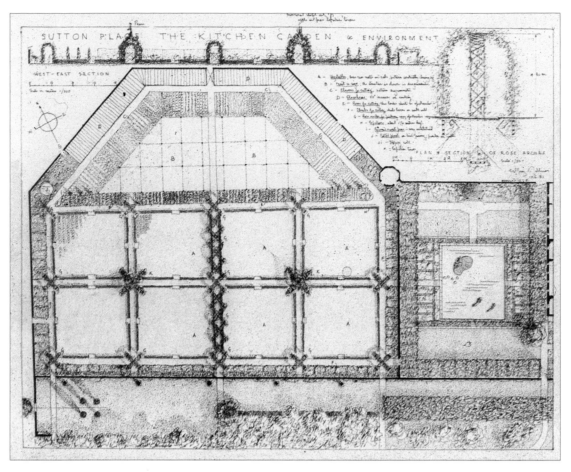

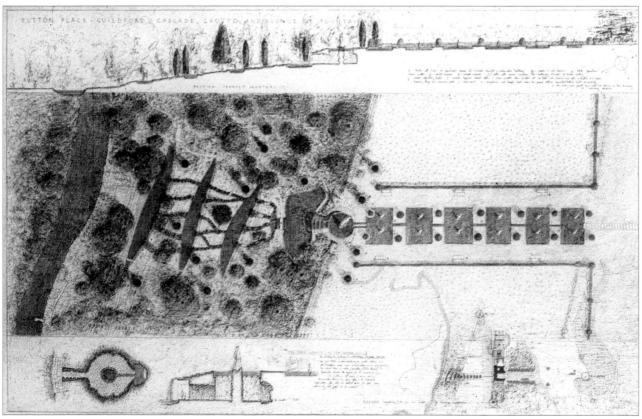

style – dug by modern methods, banked and reinforced with modern plastics, here is technology put to the service of modern art. It reminds us though of our beginnings, how we rose from the waters, and an important part of its concept is that it is managed according to 'nature's economy' – for the benefit of a healthy community of plants, animals and birds.

From these primitive rememberings, the design comes forward in time, at least to the 17th century; on the north front of the house the plan of the gatehouse has been outlined in box, set in a terracotta frame.

It is always important never to forget that Geoffrey Jellicoe was working through the exhilarating era of the Modern Movement in the 1930s. Modern Movement houses and gardens tended to have a basis in geometry – the circle motif of St Ann's Hill at Chertsey is a prominent example. At Sutton Place the symbol is again necessary, but it is not primarily geometric, for it is the cross. The lake now lies at the foot of the cross, and the distance from the lake to the house, the crossing, is so much greater than the distance on the south side to the river again, that the symbol has become the Christian cross. The designer had remembered the turmoil between the churches in Italy and England in the 16th century, when Sutton Place was being built, and found in the cross a symbol of reassurance. It also allowed, as he had remembered from the Italian villa gardens which were made against a solid background of the Church, for the occasional excursions into fantasy and even the daunting underworld of grottoes and garden conceits. The eastern arm of the cross is now walled gardens, the Paradise Garden and the Secret or Moss Garden.

The eastern façade of the house is simple and beautiful, with dark red bricks in contrast to stone mullions around windows and garden door. The house has been cut off from the Paradise Garden by a moat, or fragment of stylised moat, which is to be crossed by stepping stones to reach the garden. The moat both breaks the time-span between the old house and the new garden, and provides that element of challenge that intrigues the human mind, teasing it into any pleasure, let alone paradise itself. The detailing of the balustrades beside the moat (which seems rather strident and modern) is taken directly from Geoffrey Jellicoe's long held love for Giovanni Bellini's 'The Allegory of Souls', where the balustrade unites the past and present, the familiar and the unfamiliar.

The Paradise Garden is a pleasure garden; it is a little eastern in concept yet very English. The paths, in amusing patterns of brick and stone, weave through treillages and arbours covered in honeysuckles and roses and around small grass glades and Susan Jellicoe's romantic plantings of fragrant old roses, drifts of bergenias, acanthus, geraniums, lavenders, irises, lilies and gypsophilas. There is the sound of bird song, the hum of bees and the spattering of water on stones; it is pure delight.

The second enclosure, the Secret or Moss Garden, is darker, dominated by a great plane tree, shaded and mysterious. Many prosaic English visitors find it a little disturbing, as it symbolises rather dark, Victorian yearnings – illustrated

The Magritte Avenue plays on the perception of scale. The avenue was inspired by Stanley Seeger's purchase of the giant vases at the Mentmore sale and Jellicoe's amusement at the way the artist parodies the quality of scale – the stock in trade of all architects and designers.

in a painting in the Stanley Seeger collection by Atkinson Grimshaw called 'Midsummer Night' which shows a buxom white fairy hovering over a dark garden. In flower terms this garden is to have a carpet of wild flowers, around a circle of moss: drifts of Queen Anne's lace, wild scabious, anemones, bluebells and wild foxgloves – the flowers of a child's nature book. The preparation necessary to recall this once-common idyll is salutary – the area was completely cleared of 'weeds' by chemical means, pop-up irrigation was installed for the moss areas, which were planted by laying turfs of *Leucobryum glaucum*. The new birch and hazel trees were planted into pits.

The path from the Moss Garden leads through a gate beneath the new gazebo which guards the corner of the wall. One emerges into the light and space of the southward aspect of the house; across the lawn that Lady Northcliffe had made the woods and fields of the Wey valley fall away. Spanning the whole south front of the house and beyond is the new stone path which Geoffrey Jellicoe designed as the firm cross axis which holds the garden together. Along the South Walk one first passes under a laburnum tunnel, then Susan Jellicoe's mixed border in the Jekyll tradition, set against the wall of the Paradise Garden, takes over. In summer the walk is lined with lemon trees in

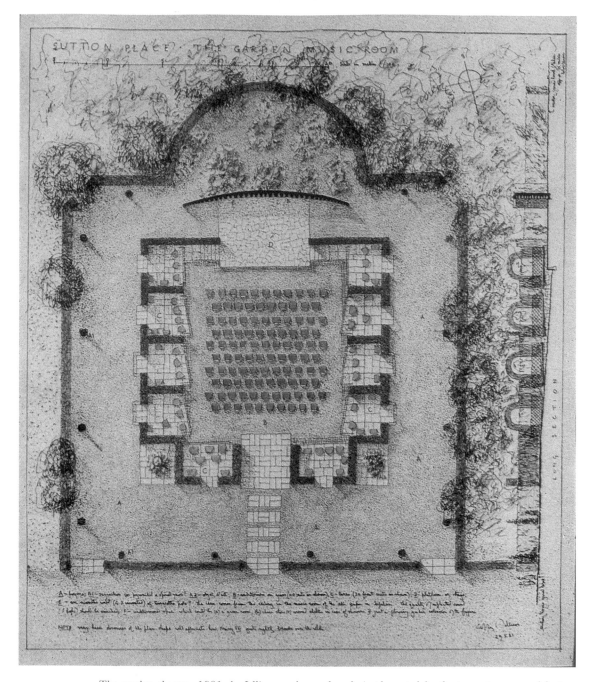

The garden theatre, 1981, by Jellicoe and now largely implemented by the present owners of Sutton Place.

tubs, and at the centre of the house's south front, in the recess of the window bays, is a small plot of exquisite planting, the Impressionist Garden, which seems always to be exquisite however the changes are rung, with attention to the mix of Impressionist colours – vivid reds and blues and soft yellows.

From the centre of the south front Lady Northcliffe's yews march across the lawn, until the land falls steeply into the river's valley. For this part of the garden, Geoffrey Jellicoe uses his most fantastic ideas, which he has brought forward from the days of the grotto builders of the Picturesque, who constructed eerie delights in Surrey, at Painshill for Charles Hamilton, and at

The Swimming Pool Garden – The Miró Mirror – with its pool based on the work of Joan Miró.

Oatlands at Weybridge, as well as from his memories of the water gardens of the Italian villas. He projects an avenue of fountains between the yews to the Persephone fountain which stands above a grotto; the floor of this fountain is glass which will light the grotto underneath, but to get into the grotto one has to pass under the fall of water. A second, more mysterious, grotto chamber is reached by a dark, wet tunnel, where a giant head of Pluto consumes the water of life. Redemption comes from Nature, and once outside the grotto's shade the water breaks into harmless rills and little falls down a prettily planted slope, to where a punt is moored for an idyllic afternoon on the river.

Back at the house, the terrace walk continues westwards; looking along the south front to the gazebo the vista shimmers, the house cannot be accurately assessed because of the ripples of light and shade, its vertical face of mellow bricks balanced by the green lawn. Turn again, and the senses are confused by a row of five gigantic vases ('rather heroic and pompous vases' said Jellicoe) of Roman origin, which came from the sale of Mentmore in Buckinghamshire. The scale is totally at odds with the comforting Tudor house and this discrepancy reminded Jellicoe of the painter Magritte. He ranged the vases along the west end of the walk and closed the vista with a square window in the wall; for the curious, who seek the view backwards through the window, the reward is a sharp comment on our century's misunderstanding of the values of scale, which Magritte's work illustrates for us.

The walled gardens on the west side of the house, are again comforting places. The enclosure nearest the house, almost square, with squares of brick retaining walls emphasising its order, has been made into the Swimming Pool Garden. The rectangular pool reflects the light, and there are stepping stones across it to an anchored sunning raft, with two smaller rafts that 'float by promiscuously' in Jellicoe's design. His inspiration for the pool was another of his long admired artist friends, Joan Miró, and the pool is to be known as the Miró Mirror.

The former Kitchen Garden is still that, beautifully organised by Jellicoe into neat squares, with paths covered by flowery trellis-work. It is a fruitful, practical and wholly comfortable place to be.

The climax of this sequence of designs that journey through space and time is the most spectacular. Out again among the over-sized vases, there is an escape hatch from the Magritte walk into a green and shady copse. The path curves through the shade of yews and hollies, and emerges on to a dappled lawn; emerging from the darkness one catches a glimpse of bright whiteness, the first hint of what reveals itself as the almost unbelievable Ben Nicholson wall, a materialisation in Carrara marble of one of his now legendary 'White Reliefs' of the 1930s. This, his last major work, is set on the other side of an existing lily pond which reflects its majesty; wall and pool are surrounded by hedges, giving a stage to pace, to stand back, go forward, to savour, contemplate and marvel, and to watch the reactions of others. The wall was unveiled not long after Nicholson's death in early 1982, and it is a triumph for Geoffrey Jellicoe's allegiance to Nicholson's work over the years, and to his own belief that art can be expressed in landscape terms. Of the wall he has written in *Sutton Place*: 'I think Ben has brought to earth something of the infinity of the world that lies around us all. This is done in a matter of just a few lines carved out of Carrara marble. No compromise, putting the truth; in fact let us say you have arrived at the truth'.

For the first half of the 1980s decade, inspired by the ownership of Stanley Seeger, the garden that has been described here was made a reality, with the exception of the grotto and cascades. It was a remarkable feat of indulgence by Mr Seeger and the Sutton Place Heritage Trust, in that he assumed the role of a client almost in the 18th century manner, and it was certain that Geoffrey Jellicoe revelled in his commonality of experience with the great designers of the past. It was surely his due. However, this being the 20th century and not the 18th, time and circumstance have a way of galloping out of control rather than keeping a steady gait, and, despite his professions of permanence and feelings of having come home to Sutton Place, Stanley Seeger parted company with the house and garden. There was an ineffable sadness in that his personal memories were filtered into the design, and the paintings and sculptures that he collected – which so expressed Jellicoe's own artistic loyalties – were removed from the house,

This detail of the Impressionist Garden shows the wisdom of siting this small area of planting where it could be seen in such delightful contrast with the detailing of the house.

and from their reflections in garden metaphors. Now there was no chance at all that Henry Moore's 'Divided Oval', magnified eight times and cast in bronze, would sit beside the lake designed for it, echoing the presence of the exquisite original in Carrara marble, inside the house, or what would be the fate of the Nicholson Wall?

This was held in the balance for some time whilst the house and gardens changed hands in 1986, until it emerged that, more than remarkably for these times, Sutton Place had found an even more indulgent ownership in the Sutton Place Foundation. This Foundation has carried out extensive restoration to the house, said to be the most serious work undertaken since Sir Richard Weston built it, and has filled it with furniture of the correct period and a fabulous collection, particularly of pre-Raphaelite, paintings and sculptures. Moreover the Foundation has lavished care on the gardens, which are now beautifully maintained by a large and devoted staff. Though there is some sadness that Geoffrey Jellicoe was not recalled to tend his designs, in general these have been carefully maintained and protected. There are losses, the Moss Garden has not been kept, and the Pool Garden – never completely successful even in its designer's estimation, has lost the Miró connotations. But there are also compensations, the Theatre Garden which Jellicoe designed, has been fully implemented and is used for summer concerts and performances, and the Kitchen Garden, now called

The Nicholson Wall. This was the artist's last major work, created specifically for this setting at Geoffrey Jellicoe's request and intended as the climax to the allegorical fantasy of Sutton Place's garden. Of this work of art in his garden, Geoffrey Jellicoe has written: 'I think Ben has brought to earth something of the infinity of the world that lies around us all. This is done in a matter of just a few lines carved out of Carrara marble. No compromise, putting the truth; in fact let us say you have arrived at the truth'.

The West Walled Garden, is filled with vegetables and roses in lavish display.

A great part of Jellicoe's original conception for Sutton Place was that it should represent the surge towards environmentally-sensitive plantings and ecologically-planned habitats; to this end he had worked closely with Marion Thompson, who had evaluated the flora and fauna of the parkland and garden. The lake was given a nesting island and reed-bed fringing, the grass-seed mixtures were carefully chosen and a variable cutting regime was built into the management plan, and native, food-bearing trees and shrubs were planted. The new owners have extended this ecologically-friendly regime to the Wild Garden and wilder areas south of the formal gardens; a collection of fruit trees, including old varieties of apples and pears now blossoms in 'ornamental meadows' of spring flowering enchantment.

The Nicholson Wall, intact and as supreme as ever, reigns over the healthy maturity of Sir Geoffrey Jellicoe's great garden, which I still maintain, is the most interesting garden made in the twentieth century. He could happily design unnumbered opportunities for plantings, especially the kind of unforced prettiness, of post-Jekyllian pedigree, of which Susan Jellicoe was such a brilliant exponent. Because it is a large garden made up of small gardens, it both echoes our traditional favourites – Barrington Court, Sissinghurst Castle among them – and holds ideas, solutions and comforts for all of us who garden in small gardens. On a prosaic level, the vigour of the roses, herbaceous borders and vegetables in the West Walled Garden, perhaps helps to answer the question that must be posed at the end of such a book as this – What kind of garden should be made now, as a garden to carry the best of this century into the next? Undoubtedly the image which shines the brightest is of a potager – a garden that mixes the good things of life, herbs, vegetables and fruit and flowers; the pink and yellow cabbages and Ruby Chard of Rosemary Verey's decorative vegetable plot at Barnsley House, polished by the whims of famous chefs, and demonstrated so ably at Barnsdale by Geoff Hamilton on television, comes winging down to us through the entire century. And from where? From Gertrude Jekyll's flowers, fruit and vegetables in the potager at Orchards, so long ago. Now that the quality of our food, the very stuff of life, is of such concern to us, gardens have to return to a useful role, albeit decorative and emotionally satisfyingly at the same time.

Finally, on the emotional and fantastical level, Sutton Place holds, for those who care to divine them, the memories of myth and legends, the evocation of other arts, the transformation of forms and textures, scents and colours into myriad jewels of the imagination. If our gardens are the essential link between our earthborn selves and the limitless adventurings of our technological future, then the 21st century talisman will surely be such a garden.

Acknowledgements

The author and publishers would like to acknowledge with thanks the new photographs for this edition, especially photographs by Stephen King of the restoration work at Munstead Wood, and by Geraldine Andrews, Charlotte Wood, Peter Greenhalf and Tim Ferguson. The Jekyll Collection from the College of Environmental Design at Berkeley, California has been available in this country for some time and now improved plans can be acquired from Surrey Gardens Trust (Tel: 0181 541 9419) or the Surrey History Centre at Woking (Tel: 01483 594594). Since the deaths of Sir Geoffrey and Lady Jellicoe, his material, plans and photographs have been divided between the Landscape Institute, the RIBA Library and Drawings Collection and the library of Thames University's Department of Landscape at Dartford. The Antique Collectors' Club has also become a source as a result of publishing and reprinting Sir Geoffrey Jellicoe's new and earlier works.

Acknowledgements and sources for the illustrations are as follows:-

Chapter One. Munstead Wood.
Pages
6, 10, 11, 43	Geraldine Andrews.
7, 14, 22-23, 35	Stephen King.
13	Orford Country Life/Lanning Roper Papers/author's collection.
15, 16, 17	From F. Jekyll, *A Memoir*, 1934 (author's collection).
18 (top), 19 (top)	Photographs John Gill (from original edition).
18(below), 19 (below)	Jekyll Collection, College of Environmental Design, Berkeley,
24, 29 (top), 37, 40 (both)	California.
26 (top), 36	From *Gardens for Small Country Houses*, 1912 (ACC).
26 (below)	Diana Steel.
26, 30, 31	From paintings by Helen Allingham.
28, 32, 33	From *Children and Gardens*, 1908 (ACC).
34	Tim Ferguson.
38, 39	Peter Greenhalf.
41	*Country Life.*
42	The author.
45	Lutyens Family Papers, RIBA Library Collection.

Chapter Two. The Arts and Crafts Garden.
46, 47, 48, 60, 61,	The author.
64 (below), 70, 71, 74, 75	
49, 52, 55, 56, 57, 64 (top), 65, 77	RIBA Library Drawings Collection.
53	From a painting by George Samuel Elgood.
54	As caption.
58, 59, 76	Jekyll Collection, Berkeley, California.
58 (below)	See caption.
62	From *Gardens for Small Country Houses*, 1912 (ACC).
63, 72	Adapted from *Gardens of a Golden Afternoon*.
66 (both), 67(top)	From *Houses and Gardens*, 1906 (ACC). All by M.H. Baillie Scott.
67 (below)	Charlotte Wood.
68, 69	See caption.
73	*Country Life.*

Chapter Three. Rodmarton Manor.
78, 87 (both), 91	The author.
79, 82, 83, 86	Geraldine Andrews.
80, 81, 84, 85,	*Country Life.*
88, 89 (both), 90, 93	Jekyll Collection, Berkeley, California.

Chapter Four. An Italian Affair.
94, 99, 100, 107, 116	Harry Smith Photographic Collection.
95, 114, 115, 118, 119	The author.
97, 108 (top)	RIBA Library Drawings Collection.
98, 102, 103	Geraldine Andrews.
101, 104, 105, 112, 113, 117	*Country Life.*
106	Howletts and Port Lympne Estate. Photograph by Rod Williams.
108 (below)	Ken and Kate Baynes, Gordon Russell, 1980.
109, 110	Diana Steel.
111	Geoffrey Jellicoe.

Chapter Five. Modern Movement Gardens.
122 (both), 127, 145, 147	The author.
123, 126, 131 (above),	RIBA Library Drawings Collection.
124, 125, 130, 131 (below), 133 (top)	*Country Life.*
140, 141, 143, 144	
132	Raymond McGrath, *Twentieth Century Gardens,* 1934.
133 (below), 134, 135,	Tunnard, *Gardens in the Modern Landscape,* 1938.
136, 137 (top), 138, 139	
137 (below)	The Landscape Institute.

Chapter Six. Sissinghurst Castle, 1930-1962.
148, 156, 157, 165,	Diana Steel.
149, 160 (top), 161 (top),	Harry Smith Photographic Collection.
162, 163,	
168, 171, 172, 173 (top, below left)	
160 (below), 161 (below),	Geraldine Andrews
172, 173 (below right)	
150	Nigel Nicolson, Sissinghurst Castle.
151, 155	*Country Life.*
152, 153, 164 (both), 169, 170	The author.
158	Stuart and Christine Page/The National Trust.
159	Aerofilms Ltd.

Chapter Seven. Hidcote Manor and the 'New Georgian' Gardens.
176, 180, 181, 184	Geraldine Andrews.
188 (above), 189, 190	
177	John Steel.
178, 179, 185, 186, 187, 191,	*Country Life*
194, 195, 203, 207	
183	The National Trust.
188 (below), 192, 197, 204, 205	The author.
193	Lanning Roper Papers. Lindley Library. Royal Horticultural Society.
196	Harry Smith Photographic Collection.
199	Lanning Roper Papers/author's collection.
200, 201	Peter Greenhalf.
202 (top)	Michael Warren.
(below, left and centre)	Laurence Whistler.
(below, right)	Norman Stevens RA, Gordon House and the Royal Academy.

Chapter Eight. The Post-Modern Garden.
208	Peter Aldington.
209	Geoffrey Jellicoe.
210	Tunnard, *Gardens in the Modern Landscape,* 1948 edition.
212 (top)	Burle Marx.
213	Marion Thompson.
214	From *Landscape Design,* February 1973, Michael Laurie.
215, 217, 218, 219	Peter Shepheard, *Modern Gardens,* 1950.
217	Peter Shepheard/RIBA Library Drawings Collection.
220, 22	Drawn by E.W. Fenton for the Festival of Britain programme/brochure, 1951.
222 (top)	Photograph Susan Jellicoe.
(below and p.223)	Geoffrey Jellicoe.
224, 232, 233, 235	The author.
225	Geraldine Andrews.
227	Sylvia Crowe.
228, 229 (top)	Michael Branch.
229 (centre)	Anthony du Gard Pasley.
(below and p.230)	John Brookes.
236, 237	William Gillespie and Partners.
238	Merseyside Development Corporation/John Mills Photography.
239	Preben Jakobsen.

Chapter Nine. Geoffrey Jellicoe and the Garden of the Mind.
240, 241	The author.
243, 254, 255, 259	Susan Jellicoe.
244, 245, 252, 253 (below)	Diana Steel.
246, 247, 248	From plans by Geoffrey Jellicoe.
249	Geraldine Andrews.
250	Jeremy Lewison ed., *Circle: Constructivist Art in Britain 1934-40,* Kettle's Yard, Cambridge, 1982.
253 (above)	The author, by kind permission of the Barbara Hepworth Museum.
256, 257	Peter Greenhalf.

Chapter Ten. Sutton Place.
260, 267 (below), 271, 275,	Author's collection.
261, 269 (top), 277	Sue Bond.
262, 263, 279,	Sue Bond (author's collection).
264, 265	Formerly Sutton Place Heritage Trust, now Geoffrey Jellicoe Papers.
266	Susan Jellicoe.
267 (top)	Jellicoe, *Studies in Landscape Design,* vol.1, 1960.
268, 272, 273, 276	Formerly Sutton Place Heritage Trust, now Geoffrey Jellicoe Papers.
269 (below), 280	Geraldine Andrews.
270	Stanley Seeger Collection.

Index

Page numbers in **bold** refer to illustrations